GLORIOUS TECHNICOLOR ®

TECHNICO
MOTION PIC
CORPORA

1006

GLORIOUS TECHNICOLOR

The Movies' Magic Rainbow

Fred E. Basten

SOUTH BRUNSWICK AND NEW YORK: A. S. BARNES AND COMPANY
LONDON: THOMAS YOSELOFF LTD

A. S. Barnes and Co., Inc.
Cranbury, New Jersey 08512

Thomas Yoseloff Ltd
Magdalen House
136-148 Tooley Street
London SE1 2TT, England

Library of Congress Cataloging in Publication Data

Basten, Fred E
   Glorious Technicolor: the movies' magic rainbow.

   Filmography: p.
   Bibliography: p.
   Includes index.
   1. Moving-pictures—United States—History.
2. Color cinematography. 3. Moving-pictures—Catalogs.
I. Title.
PN1993.5.U6B315   1979   791.43′02′0973   78-67469
ISBN 0-498-02317-6

PRINTED IN THE UNITED STATES OF AMERICA

This book is dedicated
to the millions of people
who first had their eyes dazzled
by Technicolor in the 1930s and 1940s
. . . and to the future millions
who probably will never see that glorious color
on the motion picture screen.

Contents

Foreword

Remember that wonderful moment in *The Wizard of Oz* when Judy Garland, as Dorothy Gale, opened the front door of her Kansas home and saw Munchkinland for the very first time? Imagine how that scene would have looked if the screen hadn't changed from black-and-white to full, glorious Technicolor.

Try to imagine *Gone With the Wind* without Technicolor. Or *Fantasia*. Or *Ben-Hur*. Or Betty Grable. Without Technicolor, those special movie memories, old and new, would not be the same.

The history of motion pictures is filled with innovations. Only two, however, stand out as the most important of progressive changes: sound and color. In their unique ways, both stirred shock waves around the world.

Technicolor was responsible for the color revolution. In the early days, when World War I grabbed all the headlines, movies were still called "the nickel show." The new chromatic process made an impact on the public in the 1920s but it wasn't until the following decade that full-color Technicolor, as we know it today, became the leader in the great sweep to color production. In doing so, the Technicolor headquarters in Hollywood became the Vatican of color motion pictures. From time to time, other color processes came along but none matched the technical perfection or public acceptance of Technicolor.

To film fans, particularly during Hollywood's "glory years," Technicolor meant glamour, spectacle and excitement. To the businessmen in the industry, it meant bigger box office returns. To the artists, the film directors, the writers and actors, it was a great new medium in which they could better express themselves.

But Technicolor was—and is—much more. It is also research and technicians and artistic advances which for over sixty years have played a major role in the direction of motion pictures and, now, television. In that regard, Technicolor's contributions are certainly the greatest of all.

Robert L. Surtees, A.S.C.

(Mr. Surtees, a member of the American Society of Cinematographers, has been honored by the Academy of Motion Picture Arts and Sciences with sixteen Academy nominations and three Oscars for his outstanding works in motion picture cinematography. His films include *King Solomon's Mines*, *Quo Vadis*, *Oklahoma!*, *Ben-Hur*, *Mutiny on the Bounty*, *The Sting*, *A Star Is Born* and *The Turning Point*.)

Acknowledgments

SPECIAL THANKS to three special people: *Robert Osborne* for his enthusiasm and educated, editorial eye; *Tom Tarr* for his patience and dedication to a long-time dream; and *Lou Valentino* for his generous assistance in locating many rare and treasured stills.

I am also most grateful to the following individuals, studios and institutions for their support and cooperation:

Joseph Adelman
Richard Avedon
Roy Bishop
Maureen O'Hara Blair
Tom Bodley
Janet Leigh Brandt
Herb Bridges
Robert Buckley
Gifford Chamberlain
Bill Chapman
David Chierichetti
Carol Childs
William Clothier
Florence Cole
Martin M. Cooper
Tom Coughlin
Loren Dahl
Mary Lawrence Daves
Corinne DeLuca
E. A. Eldred
Robert Epstein

Daniel L. Fapp
Rhonda Fleming
George Folsey
Jet Fore
Wendy Foster
Dore Freeman
Kenneth Galente
Jessie Garcia
Robert Goodfried
Dick Guthrie
Cecilia DeMille Harper
Christine Hawrylak
Don Hesse
Richard Hudson
Tom A. Jones
Eleanor Kalmus
Norm Kaphan
David Keith
Gene Kelly
Arthur Kelman
Marilyn Kemper

Jack Kingsley
John Kobal
Mervyn LeRoy
Helen LeVarre
Mort Lickter
Audrey Malkin
Peter C. Martin
Lois McClelland
Walter M. Mirisch
Ray Moyer
Gunnard Nelson
Skip Nicholson
Marc Pevers
Audrey Plant
Charles Powell
Michael Roshkind
Dr. Rod Ryan
Jack Sattinger
S. Arthur Schimmel
Joseph Schmit
John J. Schmitz

Margaret Scully
Tom Seehof
Danny Selznick
Larry Sher
Keith T. Smith
Alan Solomon
Robert L. Surtees
Dick Tatro
Russel Twisk
Ephraim M. Vishniac
Rex Waggoner
Murray Weissman
L. Arnold Weissberger
Lyle Walker
Earl Witscher
Mrs. Jack Wrather

Allied Artists, American Broadcasting Company, Avco Embassy, CBS Entertainment, Columbia Pictures, Walt Disney Productions, Goldwyn Studios, Hughes Productions, Metro-Goldwyn-Mayer, Modern Sound Pictures, Motown Record Corporation, National Telefilm Associates, Paramount Pictures, P.C. Films Corporation, the Rank Organization, RKO General Pictures, Security Pacific National Bank, Twentieth Century-Fox, United Artists, Universal Pictures, and Warner Bros.

UCLA Film Archives, UCLA Theater Arts Library, USC Special Collections Library, New York Public Library, M.I.T. Technique, George Eastman House (International Museum of Photography), British Film Institute, BBB Publications, Larry Edmunds Bookstore, Collector's Bookstore, Hollywood Revue, Eddie Brandt's Saturday Matinee, Academy of Motion Picture Arts & Sciences Library, and Technicolor, Inc.

Introduction

Color has fascinated mankind since Adam and Eve first spotted the brilliant red apple among the lush greens of the Garden of Eden. Despite that fascination, and influence over untold civilizations, the science of color, particularly in the field of photography, remained a mystery for centuries.

It wasn't until the release of a publication in 1704 that the foundations were established. In that year Sir Isaac Newton, accredited with the theory of color, discovered the components of light and color by means of a prism held up to sunlight. Through the prism he passed a narrow beam of light onto a screen and produced a colored band or spectrum.

In 1801, Professor Thomas Young, English physician and physicist, proposed his theory that the retina of the human eye has three sets of nerve fibers, one giving the sensation of red, one of green, and one of blue-violet. In 1839, the science of photography was created by the French painter and inventor, Louis Jacques Daguerre.

New developments followed. In 1855, the basic principles underlying color photography were established when an English physicist named James Clerk Maxwell demonstrated his classic experiment before London's Royal Institute. He simply made three still photographs of an object—one through a blue filter, one through a green filter, and one through a red filter—then projected lantern-slide positives of the three on top of the other, each screened by its appropriate filter, and recreated (or "rebuilt") the original colors of the object. Basic as the experiment was, it was hailed as creating a new era in the history of photography.

Movies in color had been the ultimate dream of film-makers. In 1873, by a happy accident, H. W. Vogel discovered the color sensitizing of photographic emulsions by means of dyes. Four years later, in 1877, Emile Reynaud patented an apparatus for projecting a strip of hand-painted pictures in apparent movement.

Although the earliest patent for color films was recorded in 1897 by Germany's H. Isensee, whose invention used a disc of colored glass which rotated before a projector lens, the first film made for screen projection (by C. Francis Jenkins) was shown three years earlier. The film, in color, contained individual hand-tinted frames.

That same year, Thomas A. Edison, the pioneer of the motion picture in America, produced a color film of a stage success, *Annabell's Butterfly Dance*, using a system he called the Kinetoscope (actually a "peep show" machine). The Edison exhibition, the first public showing of motion pictures for a fee, took place on April 14, 1894, at the Holland Brothers Kinetoscope Parlor, 1155 Broadway in New York City. The entire thirty-five foot length of the Edison Company release was also colored by hand, frame by frame, so that the white material of the dancer's flowing costume changed hue during the sequence.

The following year, the brothers Lumière projected motion pictures on a large screen for the first time. And Robert Paul, the pioneer English producer and manufacturer of cinema equipment, exhibited a seven-reel production of *The Miracle*. Each of his film's 112,000 frames was hand-colored.

Audiences for these exhibitions were limited, however. The first public projection of film on a large screen was shown in Edison Vitascope at Koster & Bial's Music Hall, an auditorium on 34th Street west of Broadway, Herald Square, in New York City on April 23, 1896. The screen measured twenty feet and was enclosed in a gilded frame.

In the late 1890s, several short French films were released in color versions, hand-tinted by an assembly line of workers employed to paint the individual frames of film one color at a time. Georges Melies, noted for his "trick" productions, used this process on such turn-of-the-century films as *An Astronomer's Dream*, *A Trip to the Moon*, *Transformation*, and *The Flower Fairy*.

Beginning in 1905, a technique of hand-stenciling color directly onto film was first used by Charles Pathe in short subjects (*Aloha Land*, *Land O'Lea*). The method was tedious but the results were often stunning. Pathe's process, called Pathecolor, was one of the first to be identified commercially and was used, starting in 1914, in a series of colorful full-length productions. Among them were *A Rose Among the Briars*, *The Life of Our Savior*, *The Three Masks*, and *Cyrano de Bergerac*. Of *Cyrano*, one New York critic noted: "The characters appear in eye-smashing creations, consisting of purple trousers, pink shirts and green capes or blue gowns, yellow hats and indigo hose." The reviewer added that the film possessed "all the artistic effectiveness of a succession of penny postal cards."

The truly photographic color process received its initial praise as early as November, 1910, when a British firm, Kinemacolor, startled the world with its first film, *Birth of a Flower*. The company followed with a string of major productions: *The Durbar at Delhi*, *By Order of Napoleon* and *The Coronation of George V*. While Kinemacolor was hailed in Europe, its future was limited. The process utilized alternating frames of red and green which were projected through a rotating color filter on the projector to a special "color fixed" screen. The equipment was cumbersome, and the continual flickering of the projected images, which gave rise to the expression "flickers," proved tiresome to audiences' eyes.

Another process was developed by Max Handschiegl, a noted St. Louis engraver, who adapted the principles of his trade to motion pictures. Finished productions were brought to Handschiegl; he would then etch, print, or hand block a "register print" of the portions of the film selected for color treatment. The result of his work became the "color plate," similar to the plates used in lithography. Examples of the Handschiegl process can be seen in sequences within D.W. Griffith's *The Birth of a Nation* (1915) and *Intolerance* (1916), Cecil B. DeMille's *Joan the Woman* (1917), Douglas Fairbanks's *The Three Musketeers* (1921), and *When Knighthood Was In Flower* (1922), starring Marion Davies.

The existing methods, to date, of applying color to film were not only time-consuming and laborious, they were expensive. A faster, more practical system had to be found to make color available. The answers were found in "tinting" (a process that had already seen limited use as early as 1907 in Edison's tinted short subject *The Teddy Bears*) and "toning."

The tinting process involved the dyeing of the black-and-white film so that the entire image would be colored by any one of eleven standard dye colors. Toning employed a chemical treatment to black-and-white film to give it a brown-and-white (sepia) look, or other single-hued tone.

During the 1920s, more than one hundred and fifty feature films were released in either tinted or toned color. While the two processes achieved roughly the same effect as placing a piece of colored cellophane over a black-and-white television screen, they did create a mood, particularly in sequences within films. For example, the fire segments in *Dante's Inferno* (1924) were appropriately red, the water scenes in *The River Pirate* (1928) projected in blue, and *The Play Girl* (1928) had scenes in lavender. The treatment proved so successful that the practice continued, in selected instances, for many years, particularly in sepia-tinted western films. Among the more notable latterday achievements using these techniques were the sepia tones of Twentieth Century-Fox's *The Rains Came*

(1939), United Artists' *Of Mice and Men* (1940), Metro-Goldwyn-Mayer's *Ziegfeld Girl* (1941) and *Tortilla Flat* (1942), the green-tinted storm sequences in David O. Selznick's *Portrait of Jennie* (1948), and the multiple tints in RKO's *Mighty Joe Young* (1949).

Color in motion pictures, in one form or another, seemed certain. Technicians and movie men, both in the United States and in Europe, were announcing new discoveries at a rapid rate. Frederick Marshall Lee and Raymond Turner of England developed the first practical color projector and film. William Friese-Greene made news with his Biocolor. The Sanger-Shepherd process was unveiled, as were the processes of McDonough, Lippman, Gaumont, Brewster, Douglas and Keller-Dorian. Coined names were in vogue: Kromoscope, Cinechrome, Chronochrome, Prizma, Zoechrome, Kelleycolor, Colorcraft, Polychromide, Kodachrome and others.

While many of the systems were praised, in one aspect or another, they all had their problems. Registration or focusing was sometimes faulty; color was often harsh or crude and not natural, therefore distracting and visually fatiguing. Too, equipment and/or projection occasionally proved difficult. But perhaps the biggest drawback of all was that not one of the multi-color processes could be made available on a commercial basis. Some of the developers had no trouble making small lengths of high quality color film. Producing a number of multiple-reel prints for mass distribution was another story. And so, despite their noble efforts, not one of them fully realized the dream of creating totally acceptable motion pictures in natural color. It remained for a determined and dedicated chemical engineer from Massachusetts, and his associates, to bring that dream to life.

Part I

The Technicolor Years

"Up to now, the moving picture industry has been like an artist who was allowed only to use pencil or charcoal. Now Technicolor has given us paints."

Director Rouben Mamoulian, 1935

1 How It All Began

Herbert Thomas Kalmus was born in the town of Chelsea, Massachusetts, on November 9, 1881. His father, Benjamin, and mother, the former Ada Isabelle Gurney, had strong musical interests and wanted their son to become a great pianist. That ambition came to a halt when teenaged Herbert stopped a baseball with the end of his finger.

With his hoped-for career in music finished, Herbert Kalmus divided his time between high school studies and part-time work. He found a three-dollar-a-week job in a local carpet store, and later supplemented his earnings with bookkeeping assignments. By his eighteenth birthday, he had managed to save five hundred dollars. To his parents delight, he decided to spend it on a college education. Because he lacked the necessary requirements in Latin, he was unable to get into Harvard, Yale, or any other liberal arts college. His interests were not scientific, but he applied for admittance to the Massachusetts Institute of Technology anyway—and he was accepted.

The young man had a flair for figures, which was one reason why so many of the intricate musical compositions he once mastered had captured his interests. Now he found a substitute in physics and chemistry, and the creativeness of experimentation and invention was unchallenged. Outside his studies, he made many new friends, not only with his classmates but among the faculty members as well. One of these acquaintances was a young redheaded art student named Natalie Dunfee, whom he married on July 23, 1902. The new Mrs. Kalmus, and a number of other associations made while in college would become instrumental in his ultimate corporate success.

Herbert Kalmus received his Bachelor of Science degree from M.I.T. in 1904 and soon left on his first trip to California where he served as principal of University School, a boys' school, in San Francisco. But the students thought his Boston accent was comic and he stayed only until 1905. Probably just as well, for a year later the infamous earthquake and fire destroyed the property.

With Daniel Frost Comstock, a member of his class at M.I.T., he went to Europe on a graduate fellowship. He received his doctorate from the University of Zurich, while Comstock received his from Basel. After returning to the United States, they both held posts at their alma mater. After receiving his doctorate, Dr. Kalmus served as a research associate (1906-07), an instructor (1907-10), and an Assistant Professor of Physics (1910-12). For three years, starting in 1913, he held dual positions: Professor of Electro-Chemistry and Metallurgy at Queen's University in Ontario,

Dr. Herbert T. Kalmus (second from right, front row) stands with members of his M.I.T. graduating class in 1904.

Canada, and Director of the Research Laboratory of Electro-Chemistry and Metallurgy for the Canadian Government. He also had a side interest. It was that enterprise that changed the course of his life.

In 1912, Dr. Kalmus formed the firm of Kalmus, Comstock & Wescott in partnership with Daniel Comstock and W. Burton Wescott. Mr. Wescott was not a classmate at M.I.T., nor even a college graduate, but he was a mechanical genius. The company functioned as an industrial research and development council, offering services on any problem of scientific nature. One of its first clients was an independent group of abrasive manufacturers who felt threatened because they could not compete with the process being used by the giant Carborundum Company. Kalmus, Comstock & Wescott saved the group by developing a similar process which, like Carborundum's, produced silicon carbide, yet did not infringe on existing patents. For their reward, the consulting firm took a share of the business. Other clients soon followed. Before long, the young company had an outstanding reputation and enviable earnings.

One day, toward the end of 1912, William H. Coolidge, a Boston corporation lawyer and investor, arrived at the office of Kalmus, Comstock & Wescott with a new movie projector called a Vanoscope. The inventor had brought it to Mr. Coolidge saying that the discovery, with its rotating mirrors, would revolutionize motion pictures by taking the flicker out of "the flickers." The lawyer and his associates were willing to invest one million dollars in the invention if it would indeed do the job. Kalmus, Comstock & Wescott made some tests on the gadget and reported that it was not practical. Undaunted, the inventor made refinements on the Vanoscope and returned to Mr. Coolidge for backing. Again, tests were run—this time more exhaustive—and the same conclusion was reached.

By now, Dr. Kalmus and his partners, having become intrigued with motion pictures, had begun work on a new type of camera. They were not interested in taking something out of movies, however. They wanted to put something in: color. If Mr. Coolidge wanted to invest a large sum of money, Dr. Kalmus reasoned, why not use it to finance his firm in the development of color moving pictures? After all, there were no practical color films in American theaters. The Kinemacolor Company had a process, but it could only photograph slow-moving objects without annoying flashes of color appearing on the screen. And, as with all other systems that had tried and failed, the pictures caused pronounced eye strain.

To Mr. Coolidge, the idea was tempting. The new camera, designed by Daniel Comstock, could photograph a scene in two colors, red and green, simultaneously. A short test run projected on a screen was all that the lawyer needed to be sufficiently impressed. He advanced the trio of scientists ten thousand dollars and told them to move ahead. And so, in 1915, the firm of Kalmus, Comstock & Wescott found itself with a new client: the Technicolor Motion Picture Corporation.

The name *Technicolor* was selected by Drs. Kalmus and Comstock as a tribute to "Tech," their alma mater. It was some time, however, before the general public became aware of it. Not so with the young company's early troubles.

The problem of developing a natural-looking color process, and of ultimately projecting it with standardized equipment, was clear from the fact that the principles of color had been known for so many years without ever having been solved. There was also the obvious point that so many individuals and groups had

Dr. Daniel Frost Comstock (circled) is surrounded by fellow classmates in 1904 M.I.T. graduation photo.

been unsuccessful in their attempts.

Technical problems were only part of the difficulty. In later years, one of Dr. Comstock's favorite quotes was itself a quote from one of America's early photographic color experts: "No independent group will ever develop practical motion pictures in natural color, the problem is too hard and will require too much money; the job will have to be done in the laboratories of a large company where large sums can be spent slowly."

Technicolor was a small company with not unlimited resources, and so the task was like a very complicated picture puzzle where the pieces were technical, financial and human. "Throughout the industry," Dr. Comstock recalled, "the 'it can't be done' atmosphere was general. It even extended to the actors who appeared in our first picture. Their attitude was 'This picture will never reach the screen. No color ever does'."

Leonard Troland had been a student of Dr. Comstock's before joining Technicolor.

Bronze plaque commemorates the founding of the Technicolor Corporation in 1915. Years later, it was mounted at the entrance to the sprawling Hollywood plant.

Working within this atmosphere became even more of a challenge, forcing Technicolor into a series of strategic moves that might never have been considered under more positive conditions. A plan called "progressive step development" was initiated. "The essence of this strategy," according to Dr. Comstock, "was to plan, as far as could be seen ahead, in a series of steps, each move—not requiring too much money or time and, at the end of each step, to show *convincing pictures on the screen.*"

It was characteristic of this scheme that in moving ahead much of the equipment and technique of the previous step be utilized, eliminating, as much as possible, back-tracking or wasted time and money. The program also minimized the risk to the investors and made continuous progress possible. (It should be noted that from the very beginning Technicolor's main goal was the development of the ultimate three-color-component process, which was theoretically capable of perfect color rendering. Dr. Comstock later remarked, however, that there was not the slightest chance of achieving color pictures as we know them today in a single step of development.)

Two other factors had a profound bearing on

One of the earliest Technicolor cameras, ca 1916. This historic model exposed two frames of film at the same time, one sensitive to red, the other green.

Interior view of an early Technicolor two-color camera. The small dark squares in the center area are the two apertures through which light entered to expose the film.

Technicolor's earliest laboratory was housed inside a railway car. It contained all the necessary equipment for processing negative and positive film, making control measurements and tests.

Technicolor's progress during its first days. Dr. Comstock credited "the rare wisdom of Dr. Kalmus . . ." who gave uniform encouragement to the technical staff.

"We had a number of bad technical emergencies," he related, "and some fiascos, and nearly any executive leader would have felt it necessary to be extremely critical at times. Dr. Kalmus acted as if he thought, 'If you can't do it, it can't be done.' This attitude was very inspiring to the technical group and must have been a unique executive attitude in the history of a large new enterprise."

Technicolor was also fortunate in being able to acquire the services of three of Dr. Comstock's most brilliant students in the Physics Department at M.I.T. These men, Leonard Troland, Joseph Arthur Ball and Eastman Weaver, all made notable and original technical contributions to the development of the process.

The work on "Technicolor Process Number One" took place in Boston in the company's first laboratory, a railway car. The facility was completely equipped with a photochemical laboratory, darkrooms, fire-proof safes, power plant, offices, and all the machinery and apparatus necessary for carrying on a number of processes on a small commercial scale. Considering the space, the scope of operations was impressive: sensitiz-

The printing room aboard Technicolor's laboratory on wheels.

ing, testing, perforating, developing, washing, fixing and drying negative; printing, developing, washing, fixing and drying positive; washing and conditioning air; filtering and cooling water; examining and splicing film; and making control measurement tests.

The enlarged staff and the new laboratory with its costly equipment put added pressures on Mr. Coolidge and the other investors. Their initial ten thousand dollar investment had increased considerably and the hoped-for commercial breakthrough did not appear to be in the immediate future. It was up to Dr. Kalmus to pacify the moneymen. His business ability showed itself time and again, not only in stretching the existing funds but in keeping new cash coming in. Dr. Comstock and Mr. Wescott were credited with the bulk of early patents, but Herbert T. Kalmus directed the production.

By late 1916, enough progress had been made on "Technicolor Process Number One" that the principals felt confident enough to produce a feature picture. The backers were naturally enthused. Finally they were going to see more than short tests. Hopefully the finished product would recoup at least some of their mounting investment. A script was developed from a seven part story by Anthony J. Kelly. It was called *The Gulf Between* and several players, Grace Darmond, Niles Welch and Herbert Fortier, were signed for the leading roles.

For economical reasons, the production shaped up as a modest venture. Nevertheless, to everyone associated with the fledgling color concern, it was to be a milestone event.

2 The First Film

In early 1917, Technicolor's portable laboratory was set in motion. The refurbished railroad car was on its way from Boston to Jacksonville, Florida, rolling over hundreds of miles of tracks to an isolated spot where the filming of *The Gulf Between* was to take place. Florida seemed the ideal location. The film-makers could take advantage of the bright sunlight, which was necessary for color photography, as well as the semi-tropical vegetation, a key background element for the story.

The production staff included Dr. Kalmus and his wife, Natalie; C.A. "Doc" Willat, formerly of the New York Motion Picture Corporation and Willat Studios and Laboratory, the production supervisor; Dr. Comstock; Mr. Wescott; Mr. Ball; and a new colleague, Professor E.J. Wall, who had done considerable work with color photography at the University of Syracuse. Both the staff and the cast were housed in a pullman car that had been hitched onto the back of the laboratory.

Dr. Comstock did not travel with the original party. He had remained in Boston to continue development of a projection system and was not scheduled to arrive until well into production. Those plans backfired when he received an urgent call from Florida asking him to come south immediately. When he reached Jacksonville, he found an exhausted staff. A distressing problem had occurred with the film itself. It could not be sensitized. (Sensitizing, or treating, was necessary at that time because of the non-existence of good color negative of fast enough speed. Without it, even in

Jacksonville in the cloudless noonday sun, a close-up of a girl wearing a sunbonnet would develop showing her face with a black halo around it.)

The Jacksonville operations were costing six thousand dollars a week. "I remember vividly," Dr. Comstock noted, "when they called me to come down. They said, 'If you can get things going in two weeks to a day, we will go on. Otherwise, we will have to close up.' There was obviously no time to do anything but feed the right kind of chemical 'medicine' to the sensitizing machine."

Dr. Comstock had long sessions with Professor Wall and others. They tried various solutions, almost in desperation, only to find that if they cured one problem, they caused another. Day after day passed without success. The cast and crew were growing restless and the budget was slowly being drained. The crisis didn't end until it was almost too late. Only thirty-six hours remained when the problem was solved.

The Gulf Between resumed production, and Dr. Comstock and Mr. Wescott returned to Boston to continue work on the projection system. The camera used in "Technicolor Process Number One" made a simultaneous exposure of red and green negatives by means of a prism (an important innovation in the process), which divided the light as it entered the camera. This necessitated the development of a new projector equipped with two apertures for adding color to the film—one with a green filter and the other with a

The Gulf Between, shot on location outside Jacksonville, Florida, featured Niles Welch, Grace Darmond and Herbert Fortier in leading roles.

red filter.

The problem of illuminating the two film apertures in the projector with continuous equality at one time seemed insurmountable. Indeed, one of the fundamental difficulties that beset and discouraged numerous investigators in the field of color photography had been the unsteadiness and inadequacy of the contemporary arc lamps, which were used as a source of light for the projection of all motion pictures. The firm of Kalmus, Comstock & Wescott felt at an early stage it essential that an improved arc be developed to provide brighter light and, of equal importance, steadier light.

Projection of the two apertures onto the screen in register also proved to be troublesome. According to Dr. Comstock, "The register adjustment had to be made from the projection booth and this was relatively far away from the screen. The necessary adjustment was of extreme delicacy and an adjustment in the

relative position between the two projector lenses would have been 'going at it' the wrong way. The relative position must be 'massively fixed' or great trouble could be expected."

A set of special register glasses was developed for superimposed fine adjustment. This permitted register correction without trying to change lens position. Register adjustment was still difficult, but it was possible.

The Gulf Between was completed in the summer of 1917 and screened before an invited audience at Aeolian Hall in New York City on September 21. Motion Picture News, in its review of October 6, cited the film as "unquestionably the finest natural color picture ever produced. The process . . . results in the absence of all 'fringe,' absence of eye strain and produces colors that are really natural. The invitation audience . . . was moved time and again to burst into

Herbert Fortier, Grace Darmond and Niles Welch in *The Gulf Between*, 1917.

The office aboard Technicolor's rolling lab.

applause of the sort that lasted long. The final shot, showing the sun setting over the water is beautiful—mindful of a Japanese painting."

The October 6 edition of *Motion Picture World* called Technicolor "vastly superior to any of its predecessors. This was quickly comprehended by a large body of spectators that comprised many of the most prominent men in the moving picture industry, and the outbursts of applause were frequent, as different scenes of uncommon beauty were shown. The new process throws upon the screen a continual succession of pictures in natural colors that copy nature with the fidelity of a finely executed oil painting. Many of the landscapes and water scenes are of remarkable coolness."

The critics were not totally complimentary, how-

ever. *Motion Picture News* added: "the camera work—the all important angle of production in this case—is all O.K. with the exception that in quite a number of the scenes it lacks definition. There is a perceptible haze, ever so slight, but still perceptible . . ."

Motion Picture World went even further.

The interiors and the human element are not so well done, the men and women in particular having a more or less painted or chromo effect. The faces are most successful in the close-ups. When the figures retreat to any distance, it is difficult to distinguish their expression. Another defect is a slight blur of color, as the shift is made from one scene to another.

Briefly, while the process shows great advancement and has much to commend it, perfection has not been reached . . . That all forms of screen drama will ever best be shown in color is more than a doubtful question. The black-and-white animated picture is frankly a photograph and is understood as such by the spectator . . . Spectacular production should offer a promising field for this color method . . . As for drama, that is the product of the playwright. Even the advent of the photoplay has not altered the value of Dumas' recipe for the practice of his art: 'All I want is four scenes, four boards, two actors and a passion.'

Had it not been for the unveiling of the new color process, *The Gulf Between* would have been virtually ignored. Reviewers said the story was "long and drawn out . . . almost without suspense . . . and weak in plot" but praised the work of the cast as "a high order of merit."

Technicolor's first public showing, at Aeolian Hall, left a deep impression on Dr. Kalmus. Years later, he recalled that Friday morning in September.

Early Technicolor developing machines, probably the only ones ever installed within a railroad car.

27

The first public viewing of a Technicolor process, an exhibition of *The Gulf Between,* was held at New York's Aeolian Hall on September 21, 1917.

Prior to the running of our film, I was asked to expound on the marvels of the new Technicolor process which was soon to be launched upon the public and which it was alleged by many could hardly do less than revolutionize their favorite form of entertainment.

The Gulf Between had been preceded by *The Glorious Adventure,* a feature picture made in England by the Kinemacolor Process. Since Kinemacolor photographed the color components by successive exposure, it was nothing for a horse to have two tails, one red and one green, and color 'fringes' were visible whenever there was rapid motion. The Technicolor slogan was two simultaneous exposures from the same point of view, hence geometrically identical components and no fringes.

We were, of course, introducing color by projecting through two apertures, each with a color filter, bringing the two components into register on the screen by means of a thin adjusting glass element . . . During the showing (at Aeolian Hall) something happened to the adjusting element and, in spite of the frantic efforts of the projectionists, it refused to adjust. And so I displayed fringes wider than anybody had ever before seen. Both the audience and the press were very kind but it didn't help my immediate dilemma or afford an explanation to our financial angels.

The final blow occurred not much later. Arrangements had been made with the Klaw and Erlanger theater chain to exhibit *The Gulf Between* for one week in each of a group of large American cities. One night in Buffalo, New York, things went from bad to worse, not only on the screen but in the projection booth. Dr. Kalmus, who was in the theater, did not like what he saw and made a snap decision. "I decided that such special attachments on the projector required an operator who was a cross between a college professor and an acrobat . . . Technicolor then and there abandoned 'additive' processes and special attachments on the projector."

Once again, the "it can't be done" forces raised their voices. Technicolor, the upstart, had also failed to field a workable color process. The Technicolor laboratory in Boston, however, was not a scene of depression. Everyone there felt that their accomplishments to date, good or bad, were simply a part of the early strategy. Besides, there was an encouraging note. Progress had already been made on the second project. Hopefully, this one would end the battlecry of the skeptics.

3 HOLLYWOOD

From the standpoint of color, the screen appearance of *The Gulf Between* had been sufficiently impressive to encourage the development of color "on the film" so that an ordinary projector could be used in the theaters. Instead of having two separate beams of color light going through two separate pictures in the projector, which had to be registered on the screen, the goal was to perfect a process that could contain both components of the picture printed from the negative in register on the positive film.

With increased activity in all departments, the laboratory on wheels became too confining. Additional space for a pilot plant was obtained in the basement of the building occupied by the Technicolor engineers, Kalmus, Comstock & Wescott, on Brookline Avenue in Boston. There, "Technicolor Process Number Two," a two-component substractive process, was developed. This was largely achieved under the direction of Dr. Leonard T. Troland, who later became Technicolor's research director.

As Dr. Kalmus described it, the new process was accomplished by "making two separate 'relief' images. By a relief image I mean that instead of having silver deposits constituting the image of the picture as printed from the negative, hills and valleys are etched in the gelatin giving a relief image corresponding with the image of the picture. Two such relief images, one each for the red and green components were welded together back to back in register. Then the two sides, one after the other, were floated over baths of the respective dyes and dried. Thus, we made a double-coated relief image in dyes."

The new process used a specially constructed camera equipped with a split-beam system so that two exposures of the same scene could be made simultaneously through the single lens. The image was relayed from the lens to a prism which split the beam into two portions and filtered the rays to form red and green images on the film.

Research on "Technocolor Process Number Two" was begun in 1918. By 1920, the money that Mr. Coolidge and his associates had invested in developing an acceptable color process had run close to $400,000. Since not a penny had been returned in profits, they withdrew their support.

Dr. Kalmus made a quick trip to New York City, where he managed to intrigue William Travers Jerome, the famed trial lawyer who prosecuted Harry Kendall Thaw for the killing of Stanford White. Mr. Jerome, in turn, interested two advertising executives, A.W. Erickson and Harrison K. McCann, who each brought in several of their own clients (their agencies did not merge until 1930). The new investors included William Hamlin Childs and Eversley Childs, makers of Bon Ami; Albert W. Hawkes of Congoleum-Nairn; and John McHugh, of (what was at that time) the Chase National Bank.

With substantial backing now guaranteed, the work on Technicolor's new process could proceed without interruption. And progress was being made. A number

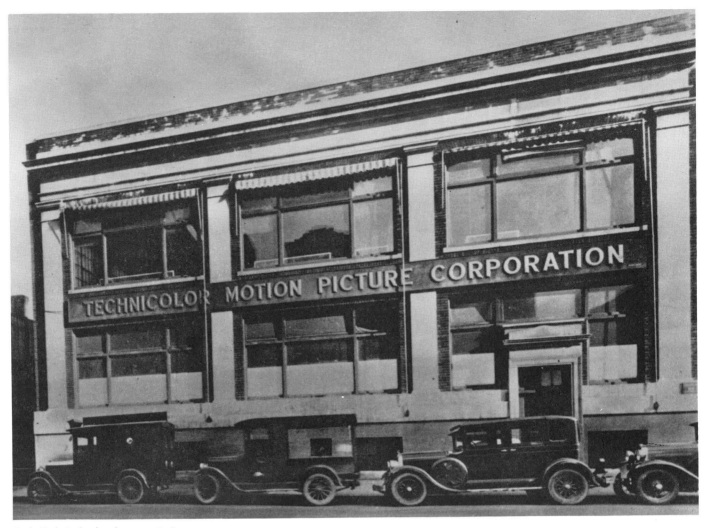

Early Technicolor headquarters in Boston.

of tests had been run, problems noted and refined.

Dr. Comstock recorded an interesting episode that took place during this period. He had just privately shown a sample run of film to Edgar Selwyn, the successful Broadway stage producer who, with his brother Archibald, had joined with Samuel Goldfish (later Goldwyn, a contraction of the two family names) in the formation of Goldwyn Pictures in 1916.

"You know what the public wants," Dr. Comstock told him, "and we want to get your comments and advice regarding these pictures."

Mr. Selwyn replied, "I would be glad to help, but if I really knew what the public wanted I would have nearly all the money in the world in a few years. But I know what you mean. Perhaps I know a little more than you do." The producer paused for a moment, then went on. "If you want me to be frank, this is what I think. The drama is the center of human interest, not flower gardens and dresses. The human being is the center of the drama. The face is the center of the human being. And the eyes are the center of the face. If a process is not sharp enough to show clearly the whites

of a person's eyes at a reasonable distance, it isn't any good no matter what it is. Your pictures need to be a little sharper."

"All right," Dr. Comstock said, "we'll make them sharper. But what about the color?"

Mr. Selwyn smiled. "The color is better than it need be. Your process is a two-color-component process. Some day you will have to add a third color component but not now. Forget about improving the colors for the present. You have troubles enough."

By 1922, the Technicolor process had reached a level that "will surprise many people," as Dr. Comstock put it. The doctor's confidence was bolstered by the fact that, while only two colors (red and green) were being used, they each contributed roughly half of the whole spectrum of color—the precise split arranged so that mixing the two in the right proportions showed a very pleasing flesh tint. Too, he was satisfied that the sharpness problem had been corrected. He no longer worried about seeing "the whites of a person's eyes at a reasonable distance."

Encouragement came from another source as well.

Anna May Wong in *The Toll Of The Sea*, first Technicolor production filmed in Hollywood, 1922.

Mr. Jerome, the lawyer and investor, had contacted Dr. Kalmus to introduce him to three men who were fascinated with the idea of color. They balked at putting any money into the project but offered their assistance should it ever be needed. The trio included movie magnates Marcus Loew and Nicholas M. Schenck of Loew's, Inc., and Joseph M. Schenck.

The alliance could not have been more timely. Technicolor was making plans to produce its second film, and its first in the new process. The three new associates immediately made good their word. It was decided to film the picture in Hollywood under the general supervision of Joseph M. Schenck. A photoplay called *The Toll of the Sea*, a Chinese version of *Madam Butterfly*, was selected. Thanks to Mr. Schenck, Technicolor was given the use of his studio's facilities, a director (Chester Franklin), and even the star of the picture (Anna May Wong)—without charge.

One of the greatest difficulties encountered during the making of *The Toll of the Sea*, according to Dr. Comstock, was to get the actors, including Miss Wong and male lead Kenneth Harlan, to treat their work

seriously. As on the first production, the players' attitude was, "This picture will never reach the screen."

But reach the screen it did, Nicholas Schenck having arranged for the release through the Metro Film Company. The premiere showing was held at the Rialto Theater in New York during the week of November 26, 1922. (Insufficient laboratory space in Boston, coupled with the great demand for bookings, created a slowdown in quantity prints, delaying the general release in the United States until the following year.)

The Toll of the Sea was shown in thousands of theaters across the country and received high praise from critics everywhere, among them the esteemed artists Maxfield Parrish and Charles Dana Gibson. The general manager of Metro wrote, "I would lay great stress on the fact that *The Toll of the Sea* has been universally accepted as the perfect motion picture in natural colors." (Dr. Comstock, recalling the comment years later, said, "Of course, any really new product is a novelty and the public is far less critical at the start than it is sure to be years later.")

Every phase of the color work in the film was carefully watched by executives of the industry. Adolph Zukor of Famous Players-Lasky Corporation sent a note of congratulations. Producer-director Rex Ingram, who was in the midst of producing *The Prisoner of Zenda* for Metro Pictures, wired Mr. Loew for permission to scrap all the black-and-white scenes already shot on the picture and begin again in Technicolor. D.W. Griffith expressed an interest in color for a proposed version of *Faust*. And Douglas Fairbanks telephoned about producing a feature some day.

The "novelty" proved its earning power, grossing more than $250,000, of which Technicolor received approximately $165,000. "Our first adventure in Hollywood seemed successful," wrote Dr. Kalmus. "Thus far we had made only one feature and several inserts (sequences for Cecil B. DeMille's 1923 version of *The Ten Commandments*, shot by Technicolor's Ray Rennahan, which the director agreed to use only after seeing them). We were told that with prints as good as we were manufacturing, if offered at eight cents per foot, the industry would rush to color."

Cost was a major drawback, however. Technicolor had no adequate means of giving rush print service and the company was charging twenty cents per foot for release prints. But steps were being taken to help correct the situation. Plant Number Two (buildings were designated by number as constructed) was being built in Boston in a building adjoining the Pilot Plant.

The new facility would be able to handle approximately one million feet of prints per month. And in April, 1923, a team of Technicolor's top technicians ("Doc" Willat, J.A. Ball and G.A. Cave) was sent to the West Coast to establish a small laboratory and photographic unit. A rented building in Hollywood served as headquarters.

Despite Technicolor's efforts to make its services more available, and marketable at a more realistic rate, other problems began to surface. Theaters around the country began to report on the mounting complaints of their projectionists. Technicolor's film, actually two films cemented back to back to give the combinations of colors, "cupped" as it sped through the projectors—first one way, then the other. The men in the booths tired of the constant adjustments necessary to keep the picture in focus on the screen. Another problem concerned working conditions on the set. Slow-speed film required high-intensity lighting to capture color. Actors not only had to endure the heat and glare of the sun but banks of baking kleig lights, as well.

These objections failed to discourage one major Hollywood producer. In November, 1923, Jesse L. Lasky and Dr. Kalmus agreed on the terms of a contract between Technicolor Motion Picture Corporation and Famous Players-Lasky Corporation for the production of Zane Grey's *Wanderer of the Wasteland*—to be shot out-of-doors without artificial lighting. Dr. Kalmus related:

We were told by Mr. Lasky, that they had appropriated not more for this picture than they would have for the same picture in black-and-white. Also, that the time schedule allowed for photographing was identical with what it would have been in black-and-white. The photography was to be done by our cameras in the hands of our technical staff, following a budget and a time schedule laid out for them by Famous Players. Rush prints and the quality of negatives were to be checked by them each day.

During the six weeks of photography our entire staff worked from early morning to late at night, including Sundays and holidays. At one time we were accumulating negatives which we did not dare to develop because of inadequate facilities in our rented laboratory. A few of us in Technicolor carried the terrorizing thought that there was no positive assurance that we would finally obtain commercial negative, and that the entire Famous Players investment might be lost. However, Mr. Lasky was not permitted to share that doubt. His confidence and help during the darkest hours were really marvelous and finally the cut negative emerged satisfactorily. We delivered approximately one hundred and seventy-five prints which were shown in several thousand theaters over the country.

Nevertheless, there were reasons why we could not obtain a volume of business. Every producer in Hollywood knew that the first important production by the Technicolor process under actual motion picture conditions and not controlled by the Technicolor company, had just been completed by Famous Players-Lasky Corporation. A considerable group of producers expressed themselves as interested, but were waiting to see the outcome. Another group believed the process to be practical and might have paid our then price of fifteen cents a foot, but considered it impracticable to send the daily work to Boston for rush prints.

Striving to make the services of his company as convenient as possible, Dr. Kalmus approved construction of a small plant at 1006 North Cole Avenue in Hollywood. The new building served primarily for the purpose of developing negatives, making rush prints, and providing a California headquarters for Technicolor.

Wanderer of the Wasteland, starring Jack Holt, Noah Beery, Richard Neill, and Billie Dove, provided an enormous boost for the Technicolor process with the movie-makers and the general public. Aside from the expense, Mr. Lasky expressed genuine pleasure with the new dimension and all that it brought to his production. "I particularly remember the dramatic use we made of color in one scene where the hero, tracking down the wounded villain who has concealed himself in a gold-mine stamp mill, notices a trickle of muddy water flowing from the mill sluiceway slowly turning red—and it thus led to the hideout of his quarry."

Wanderer of The Wasteland, shot in 1924, provided an enormous boost for early two-color Technicolor and prompted *Variety* to note: "Color is the biggest step in pictures since the close-up was first used." (Above) Anna Q. Nilsson, Gail Patrick and Edward Ellis in the 1935 remake.

The Technicolor plant at 1006 North Cole in Hollywood.

Cytherea (1924), with Lewis Stone, featured two Technicolor dream sequences. The film marked Technicolor's first experience in photographing an interior set with artificial light.

Neither *The Toll of the Sea, Wanderer of the Wasteland,* or any of the sequences made until the middle of 1924, had given the Technicolor people any experience photographing an interior set on an artificially lighted stage. Everything, to date, had been filmed out-of-doors with the aid of natural lighting. The staff was therefore enthusiastic when the company received a contract to shoot two dream sequences for the Samuel Goldwyn feature *Cytherea.*

The film was shot in Hollywood for First National Pictures under the direction of George Fitzmaurice. In its review of May 26, 1924, the *New York Times* said of *Cytherea's* color: "There are some exquisite sequences of color photography in which one enjoys the sight of the varied hues and tints of Cuban costumes and scenery . . . These are not only beautifully photographed, but they are introduced most realistically . . ."

Technicolor's first experience with indoor shooting was termed a success. Still, the studios continued to be cautious. The company was currently involved in only one production, M-G-M's original *Ben-Hur,* filming in

33

Technicolor sequences were filmed for *Ben-Hur*, one of the early lavish productions, starring Carmel Myers and Ramon Novarro, 1926. The final release print contained little of the tinted footage, however.

Rome. Six men and four cameras had been sent overseas. But upon release in 1926 the feature contained little of that footage. It was a puzzling situation. Hollywood was churning out hundreds of films, yet few producers were willing to take a chance with color. The movie town was still young. The area was bustling with energetic, bright people filled with fresh ideas. Everyone wanted to be first with a new approach, to build a name and a reputation.

What could be more naturally suited for motion pictures than color? While black-and-white films seemed to satisfy most of the demands of the moviegoers and movie-makers, Dr. Kalmus knew that there was a vast audience that had yet to be exposed to his product—and he leveled part of the blame directly at the studios. "From my own point of view," he stated, "they have never yet seriously undertaken any color work. By seriously, I mean with adequate preparation by people who are ambitious to do great work and who are at the same time sympathetic."

The doctor also felt that Technicolor needed a major personality to endorse it, one that would lend stature and marquee value. The movies had established a long list of powerful names: Gloria Swanson, Mary Pickford, Douglas Fairbanks, Rudolph Valentino, Colleen Moore, Harold Lloyd, Buster Keaton, Charlie Chaplin, William S. Hart, Tom Mix, John Gilbert, Pola Negri. And more. Trying to lure any one of them into a color production would not be easy, Dr. Kalmus knew. But the fact remained: Technicolor needed a star.

That hurdle was not as awesome as anticipated. In early 1925, Dr. Kalmus received a phone call in Boston from one of the greatest stars of silent films, Douglas

Fairbanks. Mr. Fairbanks indicated that he had found a vehicle, *The Black Pirate*, and wanted to make good his promise of two years earlier. He had the idea, the doctor reported:

that the screen had never caught and reflected the real spirit of piracy as one finds it in the books of Robert Louis Stevenson, or the paintings of Howard Pyle, and that he could catch it by the use of color. He said, 'This ingredient has been tried and rejected countless times. It has always met overwhelming objections. Not only has the process of color motion picture photography never been perfected, but there has been a grave doubt whether, even if properly developed, it would be applied without detracting more than it added to motion picture technique. The argument has been that it would tire and distract the eye, take attention from acting and facial expression, blur and confuse the action. In short, it has been felt that it would militate against the simplicity and directness which motion pictures derive from unobtrusive black-and-white. These conventional doubts have been entertained, I think, because no one has taken the trouble to dissipate them. A similar objection was raised, no doubt, when the innovation of scenery was introduced on the English stage—that it would distract attention from the actors. Personally, I could not imagine piracy without color . . .

Early Technicolor screening room, ca 1920s.

Douglas Fairbanks as *The Black Pirate*, 1926.

Adventure on the high seas: *The Black Pirate*.

The Black Pirate was to cost one million dollars, a staggering sum for the production of a motion picture in 1926. Mr. Fairbanks' attorneys, expressing natural concern, asked for a guarantee that Technicolor could deliver not only prints but satisfactory ones. A mutually satisfying agreement was reached when the engineering firm of Kalmus, Comstock & Wescott, Inc., assented to deliver prints in the event that Technicolor failed.

As production began, according to Dr. Kalmus, there was "great discussion as to the color key in which this picture would be pitched. We made test prints for Mr. Fairbanks at six different color levels, from a level with slightly more color than black-and-white, to the most garish rendering of which the Technicolor process was then capable." The star was taking no chances on this production. He spent $125,000 shooting over fifty thousand feet of film, over a four month period, to test color keys, make-up (his co-star, Billie Dove, was selected because her complexion and coloring photographed so well in *Wanderer of the Wasteland*), fabrics—and even locations.

Douglas Fairbanks originally set to work on the shore of Catalina Island and off the shore on a specially constructed pirate ship (with four of the seven Technicolor cameras then in existence) to capture moods after the manner of impressionistic paintings.

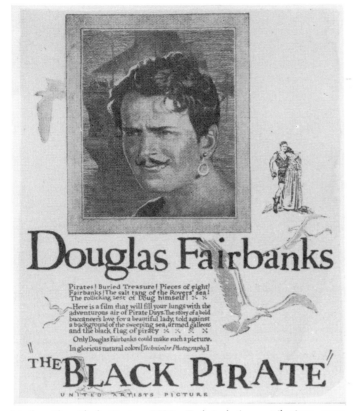

Douglas Fairbanks

Pirates! Buried Treasure! Pieces of eight!
Fairbanks! The salt tang of the Rovers' sea!
The rollicking zest of Doug himself! ✕ ✕

~Here is a film that will fill your lungs with the
adventurous air of Pirate Days. The story of a bold
buccaneer's love for a beautiful lady, told against
a background of the sweeping sea, armed galleons
and the black flag of piracy ✕ ✕ ✕ ✕

Only Douglas Fairbanks could make such a picture.
In glorious natural colors [*Technicolor Photography*]

THE "BLACK PIRATE"

UNITED ARTISTS PICTURE

Ad for *The Black Pirate*, 1926. Technicolor's contributions were downplayed in favor of star and story.

But much of that film was rejected because the backgrounds did not photograph to Mr. Fairbanks' satisfaction. Instead, most of the picture was shot on the United Artists lot, including, as Dr. Kalmus expressed it, "some of the most realistic pirate scenes aboard ship . . . all being done on a tremendous model afloat in an artificial pool which is rocked by mechanically produced waves." Henry Sharp, Mr. Fairbanks' cinematographer, worked closely with Technicolor's own cameraman, George Cave.

During the production, Dr. Kalmus kept in constant touch with his eastern office. "No description which I have had and passed on of *The Black Pirate* pictures," he wrote to Dr. Troland, "has been adequate to express how really remarkable they are. Everybody concerned is just raving about them and my own enthusiasm is beyond anything I can express. Doug and his whole organization think this picture will be epoch making."

With the completion of *The Black Pirate*, all of the key elements Dr. Kalmus felt necessary for a truly exceptional box office attraction had come together. Now, there was nothing left to do but wait for the release of the film.

4 Pirates, Vagabonds and Kings

The Black Pirate was an immediate triumph. Audiences raved, theater receipts soared, and reviewers were unanimous in their praise of Douglas Fairbanks' "glorious chromatic production." Following the film's formal opening on March 8, 1926, at New York's Selwyn Theater, attended by Mr. Fairbanks, Mary Pickford and other celebrities, the *New York Times* reported: "The unrivalled beauty of the different episodes is mindful of the paintings of the old masters."

More importantly, the still-new Technicolor process was technically applauded. "There is no sudden fringing or sparking of colors," noted the reviewer, "the outlines being always clearly defined without a single instance of the dreaded trembling 'rainbow' impinging itself upon the picture."

From its initial success, *The Black Pirate* was hailed as "another stride forward for the screen." But for Technicolor, as Dr. Kalmus was quick to admit, the film became one of the company's biggest headaches. The New York showing had been supervised by trained technicians in a controlled situation. But once prints of the film were released to outlying theaters, to be projected by virtually untrained operators, troubles mounted. Suddenly, word was out that the film was continually jumping out of focus.

It was the same old problem, "cupping," that had plagued the release of *Wanderer of the Wasteland* two years before. Only now, because of the broad distribution of *The Black Pirate*, it appeared to be more serious. Teams of men were sent about the country,

rushing new prints to theaters and returning the damaged ones to the laboratory in Boston where they were put through a debuckling process and reshipped. Because these prints were temporarily satisfactory, the popularity of *The Black Pirate* was not diminished. And while, with special attention, executives at Technicolor realized they could operate in this manner for a picture or two, it was clear that their process was not a commercial success. That point reached home even more sharply when both Jesse L. Lasky and Douglas Fairbanks (who was personally upset over the too-dark night scenes in his film) reported to Dr. Kalmus, "We have concluded not to do more Technicolor pictures for the present."

The final blow landed in early 1927. Dr. Kalmus had made a special trip to the West Coast to meet with Louis B. Mayer and Irving Thalberg at M-G-M. He memoed back to Dr. Troland:

Metro wants to do *Rose Marie* in Technicolor. At the present moment they have three writers at work endeavoring to make a real subject of it. Dozens of questions came up regarding the treatment which they answer in conferences held twice a week, but the final decision has not been reached. On our part, various technical questions arise, the last of which has to do with the amount of snow Technicolor scenes can stand in the background and foreground. I have just been running some snow shots for them in their projection rooms. A considerable portion of *Rose Marie* will be laid in the snow fields and the test snow shots we made show up very beautifully. Not twenty minutes ago Thalberg told me that he definitely had in mind to have the picture completed to show at their convention on May 1.

Rose Marie missed the target date but it was released the following year featuring Joan Crawford and James Murray—in black-and-white.

The doctor and his backers were back where they started, with a multi-million dollar investment and no customers. Clearly, their existing color system had not been accepted. It was now imperative for the company to come up with still another process, one with both color component layers on one side of the film instead of one on each side.

Dr. Kalmus once more found himself appearing before the directors of the company to appeal for more money. This time, however, he was not after financial aid for new cameras, printers, and research salaries. Armed with encouraging word on his laboratory's development of the sought-after new two-color process ("Technicolor Process Number Three") and advice from Nicholas Schenck, who felt the company should produce a picture itself to prove both quality and costs, Dr. Kalmus urged funds for production.

"When they asked me what I knew about producing a motion picture," he later recalled, "I frankly told them nothing, but at least I could start from scratch without some of the fixed ideas and prejudices concerning color that some of the Hollywood producers seemed to have accumulated."

Dr. Kalmus wanted to make short subjects, not primarily to make money but to prove to the industry that (1) there was nothing mysterious about the operation of Technicolor cameras (2) cameramen trained to work with black-and-white film could easily adapt to color (3) rush prints could be delivered promptly and (4) the job could be done efficiently and economically. A series of historical dramas, the doctor felt, would best serve this purpose.

Dr. Leonard Troland, his esteemed associate, totally disagreed as to the thematic approach and spelled out his opposition in detail.

It is obvious that we are making subjects to sell to the public for the purpose of amusing them and that our main purpose is not uplift or education. It, therefore, seems to me that we must not be high-brow in our selections and that our pictures should appeal in a fairly simple way to primitive instincts, such as sex, fear, laughter, etc. Becoming acquainted with American history is certainly not a fundamental motive of this sort, although the appeal to patriotic emotion may work under certain circumstances.

I am afraid that we are an academic or high-brow organization . . . Anything which we feel is beautiful is apt to be a flop with the public. Isn't it the best business judgement to do the old stuff that we know the public will buy, rather than try to set new standards in any domain except photography?

I should like to see us make a series of two-reel comedies of a very ordinary type so far as action goes, but Ziegfeldized to the absolute limit that the censorship will stand. Then you will be playing color's highest card so far as box office value is concerned. I am as sure of this as any psychological proposition I would dare to lay down, because I know that the high-brows will buy as well as the low-brows when it comes to sex appeal, and color has a great deal to add here. People want a laugh or a kick and not tears or historical instruction. The latter is what they desire for their children, not themselves.

I should strongly recommend that we experiment with at least one subject which is distinctly of the type which we as a high-brow group would shun and would blush to sign our names to. Such an experiment will, in my opinion, be the best box office success of all.

Dr. Kalmus listened but held firm. The first of the Technicolor two-reelers debuted during 1927. Called *The Flag*, it starred Francis X. Bushman as George Washington and Enid Bennett as Betsy Ross and told

The new Technicolor two-color camera, ca 1926.

Otto Matiesen and Agnes Ayers as Napoleon and Josephine in *The Lady of Victories,* 1927.

the creation of Old Glory. As a companion piece to Charlie Chaplin's successful black-and-white production of *The Circus*, its favorable reviews surprised no one, least of all Dr. Kalmus, who remarked, "George M. Cohan probably never produced anything more certain of applause than when George Washington unfurled the first American flag in glowing color." Immediately after its release, the doctor received a congratulatory memo from Leonard Troland, to which he replied, "I am so tremendously pleased that you liked the little picture so well and thank you for your earlier encouraging expressions with regard to it."

The Flag was followed by *Buffalo Bill's Last Fight* and *The Lady of Victories* (originally *More Than A Queen*). The latter film, an episode in the life of Napoleon and Josephine, starred Agnes Ayers and Otto Matiesen. It was factually weak but considered the finest example of color to date. In all, Technicolor produced twelve films in its *Great Events* series. The

survival of the company has been credited to the experience gained in the making of these pictures.

Despite positive nationwide reaction to the series, the studios continued to be color shy. After all, as friends and associates made clear, the films were only short subjects. Again, Nicholas Schenck stepped in. Produce a feature film, he suggested, and Metro-Goldwyn-Mayer would distribute it.

Since its release in 1923, Dr. Kalmus had been impressed with the black-and-white production of *The Covered Wagon,* a story of love, survival, and the conquering of a continent. Why not produce a love story about the Vikings, he reasoned, one with the epic qualities of fighting mutiny and storms while conquering an ocean? Jack Cunningham, who wrote *The Covered Wagon* and a number of the *Great Event* shorts, was hired to write an original screenplay for *The Viking* to star Donald Crisp and Pauline Starke. When the final reel was processed, Technicolor had spent

39

The Lady of Victories.

$325,000 on the production—and it showed. Irving Thalberg, M-G-M's wizard, liked the film so much that he decided to buy it for his studio and reimburse Technicolor for its expenses.

With the release of *The Viking* (1928), two major faults plagued the film. Although it was the first Technicolor motion picture to have synchronized music and sound effects, it was one of the last productions without audible dialogue. The second problem, and probably the most serious, was attributed to the very authenticity of the film. True to character, Leif Erickson, the Viking hero, had a long curling mustache. American audiences, at that time, preferred their idols to be smooth shaven. More than once, critics noted, the entire screen appeared to be filled with Viking whiskers.

The film's faults aside, *The Viking* was heralded as an excellent color job and opened a few influential eyes. Technicolor had again proven itself and, in the process, demonstrated that decreased costs were possible. Warner Bros. and M-G-M began planning their own short subjects in Technicolor, to be produced on a regular basis, and scheduled color sequences for two important films, *The Broadway Melody* and *The Desert Song*. The powers at Paramount, more than satisfied

Donald Crisp as *The Viking*, 1928.

Pauline Starke in *The Viking*.

with the results they had seen, signed for a feature-length production called *Redskin*. The studios, at last, were becoming color-conscious.

It was up to Jack L. Warner, however, to take the plunge on a grand scale. Warner, whose brilliant experiments with talking pictures turned Warner Bros. from a company that made $30,000 in 1927 into one that earned over $17 million in 1929, was naturally receptive to another new cinema idea. Once he caught sight of the extra profits that color conferred to *The Desert Song*, he signed contracts calling for more than twenty full-color features. The package included *On With The Show*, the first all-talking, all-color picture, and *Gold Diggers of Broadway*, a movie gem which grossed over $3.5 million (the then-reigning boxoffice champion was Warner's *The Singing Fool*, with a top of $5 million).

Just as Jack Warner's success with the "talkies" led other studios to abandon the silent film, his color

creations started a new trend. Producers swarmed upon Dr. Kalmus and his facilities, waving cash and demanding footage. "As evidence of the increased color-mindedness throughout the industry," the doctor recorded, "Technicolor had contracts for the ten months beginning March, 1929, covering the photography and delivery of prints of the footage equivalent of approximately seventeen feature-length productions. This required a doubling of the Hollywood capacity which was accomplished in August, 1929. For the year 1930, Technicolor had closed contracts for thirty-six feature-length productions . . ."

During this boom period the company was pressed to such an extent that cameras operated day and night. Laboratory crews, not equipped to handle one-tenth of the volume they actually turned out, worked three eight-hour shifts. At one time, the extremely delicate process of printing the film was carried on amid the debris of falling bricks and the roar of riveters' guns in a

41

If rainbows were black and white

Suppose that, since the world began, rainbows had been black and white! And flowers; and trees; Alpine sunsets; the Grand Canyon and the Bay of Naples; the eyes and lips and hair of pretty girls!

Then suppose that, one day, a new kind of rainbow arched the sky with all the colors of the spectrum—that a hitherto undreamt-of sunset spread a mantle of rich gold over the hills.

In "Song of the West" Warner Brothers present all the magnificent beauty of nature, in Technicolor.

Literally, that is what happened to the motion picture screen. Technicolor has painted for the millions of motion picture "fans" a new world — the world as it really is, in all its natural color.

Yesterday is an old story in the annals of the "movies." For yesterday motion pictures were silent. And...yesterday motion pictures were black-and-white.

Today you hear voices, singing, the playing of great orchestras. Today you see the stars, the costumes, the settings—in natural color — in Technicolor.

DOLORES COSTELLO, lovely Warner Brothers star, is even more charming than ever, in Technicolor.

Technicolor *is* natural color

SOME OF THE TECHNICOLOR PRODUCTIONS

DIXIANA, with Bebe Daniels (Radio); GLORIFYING the AMERICAN GIRL, with Mary Eaton. Eddie Cantor, Helen Morgan, Rudy Vallee in revue (Paramount); GOLDEN DAWN, with Walter Woolf, Vivienne Segal (Warner Bros.); HOLD EVERYTHING, with Winnie Lightner, Georges Carpentier, Joe E. Brown (Warner Bros.); PARAMOUNT on PARADE, all-star revue (Paramount); The ROGUE'S SONG, with Lawrence Tibbett, Catherine Dale Owen (Metro-Goldwyn-Mayer); SON of the GODS, starring Richard Barthelmess (First National); SONG of the FLAME, with Bernice Claire, Alexander Gray (First National); SONG of the WEST, with John Boles, Vivienne Segal (Warner Bros.), The VAGABOND KING, starring Dennis King (Paramount); BRIDE of the REGIMENT, with Vivienne Segal (First National); UNDER A TEXAS MOON, with Frank Fay, Noah Beery, Myrna Loy, Armida (Warner Bros.).

The Technicolor Corporation promoted its own product in consumer magazines while studio ad departments continued to minimize the color process' lure, 1930.

"Onward, onward swords against the foe! Forward, forward the lily banners go!"

IT lives again!—the thundering throb of "Song of the Vagabonds," in the glorious golden voice of Dennis King, star of Paramount's all-color musical romance, "The Vagabond King"! Once the greatest triumph of the Broadway stage, now the supreme triumph of the talking, singing screen—Paramount's New Show World. ¶ Blazing with gorgeous Technicolor throughout . . . vibrant with stirring melodies . . . packed with thrills and adventure, excitement, romance! ¶ With Broadway's favorite romantic stars, Dennis King and Jeanette MacDonald in the leading roles, and a great cast. The New Show World of Paramount at its most brilliant height! ¶ And only Paramount, with matchless resources and unrivaled man-power, could unfold before your eyes this glittering panorama of song, color and romance in all the blazing glory of the original, the greatest of all musical romances! ¶ Don't miss the outstanding eye-and-ear treat of the year. Ask your Theatre Manager now when he is planning to show "The Vagabond King". *"If it's a Paramount Picture it's the best show in town!"*

DENNIS KING
"THE VAGABOND KING"
WITH
JEANETTE MacDONALD

Warner Oland and O. P. Heggie and cast of 1000. Ludwig Berger Production. From "If I Were King" by Justin Huntley McCarthy and "The Vagabond King" by William H. Post, Brian Hooker and Rudolph Friml.

Paramount Pictures

PARAMOUNT FAMOUS LASKY CORP., ADOLPH ZUKOR, PRES., PARAMOUNT BLDG., NEW YORK CITY

On With The Show (1929), the first all talking, all color motion picture, featuring the future Dagwood Bumstead, Arthur Lake.

A portion of Technicolor's expanding Hollywood facilities, 1930.

Dr. Kalmus at his desk in Hollywood, 1930.

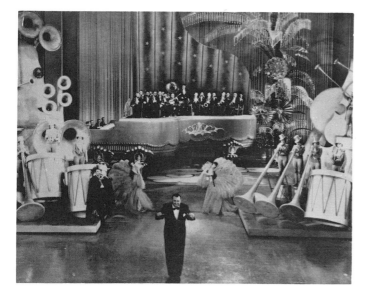

Paul Whiteman and his orchestra in *King Of Jazz*, 1930.

Maurice Chevalier and showgirls in *Paramount On Parade*, 1930.

The wedding number in *King Of Jazz*.

building in which one wall had been torn away to permit enlargement (because of the highly explosive nitrate film being used, many of the new walls were constructed of massive steel and concrete, eighteen inches thick in spots). Hundreds of new men were hastily trained to do work which properly required years of training. Many features were made which Dr. Kalmus personally counselled against, despite the fact that Technicolor's crowded schedules called for a deposit of $25,000. During this peak, the company had $1.6 million in cash payments on future contracts.

While Technicolor's facilities were being strained, so were the eyes and pocketbooks of movie fans across the country. America was in the throes of the Great Depression but theater screens offered a few hours of bright entertainment and, for the first time, a chance to see many of the top stars of the day in thrilling color—the beautiful Jeanette MacDonald in *The Vagabond King*, Paul Whiteman in *King of Jazz* (the first Technicolor film to win an Academy Award), Charles "Buddy" Rogers and Nancy Carroll in *Follow Thru*, Marilyn Miller in *Sally*, John Boles and Vivienne Segal in *Song of the West*, Irene Bordoni in *Paris* and Eddie Cantor in *Whoopee*.

The good early pictures were succeeded by mediocre and bad ones. Even in normal times and under optimum working conditions, the two-color process had serious weaknesses. Limited to shades of red and green, and their combinations, many compromises had to be made. Blue and various other hues, could not be achieved; therefore, outdoor scenes required camera angles that did not show large areas of sky or water. When it became necessary to photograph those areas, audiences saw them at dusk or dawn—or so they imagined—with the available warmer tones prevailing. Trying for added realism, dramatic effects became commonplace and many films took on a mystical quality.

Perhaps one of the most glaring casualties of two-color Technicolor can be seen in a color sequence from the movie *Irene*, starring Colleen Moore. According to producer-director Mervyn LeRoy, who had worked as a gag writer on the film, a major problem was encountered in shooting the *Alice Blue Gown* number. "Everything possible was tried to make the dress appear as blue but there was nothing anyone could do about it. Audiences had to settle for a pale green."

Technicolor alone could not be blamed for the declining quality of color feature films. The producers themselves had very little color sense, either from the standpoint of arranging esthetic compositions or acquiring a tint technique. Hollywood had gone "color mad" but little else had really changed. No one seemed to realize that a color film is simply not a black-and-white film shot in color. Everyone at the studios had grown up in a black-and-white world and did things in a black-and-white way.

There was more than casual concern at Technicolor. At the Boston lab, Dr. Troland memoed George Cave: "We are certainly having the matter of poor quality rubbed into us here. Some critics think we would better shut down on color for a year, until we get it ready for use . . . Metro particularly emphasizes the idea that we are putting out a lot of stuff which is not doing us any good."

Audiences were now growing weary of the increasing number of second-rate films with poor stories—a monotony of musicals and period pieces—that were to be saved, hopefully, by (less than perfect) color. Realizing the shortcomings of his two-color process, Dr. Kalmus reported to Technicolor's directors: "The fact that we have signed this large volume of business on the basis of our present two-color process has not altered, in my opinion, the fact that the quality of this two-color output is not sufficiently good to meet with universal approval, and hence cannot be regarded as ultimate. . . . Consequently, I feel urgently that our drive to put our process on a three-color basis as soon as possible should not in the least be abated."

Dr. Kalmus' remarks couldn't have been more timely. With dwindling theater attendance (receipts for mid-1931 were the lowest in fifteen years), the producers soon realized that Technicolor was not a cure-all for the industry. Contracts were canceled, guarantee money was refunded, and production slowed again to a few short subjects. Color pictures had once more fallen into disfavor. Technicolor, however, was not sitting quietly in its newly expanded Hollywood plant. A revolutionary new color process was in the final stages of development. The only question now was, would anyone be receptive to it?

5 All the Colors of the Rainbow

By May, 1932, Technicolor had completed its first three-component camera and had one unit of its main processing plant, shifted the previous year from Boston to Hollywood, equipped to handle a moderate amount of three-color printing. Though the new process was more expensive (cameras alone cost $30,000 each to build), it reproduced faithfully any shade or hue, indoors or out, and for the first time color movies were true and realistic. "Not only is the accuracy of tone greatly improved," Dr. Kalmus noted, "but definition is markedly better. The difference between the three-component process and the previous two-component processes is truly extraordinary."

Dr. Kalmus was aware that he could not offer his new process to one customer without offering it to all, which required many more cameras and the conversion of a greater portion of the laboratory. Too, he was continually haunted by the fact that the studios were still burning over their recent adventures into color, and wanted no part of any new product no matter how extraordinary it was.

To allow time to become better equipped (the company had learned its lesson only a few short years before), and to prove the new process beyond any doubt, the doctor sought first to try it out in the cartoon field. No cartoonist, however, wanted color. The general feeling was that animated features were good enough in black-and-white and that, of all the departments of production, cartoons could least afford the added expense.

Undaunted, Dr. Kalmus continued making the rounds of artists and animators. His dedication finally paid off. Walt Disney felt that color might make some sense in his *Silly Symphonies*, an umbrella title for a continuing series of light, whimsical fantasies. Although Disney had never used the two-color process in any of his creations, he was so impressed with the new three-color that he openly stated, "I wanted to cheer." His brother, Roy, was less enthusiastic. As financial guardian, Roy Disney felt it his duty to point out the likely hazards involved with color animation and even went so far as to try and enlist support from influential associates in an effort to discourage Walt. United Artists, distributor of the Disney shorts, shared that concern. The studio would distribute Disney's product, if he could produce one, but would not advance him any money.

Walt Disney had been working on a cartoon called *Flowers and Trees*, the nonsensical romantic adventures of two young saplings and a cantankerous old stump, when Dr. Kalmus approached him. Although nearly half the film had been completed in black-and-white, he decided to scrap the footage and have his artists begin again—this time in full color. Roy was appalled, not only at the total waste of good product but at the thought of adding another ten thousand dollars, at least, to the cartoon's cost.

In late 1932, *Flowers and Trees* premiered at Grauman's Chinese Theater in Hollywood as a companion piece to Irving Thalberg's production of

Romance blossoms between two lovers in Walt Disney's Silly Symphony, *Flowers and Trees*, the first film released in full color Technicolor.

The grand matron of the forest leads a flock of birds in song in *Flowers and Trees*. The milestone cartoon won Disney his first Academy Award in 1932.

Eugene O'Neill's *Strange Interlude*. Despite its fragile storyline and colors that tended to be somewhat washed out by today's standards, the new Technicolor turned the cartoon into a valuable property. *Flowers and Trees* became the first Disney production to win an Oscar (Best Cartoon of 1931-32).* The success of this venture and the even greater success of the all-color *Three Little Pigs*, which earned another Academy Award the following year, told Disney his instincts had been correct. Technicolor was a natural for his cartoons.

It wasn't too long before Walt Disney had signed a contract to operate on a strictly color basis, producing both the *Silly Symphonies* and *Mickey Mouse* cartoons in Technicolor. In return for Disney's pioneering with the new process, Dr. Kalmus gave him a three-year exclusive for the cartoon field. What originally appeared to be a smart move turned out to be nearly fatal.

*The Academy also recognized Technicolor's contribution by honoring the company with a Class II (Technical) Award for its Color Cartoon Process.

Disney's 1933 Technicolor success, *Three Little Pigs*.

Once the popularity of Disney's color creations had been proved, other producers began to approach Dr. Kalmus for film for their cartoons. Having to turn them down put the Technicolor chief in an awkward position. How, for example, could he refuse M-G-M the use of Technicolor? Doing so would naturally influence Mr. Mayer's decision to use the process in lengthier productions. And feature films were the real goal of the Technicolor company.

With Walt Disney's consent, the three-year exclusive was reduced to one. In the meantime, the studios and cartoonists would be allowed use of the previous two-color process. Under proper supervision and handling, everyone agreed, the old system would be satisfactory, particularly for animation. The agreement also gave Technicolor's outmoded equipment a second lease on life. The company had thirty two-color cameras on hand, all standing idle. The deal made with Disney's competition extended their usefulness one extra year.

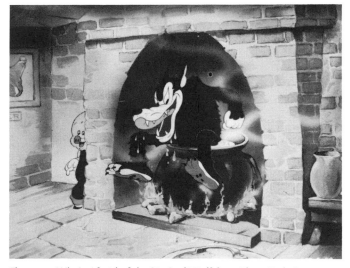

The song, *Who's Afraid of the Big Bad Wolf* from *Three Little Pigs*, swept America and helped dispel the Depression blues.

While the producers willingly admitted they had been wrong about color in cartoons, they were still certain they were right about features. Whenever Dr. Kalmus sought to break the barrier, he was asked, "How much more will it cost to produce a feature in three-color Technicolor than in black-and-white?"

His reply was simple. "You have all seen Disney's *Funny Bunnies*," he would tell them.* "You remember the huge rainbow circling across the screen to the ground and you remember the funny bunnies drawing the color of the rainbow into their paint pails and splashing the Easter eggs. You will admit that it was marvelous entertainment. Now I will ask you how much more did it cost Mr. Disney to produce that entertainment in color than it would have in black-and-white?" The answer was that it could not have been done at any cost in monochrome.

Having made his point, the doctor would then draw a similar analogy with regard to feature production, telling his skeptics:

If a script has been conceived, planned and written for black-and-white, it should not be done at all in color. The story should be chosen and the scenario written with color in mind from the start so that by its use effects are obtained, moods created, beauty and personalities emphasized, and the drama enhanced. Color should flow from sequence to sequence, supporting and giving impulse to the drama, becoming an integral part of it and not something super-added. The production cost question should be, what is additional cost for color per unit of entertainment and not per foot of negative? It needn't cost any more, of course.

The producers listened but they didn't buy.

Another breakthrough came when Merian C. Cooper and John Hay (Jock) Whitney began to show a practical interest in Technicolor. Mr. Cooper was a noted motion picture director (*King Kong*), producer (*Grass, Chang, The Four Feathers*), cinematographer (*Gow, the Head Hunter*) and former production chief at RKO-Radio Pictures. Mr. Whitney was a horse fancier, pilot, Chairman of the Board of Freeport Texas Company (sulphur producers), and the cousin of wealthy Cornelius (Sonny) Vanderbilt Whitney.

It was Merian Cooper's enthusiasm for Technicolor that first attracted Jock Whitney to the picture business. In turn, Jock Whitney interested his cousin Sonny. The result was the formation of Pioneer Pictures, Inc., organized in the spring of 1933, with

*Actual release title of the *Silly Symphonies* cartoon was *Funny Little Bunnies*.

distribution to be handled through RKO. While there was no corporate connection between Pioneer Pictures and Technicolor, a personal one was established when a large block of Technicolor stock was purchased by the two Whitneys. On May 11, 1933, Pioneer signed a contract with Technicolor calling for the production of eight films, "superfeature in character and especially featuring color."

There were still questions to be answered and to protect the fledgling studio's investment conditional clauses were inserted into the contract, among them a provision requiring extensive preliminary testing prior to production. Would the three-color process indeed capture all shades of blue? Would a leading lady with dark hair photograph against light backgrounds? Conversely, a blonde against dark backgrounds? What about make-up? And the visibility of extremely small figures in the background? Technicolor was now moving into "live" production—a far cry from the work, to date, in the cartoon field.

Exhaustive tests under various conditions were made, with the results proving more than satisfactory to Mr. Cooper and the Whitneys. Now began the hunt for a suitable feature-length property, the first story ever to be produced in the newest Technicolor process. No less than two hundred ideas were under consideration.

Don Alvarado and Steffi Duna in *La Cucaracha*, 1934.

La Cucaracha's production staff sits out of camera range (camera is "blimped" to muffle sound) as cast principals—Paul Porcasi, Steffi Duna and Don Alvarado—await resumption of filming.

La Cucaracha.

While the search for a story continued, under Jock Whitney's supervision, Pioneer Pictures' hierarchy decided to "get its feet wet" by shooting a live action two-reeler which, in a sense, would be nothing more than an expanded test of the process under actual production conditions.

A thin-plotted storyline (how a hot-tempered cantina girl maneuvers to recapture her dancer/lover) with an intriguing title, *La Cucaracha*, was chosen. Except for hiring Robert Edmond Jones, the famed stage designer whose use of colored lighting revolutionized Broadway in the 1920s, as art director and the movies' Kenneth Macgowan as producer, the film featured no big names. This was understandable inasmuch as stars were unwilling to appear not only in the new process but in short subjects as well. For the leading lady, the studio hired Steffi Duna, a fiery young singer-actress from the Tingle-Tangle, an intimate theater in Hollywood. Veteran character actor Paul Porcasi and Don

Alvarado were handed the male leads. The project garnered unexpected publicity when John Barrymore, a close friend of Mr. Jones', volunteered to play Hamlet for the lighting tests, which involved experimental placements of various colored filters over the lamps to add splashes of vivid color to the otherwise pastel mood.

Pioneer spared no expense on the production of *La Cucaracha*, spending about $65,000 (the usual short then ran about $15,000). But this initial effort from the studio was in no way intended to be "just a short." It was, in every respect, a short feature, and the industry watched its progress with interest.

As expected, when the film was released in 1934, reviewers tended to overlook the principals and plot in favor of the new Technicolor process. Said one:

. . . the colors are clear and true; when a gentleman in a close-up turns red with anger you can see the color mounting in his cheeks . . . there are now rich, deep blues and it is no longer necessary to avoid or to regret the existence of blue skies, blue water and blue costumes. The old process presented blurred outlines which were even harder on the eyes than its imperfect colors . . . . Color producers today may again mishandle their medium—but at least they will have good colors, well focused, to abuse. There

Early three-color Technicolor camera. (For detailed description of the three-color process see Appendix 4, The Technicolor Technique.)

51

Eddie Cantor in *Kid Millions*, 1934.

full-length feature. Even so, Technicolor's business was improving. Between *Flowers and Trees* and *La Cucaracha,* the company had completed work on no less than fifty productions, either cartoons, short subjects or sequences within black-and-white films. Among them were a Disney insert, *Hot Chocolate Soldier,* for M-G-M's *Hollywood Party* starring Jimmy Durante, and a sequence for the closing scene in Twentieth Century Pictures' *The House of Rothschild* with George Arliss, Boris Karloff, Robert Young, and a rising contract player named Loretta Young. Twentieth, like Warner's and M-G-M which were also timidly experimenting with Technicolor, appeared to be even less confident than the other major studios. *The House of Rothschild* footage was shot in both color (it was the first test of the new process on a very large set) and black-and-white, the latter to be substituted in all release prints depending on public reaction to the Technicolor version.

Another closing sequence to reach the screen appeared in Samuel Goldwyn's *Kid Millions* on which *Daily Variety* reported: ". . . an ice cream factory number in Technicolor is one of the finest jobs of tint-work yet turned out by the Kalmus lab, and the joint Seymour Felix-Willy Pogany handling of the colors, mass movements and girls creates a flaming crescendo for the production." The enormous popularity of comedian Eddie Cantor introduced many customers to "living color" via this film.

As Technicolor began hitting the screen in bits and pieces, the news was released that Pioneer Pictures had finally selected a vehicle for the first full-color, full-length motion picture. The property was Thackeray's classic, *Vanity Fair.* Within the year, film audiences would know it as *Becky Sharp.*

is no question that color has made *La Cucaracha* an outstanding short.

At the 1934 Oscar ceremonies, *La Cucaracha* won the Academy Award for best Comedy Short Subject.

Although Pioneer Pictures' first entry into movie production had created a stir, the studio continued to move cautiously in selecting a property for its first

6 Becky Sharp

The introduction of Technicolor's new three-color process, based on the release of *La Cucaracha*, had split the film world into two argumentative camps. On the one hand were the cinematographers, directors, art directors, and various executives who felt that natural color photography would herald an industry revolution as sweeping as the one introduced by sound. The opposition felt that, while color was interesting, it could play no really important part in the dramatic and artistic advancement of the cinema.

The color controversy spread to the general public as well—and had film fans playing a guessing game as to the vehicle for the first full-length feature. Based on reports that had reached the nation's press, the odds-on favorite had been *The Three Musketeers*, starring Francis Lederer. The selection of *Vanity Fair* surprised many people.

Becky Sharp went into production on December 3, 1934, at the RKO Pathe studio in Culver City, with Miriam Hopkins in the title role, Frances Dee as Amelia Sedley, Cedric Hardwicke as the Marquis of Steyne, Billie Burke as Lady Bareacres, and Nigel Bruce and Alan Mowbray in featured roles. Robert Edmond Jones, who worked on *La Cucaracha*, was engaged to handle settings and costumes.

Filming began on an optimistic note but a series of events occurred which soon labeled the production, as Dr. Kalmus put it, "a champion for hard luck." The original director, Lowell Sherman, was taken ill only three weeks into shooting. He died before the month ended.

Sherman's directorial credits included *She Done Him Wrong*, the 1933 film that launched Mae West's movie career, and the same year's *Morning Glory* for which Katharine Hepburn won an Academy Award. He was an elegant, witty man with a flair for the high style comedy of manners that attracted audiences during the dim Depression days. It was hoped he could restrain the dynamic Miss Hopkins, whose on-screen presence often overpowered everyone and everything in sight, in favor of the new color process.

Director Rouben Mamoulian (*Dr. Jekyll and Mr. Hyde*, 1932; *Queen Christina*, 1933) was hired to step in where Sherman had left off. But on viewing the scenes already shot, plus Technicolor demonstration film, he was not pleased. Mamoulian said:

Up to now the moving picture industry has been like an artist who was allowed only to use pencil or charcoal. Now Technicolor has given us paints. Color is an adventure—and a promise. But, at present, it is in about the same stage of development as was sound when the first talkies were made. Color is mechanically well developed but no one has used it enough to be fully conversant with the artistic technique of applying it constructively to production.

Do you remember when the first talkies came out, how carefully we recorded every slightest noise that might be 'natural'—every footstep, every rustle, every door-slam, even to eggs sizzling in a frying pan? Well, until now, color has been in exactly the same stage of development. We have had the means

Ad, 1935.

of bringing color to the screen and we have taken pains to see that it gave us plenty of color. But from now on we must be selective, using color intelligently for its dramatic, emotional values as well as for pictorial purposes. The main thing is not to get excited over color to the point where enthusiasm for color overbalances what we have already learned about film craftsmanship.

Before the cameras were to roll again on *Becky Sharp*, Rouben Mamoulian had met with Robert Edmond Jones and associate art director Wiard Ihnen. Together, a decision was reached to completely redesign the look of the film, to use color delicately, yet dramatically, rather than for a purely decorative effect.

Mamoulian's linking of color and sound was ironic. No sooner did production resume than problems were encountered in recording the audio portion. As Dr. Kalmus recalled, "Mr. Whitney (of Pioneer Pictures) suddenly found himself in the anomalous position of having to produce the first three-color Technicolor feature, of having to surmount all the hazards of color, yet being in difficulty with an aspect of the work which everyone had naturally taken for granted."

Becky Sharp soon became an expensive workshop and constant experimentation was necessary.

The picture was set in England during the days of Napoleon so it was only natural that soldiers with red coats of that period be a part of the cast. Yet early in the filming the art and color specialists discovered the dangers of injecting any of the primary colors in heavy doses.

Until the entry of the first red coat, the rushes revealed, there was something very pleasant, almost poetic, in the use of pastels and grays. But the sudden arrival of too much red was a shock. The eye caught it and held on throughout the scene.

Another illustration of the power of red, thought to be a dramatic color accent at the time, became evident in one scene where Miriam Hopkins and several other cast members were seated in the foreground. In back of them was a large vase of red roses. The flowers completely "upstaged" the performers.

Color became a scene-stealer again in a sequence where Becky, dressed in bright blue, confronted a soldier in a red coat. The result was a harsh clashing of colors, forcing the viewer to continually shift his attention.

Karl Hale, an early color specialist who followed the filming with interest, offered the film-makers this advice: "Too much color will tire one very quickly. What you learned about composition in black-and-white will not mean much in color filming if you do not watch the placement of your colors. Color itself can throw your composition all awry. It will make its own composition in spite of you.

"It seems as though it would be best to lead up into the heavier colors slowly. Attempt the softer shades, learn the value of color and expecially the placement of values. Otherwise you are merely going to have a hodgepodge of color without any central interest."

Color designer Robert Edmond Jones had these thoughts: "With the new process, the possibilities are unlimited. Rather, they are limited only by the intelligent artistry with which the color is employed . . . Up to now, of course, the industry has been anything but color-conscious. Now that we have color—and very good color—to work with, we must learn to think in terms of color. But color does not mean an abundance of color. This can not be too strongly emphasized."

Basically, *Becky Sharp* was made to prove a point: that color, in all its glory, had at last arrived upon the screen. And while chromatic effects were used with splash at times, the picture also revealed moments of great restraint and inventiveness. One now-famous sequence was superb in the way color was handled to heighten dramatic impact. The scene was the Duchess

Miriam Hopkins and Alan Mowbray in *Becky Sharp*, 1935.

The tavern scene in *Becky Sharp*.

On the set of *Becky Sharp* with Miriam Hopkins (left), director Rouben Mamoulian (seated before camera) and crew.

The Duchess of Richmond's Ball, *Becky Sharp*.

of Richmond's Ball. Napoleon's cannons had sounded at Waterloo and fear was spreading among the dancers. As the scene builds to a climax, through a series of intercut shots, the audience sees the colors shift from the coolness and sobriety of grays, blues, greens, and pale yellows to the excitement and danger of deep oranges and flaming reds. The effect was achieved, according to Director Mamoulian, by the selection of dresses and uniforms worn by the characters and the changing color of backgrounds and lights.

Becky Sharp was completed on March 20, 1935, at a cost of nearly one million dollars. On its release in late spring, the film was generally crucified as dramatic fare, classed as "dull . . . artificial . . . tedious." But *Becky Sharp* was a milestone in screen entertainment. Audiences were more attracted by its color than by its story or its characters and players. And from that standpoint alone, the film received high praise and fair

evaluation. Said the *New York Times* in its review of June 14, 1935:

Science and art, the handmaidens of the cinema, have joined hands to endow the screen with a miraculous new element in *Becky Sharp*. . . . Although its faults are too numerous to earn it distinction as a screen drama, it produces in the spectator all the excitement of standing on a peak in Darien and glimpsing a strange, beautiful and unexpected new world. As an experiment, it is a momentous event, and it may be that in a few years it will be regarded as the equal in historical importance of the first crude and wretched talking pictures. Although it is dramatically tedious, it is a gallant and distinguished outpost in an almost uncharted domain, and it is probably the most significant event of the 1935 cinema.

Certainly the photoplay, coloristically speaking, is

Cedric Hardwicke, Alam Mowbray, and Miriam Hopkins in *Becky Sharp*.

the most successful that has ever reached the screen. Vastly improved over the gaudy two-color process of four or five years ago, it possesses an extraordinary variety of tints, ranging from placid and lovely grays to hues which are vibrant with warmth and richness. This is not the coloration of natural life but a vividly pigmented dream world of artistic imagination.

The major problem, from the spectator's point of view, is the necessity for accustoming the eye to this new screen element in much the same way we were obliged to accustom the ear to the first talkies. . . . At the moment, it is impossible to view *Becky Sharp* without crowding the imagination so completely with color that the photoplay as a whole is almost meaningless. That is partly the fault of the production and partly the inevitable consequence of a phenomenon.

Said *Variety:* "Technicolor's tints offer magnificent eye entrancement to give added significance to the pre-Victorian comedy-drama for smash entertainment. . . . The color is so entrancing that it threatens at times to beguile the appreciation away from the story, and this exhibit suggests that color may have to be fed to audiences a little more moderately while they get inured to the vivid new screen process. Use of the blues especially would seem to call for more care to prevent too sharp contrasts. . . ."

Variety's comment regarding "use of the blues" was particularly meaningful. The colormen, obviously overreacting to the old two-color process' inability to record the color blue, became heavy-handed in trying to impress viewers with their new capabilities.

Other critics were plainly brutal in their evaluation of the new film, noting that the skin tones were often "over ripe" and that "there is no sex appeal in a gal who looks as if she is in the last stages of scarlatina." One even remarked that "all the actors look like roast turkeys." Within a few years, such comments would haunt Technicolor.

While the public rushed to see *Becky Sharp* and the color controversy raged, one basic fact emerged: the film did not introduce the hoped-for perfect color but it did represent a tremendous advance beyond the previous two-strip process and established the point that a true, natural color system had finally arrived that was both practical and economical.

(*Note:* Sadly, there are no known Technicolor prints of the complete version of *Becky Sharp* in existence. Because ownership of the negative passed from company to company—Astor Pictures bought the distribution rights from the Whitney family in the late 1940s—it never received the care necessary to preserve it. Unable to afford Technicolor's fees, Astor resorted to two-color Cinecolor for new prints. Today, this landmark film exists only in a process which Technicolor obsoleted.)

Frances Dee as Amelia Sedley in the silhouette scene from *Becky Sharp*.

7 Where Are the Stars?

In mid-1936, a Los Angeles newspaper reported that the respected cinematographer Hal Mohr had predicted that *The Green Pastures,* the film he was then currently shooting, would be the last major production to be filmed in black-and-white. The column further quoted him as saying he and his fellow cameramen were "storing in mothballs their hard won cinematographic arts in favor of the new chromatic medium which had bloomed overnight to dominate the Hollywood production schedule."

Carl Laemmle, the president and founder of Universal Pictures, was in Paris when he heard about the Hal Mohr item and immediately refuted the prediction. He was described as adamant when he told reporters that "most motion pictures of the future would be in black-and-white."

The truth was Mr. Mohr had never made such statements nor did he have any idea as to how they reached the paper and were accredited to him. What made the comments even more incredible was the fact that a notice in *The Hollywood Reporter,* dated August 11, 1936, listed forty-five productions in progress in Hollywood studios. Only one was shooting in color. Looking even farther ahead, *Motion Picture Herald,* noted for its reliability, reported on four hundred and eighty-five features projected for the coming production season by the ten largest companies. Of those, three were to be in color.

To date, three feature films in the new Technicolor process had been released: *Becky Sharp* in June, 1935, *The Trail of the Lonesome Pine* in March, 1936, and *The Dancing Pirate* in May, 1936. During this same period, over five hundred black-and-white films were made and released.

The early rush by movie-goers to see *Becky Sharp* generated wild optimism both at Pioneer Pictures and at Technicolor. Initially, it was heralded as a box office smash. Within weeks after the release of the picture, however, audience interest dropped sharply. *Becky Sharp* was not a financial success nor was it highly regarded as a theater attraction by exhibitors.

The Trail of the Lonesome Pine, Walter Wanger's outdoor drama with Sylvia Sidney and screen newcomers Fred MacMurray and Henry Fonda, fared much better and became a highly successful and profitable venture. But the question around Hollywood was, to what degree did color influence its popularity?

In the screenplay, the producer had a proven theatrical property, one that had been filmed earlier (1916) in black-and-white. The new version was constructed with an eye to story, unfolding of drama and entertainment content. Unusual precautions were taken to keep the color subdued and of secondary interest. "The goal we set at the start of the production and never deviated from," Mr. Wanger declared, "was to hew to the storyline and let color fall where it may."

To a great extent, Mr. Wanger and his director, Henry Hathaway, succeeded in achieving their goal. Said the *New York Times* of the production:

Color has traveled far since first it exploded on the screen last June in *Becky Sharp.* Demonstrating increased mastery of the new element, Walter

Nigel Bruce and Fred MacMurray in *The Trail of The Lonesome Pine*, 1936,
the first outdoor drama filmed in full color.

Henry Fonda on the set of *The Trail of The Lonesome Pine*. He had made his
film debut a year earlier in *The Farmer Takes A Wife*.

Sylvia Sidney and Spanky McFarland, *The Trail of The Lonesome Pine*.

Wanger's producing unit proves . . . that color need not shackle the cinema but may give it fuller expression.

Chromatically, *Trail* is far less impressive than its pioneer in the field. *Becky Sharp* employed color as stylistic accentuation of dramatic effect. It sought to imprison the rainbow in a series of carefully planned canvases that were radiantly startling, visually magnificent, attuned carefully to the mood of the picture and to the changing tempo of the action.

Trail attempts none of this. Paradoxically, it improves the case for color by lessening its importance. It accepts the spectrum as a complementary attribute of the picture, not its *raison d'etre*. In place of the vivid reds and scarlets, the brilliant purples and dazzling greens and yellows of *Becky Sharp*, it employs sober browns and blacks and deep greens. It may not be natural color but, at least, it is used more naturally. The eye, accustomed to the shadings of black and white, has less difficulty meeting the demands of the new element; the color is not a distraction but an attraction—as valuable and little more obtrusive than the musical score.

Motion Picture Herald called it ". . . one of the most important motion pictures, not simply because it is a color picture in which the art of intelligently and expertly applying hues and tints approaches perfection, rather more because of the depth and power of its motivating human interest heart-touching story, the high quality of acting provided by principals and support, finesse of direction, and worth of substantiating production features."

The general consensus seemed to be that *The Trail of the Lonesome Pine* could not be hailed as a monumental color triumph. Rather, it was a shrewdly handled picture that made money—and incidentally happened to be in color.

The Dancing Pirate, which featured Steffi Duna (of *La Cucaracha* fame), Frank Morgan and Charles Collins, didn't fare too well at the box office and proved to be Pioneer Pictures last feature. Upon release of the film, the studio was dissolved and Mr. Whitney joined with David O. Selznick in the formation of Selznick International Films.

The production missed with the critics as well, although their evaluations were positive regarding its color. *The Dancing Pirate*, said *The Hollywood Reporter*, "belongs to that fantastic school which deems anything is permissible as long as it is played against a musical background. It has gorgeous color, intelligently and sparingly used by Robert Edmond Jones, but little else to recommend it as a potentially great box office attraction. It will have to be sold almost entirely upon the novelty of color."

Many of the writers appeared overly opinionated in their evaluation of the new color technique. "One hour of color," noted one reviewer, "is too much color at one sitting. Eyes are accustomed to reading from black against white."

Wrote another: "Inclusion of color stifles the greatest of audience reactions; it does not stimulate the imagination. Color, of itself, will not impart dramatic punch."

Still another: "Individuals have definite color prejudices. One may have emphatic antipathy for greens in wearing apparel. If the star appears in a gown of green, his sympathy is immediately alienated."

One exhibitor, after a screening of *The Dancing Pirate*, offered a more objective view. "The producers missed fire here," he stated. "In making a great picture you must have names that sell at the box office." The inference was clear. Color alone could not carry a picture—nor could color lure enough customers to the ticket windows to encourage producers to jump picture costs another third by adding the involved and highly technical new process.

The top stars of the day included Shirley Temple, Clark Gable, Fred Astaire and Ginger Rogers, Dick Powell, Joan Crawford, Claudette Colbert, Jeanette MacDonald and Gary Cooper. These stars, and others, were generally under contract to the major studios, which were hesitant to use their top players in a color production. Color was still a novelty and having them appear, or even be associated with such a production, could jeopardize their futures. The smaller studios rarely had a stellar personality.

Too, established leading ladies, in particular, wanted to avoid Technicolor. Black-and-white filming had developed to such an art that a variety of subtle lighting techniques were available to establish various effects and moods. Color lighting tended to be brilliant and harsh. To obtain an image for color film, subjects had to be flooded with light from all angles.

The majority of studios opted for a "wait and see" approach and let their continuing black-and-white schedules reflect executive opinion. Seldom were the stars allowed to speak their minds although there were those who let their thoughts be known. In November of 1936, Walter Wanger, whose success with *The Trail of the Lonesome Pine* prompted him to be a color enthusiast, was searching for a leading lady to play the starring role in his production of *Vogues of 1938*. His first choice was Carole Lombard. Miss Lombard had a reputation for frankness and did not hesitate in admitting her fear of color to the press. "Sure, I'll read the story of *Vogues*," she said, "but, you know, color goes a little screwy at times and I'm not just sure I want to make a Technicolor picture."

THE FIRST
DANCING MUSICAL
IN 100% NEW
TECHNICOLOR

DANCING PIRATE

Ad, 1936.

The Technicolor camera, positioned atop a flying steel crane, films dance sequence for *Dancing Pirate*, 1936. Steffi Duna and Charles Collins, the leading players, are in foreground.

Bette Davis labeled Warner's first Technicolor production "tripe."

Carole Lombard: "Color goes a little screwy. . . ."

The fact that *Vogues of 1938* was to be a glamorous "clothes picture" seemed to be a powerful influence in getting Carole Lombard to even consider the role. But she recalled the sometimes "over ripe" tints of *Becky Sharp* and color frightened her. The role was eventually assigned to Mr. Wanger's wife-to-be, Joan Bennett.

Bette Davis, too, was an outspoken hold-out. She considered her 1936 black-and-white picture, *Satin Met A Lady*, to be a disaster and pleaded with her studio, Warner Bros., for a good property. Jack L. Warner personally sent her a script of *God's Country and the Woman*, a north woods melodrama the studio had scheduled for the following year's release. To entice Miss Davis, he emphasized that she would be co-starring with matinee idol George Brent in the studio's first three-color Technicolor feature film. The star was not at all interested and called the entire project "tripe." She held firm even after Mr. Warner returned to tell her that he had just taken an option on a then unpublished novel. If she would do *God's Country and the Woman*, the role of the book's heroine, Scarlett O'Hara, was hers. The studio placed Bette Davis on suspension.

In spite of the drawbacks, Technicolor did have one advantage that intrigued actresses: it did not project with pinpoint sharpness on the screen. To get a "soft focus" in black-and-white meant diffusing the lens. With mid-1930s Technicolor there was no need for diffusion. That point, however, was not enough to induce the likes of Joan Crawford, Greta Garbo, or Norma Shearer to desert the security of their monochromatic world. And so, whenever a major studio experimented with color, it preferred to give its newcomers a chance. Far safer, for example, to cast Frances Farmer rather than risk Claudette Colbert's career.

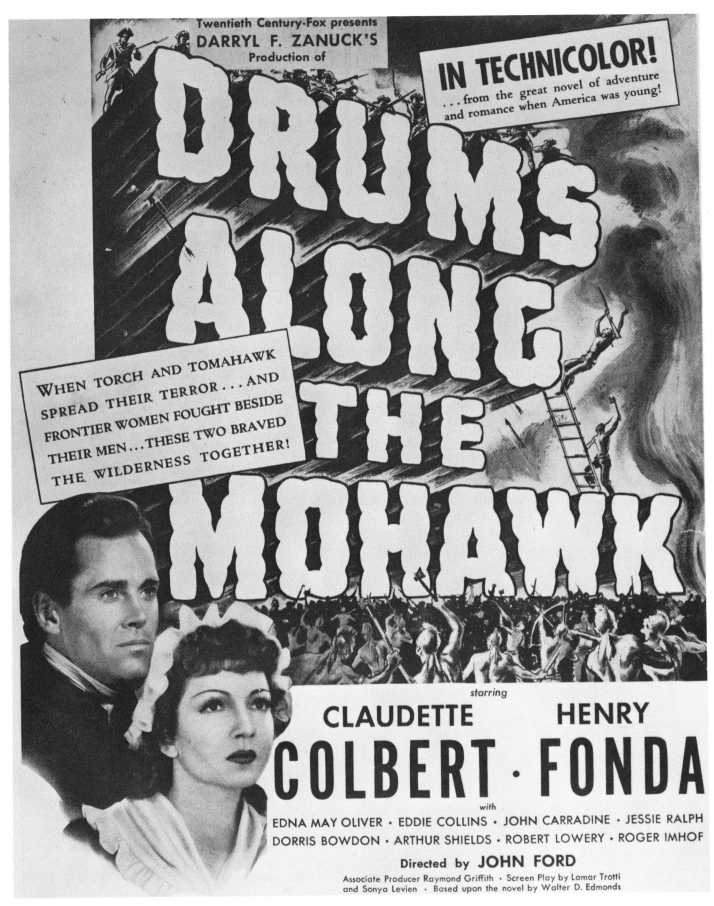

Twentieth Century-Fox presents
DARRYL F. ZANUCK'S
Production of

DRUMS ALONG THE MOHAWK

IN TECHNICOLOR!
...from the great novel of adventure and romance when America was young!

WHEN TORCH AND TOMAHAWK SPREAD THEIR TERROR...AND FRONTIER WOMEN FOUGHT BESIDE THEIR MEN...THESE TWO BRAVED THE WILDERNESS TOGETHER!

starring

CLAUDETTE **COLBERT** · HENRY **FONDA**

with

EDNA MAY OLIVER · EDDIE COLLINS · JOHN CARRADINE · JESSIE RALPH
DORRIS BOWDON · ARTHUR SHIELDS · ROBERT LOWERY · ROGER IMHOF

Directed by **JOHN FORD**

Associate Producer Raymond Griffith · Screen Play by Lamar Trotti and Sonya Levien · Based upon the novel by Walter D. Edmonds

Ad, 1939.

64

Claudette Colbert found black-and-white photography more flattering.

Miss Colbert would not even consider appearing in color films. By 1936, she was a screen veteran and a top money-maker. Her saucy hairstyle and sophisticated looks were known to millions of movie-goers. Despite her vast appeal, she had always felt that her face, with its wide-set eyes and high cheekbones, was difficult to photograph. Too, her nose was broad at its base. She was, therefore, insistent that she be photographed only from certain more flattering angles.

To further help heighten her appeal, she became a master of make-up, devising such "tricks" as running a tinted line down the center of her nose and around the base of the nostrils to minimize the broadness. With special filters and diffusion lens' on the camera, her technique was highly successful for black-and-white filming. Color was another story.

In 1939, she surprisingly agreed to appear in *Drums Along the Mohawk*, to be directed by John Ford. Mr. Ford was not one to pamper his stars, and he shot the film and the performers his own way. Claudette Colbert did not appear in another color production for sixteen years (*Texas Lady*, 1955).

Money, of course, was a major determining factor in casting. The top stars commanded large salaries. Why gamble with the added expense of Technicolor when a big name alone could virtually insure the success of a black-and-white picture?

Technicolor was in the throes of another cycle. To Dr. Kalmus, the situation was much too similar to the one that faced his company in 1925. Douglas Fairbanks had given color an important boost in that year but there was no Fairbanks on the horizon now. It was even more frustrating to know that a true, full-color process, one that photographers and moviemakers had dreamed about for over one hundred years, was finally here. People were no longer saying, "It can't be done." It could be done. It had been done.

Whatever criticisms that had been leveled at color in pictures, the doctor knew, were not insurmountable nor basically the fault of his process. The system worked. It simply needed refining—and it was up to Technicolor to prove it.

8 Revolution Behind the Scenes

Starting in the mid-1920s, Technicolor had made available a color consulting service to work with the studios and designers prior to and during film production. Now that service was not only available but required—and expanded to include the upgrading of virtually every facet involved in color photography. A contract with Technicolor was a package that included not only the rental of the three-color camera but a Technicolor cameraman who worked as an advisor to the studio's cinematographer; advice given to art directors, set directors and designers, wardrobe and property departments; use of make-up and assistance to the studio make-up departments; the requirements of special lighting equipment; and laboratory processing up to and including the final release prints. Technicolor had but one goal in mind: that of adapting the Technicolor cameras and equipment, and the use of the Technicolor process, to picture production, with the smoothest possible coordination and the fewest possible special facilities or special equipment.

THE CAMERAMEN. Technicolor's staff of cameramen were drawn from the ranks of black-and-white studio cinematographers and trained in the special requirements of color photography. They were taught to "think color" at all times, to know its limitations, to become expert in the areas of exposure and lighting, and to be able to handle any assignment, exterior or interior, that required shots ranging from a minute insect to a towering skyscraper.

Originally, the major photography on all three-color features had been handled by one of the company's cinematographers. Dr. Kalmus knew, however, that with increased use of the process, the work had to become the responsibility of the studios first cameramen. That point was obvious for a number of reasons. These men were familiar with their individual studio's special requirements; they knew the crews and how to get things done in the shortest, best possible way. Too, they were sensitive to the special photographic requirements of the stars on their lots and had the confidence and respect of the studio staffs.

At Technicolor's insistence, it became standard practice for a studio first cameraman to team with a Technicolor first cameraman. The feeling was that during the course of production the studio man would gain insight not only into the new color process but the camera and side equipment as well. Eventually, he would be on his own and would not require the assistance of a Technicolor cameraman. Said one cinematic journal: "This policy should be of great benefit to Technicolor for it will not only develop greater variety and individual style in Technicolor productions, but it will also eliminate the divided responsibility, and its inevitable friction, which seemed inseparable from the old arrangements."

Technicolor's camera crew included many of the finest cinematographers in the business. Ray Rennahan, the company's cameraman on *La Cucaracha* and *Becky Sharp*, was ultimately involved in more color productions than any other motion picture photographer and was honored with a number of Academy Awards and nominations for his work on such features as *Gone With The Wind, Blood and Sand, For Whom*

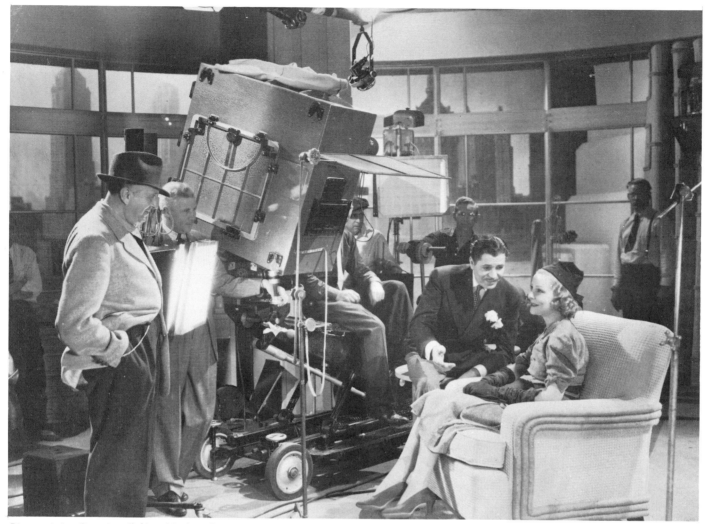

Director Irving Cummings (left) and Technicolor cameraman Ray Rennahan (standing by camera) watch as Warner Baxter and Helen Vinson rehearse a scene for *Vogues of 1938*. The camera, mounted on a moveable dolly and directly under the microphone, is protected within a special sound-proof housing.

the Bell Tolls, and *Lady In The Dark*. Over the years, others in the department were recognized for their outstanding achievements as well. Among them were: W. Howard (Duke) Greene (*The Private Lives of Elizabeth & Essex, Blossoms In the Dust, Phantom of the Opera*), Allen Davey (*Hello, Frisco, Hello, Cover Girl, Life With Father*), William V. Skall (*Northwest Passage, Reap the Wild Wind, Joan of Arc, Quo Vadis*), Wildred M. Cline (*Aloma of the South Seas*), Charles Boyle (*Anchors Aweigh*), Winton Hoch (*She Wore A Yellow Ribbon, The Quiet Man*), Art Arling (*The Yearling*) and William Snyder (*The Loves of Carmen, Jolson Sings Again*). All were members of the American Society of Cinematographers.

Since the Technicolor camera and accessory equipment were precision machinery, a staff of trained technical men was maintained to care for them. On each studio set where Technicolor cameras were in use, there was a skilled technician functioning as an assistant cameraman. Backing up these men was a group of maintenance men who, at the end of each day's shooting, returned the cameras to the Technicolor service department in Hollywood for servicing and cleaning, both mechanically and optically. The cameras were then returned to the studio, in top condition, for the next day's work. On distant locations, cameras were maintained in the field.

The big rush to the two-color process in 1929 and 1930 helped establish Technicolor as a leader in the industry. It also helped create uncertainties that were to linger through 1936. The deteriorating quality of color during the boom was, to a great extent, the result of too many untrained individuals working with an unknown. Now, with Technicolor's assistance, a new era was about to begin for Hollywood's cameramen.

COLOR COORDINATION. Mrs. Natalie Kalmus was an art student and sometime model when she and Dr.

Technicolor cameraman W. Howard (Duke) Greene.

Natalie Kalmus, Technicolor's color consultant, ca 1930s.

Plant No. 5 in Hollywood where cameras were stored and maintained.

Andre Durenceau was imported from Paris to head Technicolor's art department, a wing of the Color Advisory Service supervised by Natalie Kalmus.

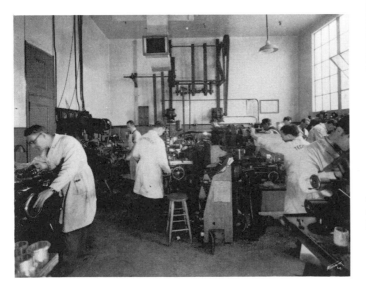

Technicolor's camera repair shop, ca 1930s.

Kalmus married during their college days. She had been attending a Boston art school, and when her husband traveled to Europe to obtain his doctorate she accompanied him and enrolled at the University of Zurich. Later, she continued her studies at Queen's University in Ontario upon his appointment to the staff.

During the early days of Technicolor, she participated in many of the color tests, working as a "stand in" for the performers and offering artistic advice on color harmonies. Natalie Kalmus was, in fact, the model toward which the first crude Technicolor camera was pointed.

In 1921, unknown to most of their associates in the industry, she and Dr. Kalmus divorced. They continued to share the same home for many years, however, and at the office their working relationship remained dedicated and unchanged.

By 1926, as part of the divorce settlement, Mrs.

Kalmus had become a integral part of the company. It was in that year that the groundwork and fundamentals were established for a Color Advisory Service. Ten years later, as head of the department, she supervised a large staff and was destined to become one of the best known and most influential of the company's personnel. Until 1948, her name appeared as "Color Consultant" within the credits of virtually every motion picture made in Technicolor.

Dr. Kalmus had a reputation for being a perfectionist. He felt that the sight, on the screen, of less than ideal or improperly used color only impeded his company's aims and progress. It was his hope that this newly strengthened department would become a keystone to Technicolor's future. As such, it became the connecting link between the studios' creative experts (the art directors, set designers and decorators, wardrobe designers, and property departments) and Technicolor during both the preparation and the shooting of a film.

The work of Mrs. Kalmus and her staff, notably

Working directly from film scripts, Mrs. Kalmus and her staff prepared color charts for each scene, using actual fabric samples and paint swatches.

longtime associates Henri Jaffa and William Fritzsche, began long before the cameras rolled. "We first receive the script for a new film," she noted, "and we carefully analyze each sequence and scene to ascertain what dominant mood or emotion is to be expressed. When this is decided, we plan to use the appropriate color or set of colors which will suggest that mood, thus actually fitting the color to the scene and augmenting its dramatic value. We then prepare a color chart, using actual samples of fabrics and materials, for the entire production—each scene, sequence, set and character being considered. This chart may be compared to a musical score, and amplifies the picture in a similar manner."

Because the early two-color pictures could reproduce color, producers often thought they should continually flaunt vivid hues before an audience. Such practices led Natalie Kalmus to develop a creed which she based on "the law of emphasis." That is, *Nothing of relative unimportance in a picture shall be emphasized.* She believed in simplicity and sought to eliminate distracting focal points within scenes, unnecessary busyness that succeeded only in disturbing a viewer's concentration or in tiring his eyes.

"Natural colors and lights do not tax the eye nearly as much as man-made colors and artificial lights," she stated. "Even when Nature indulges in a riot of beautiful colors, there are subtle harmonies which justify those colors." To that end she created a method of distinct "color separation," a term, she explained, which means "when one color is placed in front or beside another, there must be enough difference in their hues to separate one from the other photographically. If the colors are properly handled, it is possible to

Wardrobe test for Olivia de Havilland in *Gold is Where You Find It*, 1937.

make it appear as though the actors are actually standing there in person, thus creating the illusion of the third dimension."

Because of the general warm glow of flesh tints, she usually introduced the cooler tones into the backgrounds. If she found it advantageous to use warmer tones in the set, she suggested lighting that would create shadows in back of the actor. As for the performers themselves, she noted, "We plan the colors of the actors costumes with especial care. Whenever possible, we prefer to clothe them in colors that build up his or her screen personality."

Mrs. Kalmus introduced the art of modifying colors so that the eye would accept the desired shade. For instance, she discovered that, under the strong Technicolor lights, white constantly changed in value and tone, picking up and absorbing the reflections of surrounding colors. When dyed a neutral gray, however, it would appear white on film. The practice had another advantage: it eliminated glare. A stark white shirt would often cast so much reflected light that an actor's face would either be undistinguishable or lost entirely. This artful trick was not limited to costumes. Props and sets were modified in color at times as well. But clothing was the big item, so much so that Malone's Studio Service, a dry cleaners in Hollywood, made a specialty of it.

Color test for *Ramona* (1936) with Loretta Young and Don Ameche. The top rows on the color board contained monochromatic shades ranging from black to white while the bottom row had blocks of red, yellow, blue and brown in vivid tones.

Mrs. Kalmus was also a strong believer in the language of colors ("They alone speak with more eloquence than can be described by words . . .") and she often relied on it to establish a mood. But she exercised great restraint and never allowed the heavy-handed color symbolism that surfaced during the sweep of the 1920s. It was not uncommon to see the silent screen flooded with red to emphasize an actor's rage—or green to show his envy.

As the reigning Technicolor authority on color artistry, Natalie Kalmus certainly had her detractors, particularly in the latter days of her career (there was talk of overly officious behavior, drinking, even that she was color *blind*). Through it all, however, she never swayed from the beliefs she established in her department during the mid-1930s: "The principles of color, tone, and composition make a painting a fine art. The same principles will make a colored motion picture a work of art."

MAKE-UP TECHNIQUES. Prior to the development of three-color Technicolor, during the days of black-and-white and two-color movies, motion picture make-up was applied in a heavy, theatrical manner, mainly to give the skin a smooth, unblemished appearance (the covering of minor skin problems, fine lines

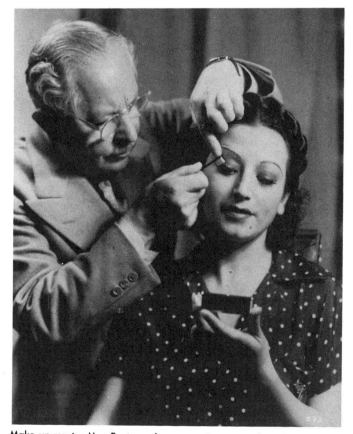

Make-up master Max Factor, whose organization perfected a new line of cosmetics specifically for full-color Technicolor in the mid-1930s.

and wrinkles). The delicate shadings that are normal in good flesh tones were not required. With the arrival of the new Technicolor process and its high sensitivity to the total color range, a radically different approach to make-up application and materials was needed.

In the mid-1930s, the Max Factor organization perfected a line of make-up expressly for the new Technicolor. Called the "T-D" series, it offered a wide range of shades, from extremely light to extremely dark, in a numbered sequence.

Sensing a possible trend toward color, research on the project had begun several years earlier in the Factor laboratories in Hollywood. Through trial and error, a new compressed "cake" substance, to be applied with a thin coat using a moist sponge, was developed to replace the previously used paste or greasepaint. The line, which eventually became famous commercially as "Pan-Cake" make-up, was first tested on guinea pigs, then on the Max Factor chemists themselves. It was not unusual for these men to wear various shades of make-up simultaneously over lengthy testing periods to measure changes, if any, in coloration due to perspiration or normal skin secretions.

The project was enormously complex, as Mr. Factor admitted:

> Previous make-ups were based on various combinations of pink, yellow and white. Well applied, they may have looked very nice to the eye but the more critical color camera unmasks it for the glaringly unnatural thing it is. In analyzing the human complexion with a spectroscope, we found that the darker pinks, or red, are present as well as certain proportions of yellow, white and blue. This is true because the skin itself is essentially a translucent covering with relatively little color of its own. So our new make-up had to be made to blend with not one but a number of colors.

The new Technicolor make-up was intended to duplicate, in tones the camera could interpret, the coloring of the underlying complexion. Radical changes in a person's coloration were avoided. Said Mr. Factor, "In black-and-white we worked with contrasts of light and shade. When making up a blonde, for example, we sought to heighten that tonal contrast by applying a rather dark make-up which gave a positive contrast to the light hair. In color, this is not the case. A blonde or brunette would use a make-up of a color in keeping with her own complexion . . . We are no longer striving for a purely artificial contrast but seeking to imitate and enhance the subject's natural coloring."

The application of make-up was the responsibility of

Banks of light flood the ballroom set for the Technicolor final sequence in
The House Of Rothschild, 1934.

the studio make-up departments, although the color cameramen could request "touch ups" when necessary. The heat of the lamps often caused problems, particularly on interior sets. Moist or oily skin surfaces, which caught or reflected color and light, had to be toned down. Other problems surfaced on exterior locations. With the actors working in bright sunshine, they usually began to sunburn and make-up changes became necessary to compensate for the gradually tanning complexions. The reverse was also true. When the cast moved indoors to continue shooting, their slowly fading tans needed attention.

During this early period, new make-up tricks were devised and honed to a high degree by the Factor group and others, notably Perc Westmore. Long faces were shortened, noses were narrowed, eyes were widened, and double chins were made to disappear. Leading men were handsome and debonair; leading ladies were beautiful and sophisticated. Glamour, in

The powerful Mole-Richardson carbon arc lamp of the mid-to-late 1930s was used in large doses as a floodlight or spotlight in both interior and exterior Technicolor cinematography.

greater doses than ever before, was in vogue.

Make-up for Technicolor had certainly not been perfected by 1936. Continual advances were made through the years to keep pace with the developments within color filming. It was a big start, however. To the film crowd, the flawless faces that began appearing on the tinted screens gave Technicolor performers a look all their own.

LIGHTS! LIGHTS! LIGHTS! Performers who had worked in Technicolor productions had one common complaint: the extreme heat of the lamps. Temperatures on the sets were so high that flowers wilted and paint blistered. Said one cameraman, "I once saw smoke rising from an actor's hair!"

The scene was a far cry from the earliest days of motion pictures when photography relied only on natural daylight to capture images on film. The very first studio, Thomas Edison's, was in fact constructed upon a giant turntable so that "the set" could be rotated to follow the sun.

Moving pictures began to mature just prior to World War I when various artistic accessories were brought into practice, such as artificial lighting to help establish mood and effect. Simple street-type lights were first used then more powerful carbon-arc floodlamps. From the theater stage, spotlamps were adapted. The Kliegl brothers of New York developed the Klieg light especially for motion pictures.

Incandescent lights gained popularity because they could be used in areas where the larger lamps could not. They provided a softer, less direct source, and they were clean. (Stages frequently had to be aired to clear the smoke from some high powered sources.) "Inkies," as they were known, were also quieter. Microphones were keenly sensitive to the sizzling, sputtering sounds of arc lights.

During the mid-1920s, "inkies" created a revolution of sorts in motion picture lighting. But all of that changed with the introduction of Technicolor's new three-strip process. It was not a move in the right direction. The new Technicolor required an exceptionally high light level to record all the colors on film—a flat, white light and plenty of it. The only source really capable of providing that output was the old-fashioned arc lamp. This time, it returned in larger doses and with it came soaring temperatures and complaints from performers.

During the development of its new color process, Technicolor had contacted several suppliers and manufacturers of cinema lighting equipment. Initially, special units of improved quality were devised and, from time to time, new designs and modifications were brought into production. Still, they did little to relieve the discomfort, nor did they permit cinematographers the hoped-for flexibility (or level of artistry) they enjoyed with black-and-white filming.

The big breakthrough came in 1939 when Technicolor announced, after a lengthy period of secret research and development, the discovery of a new, faster film which would yield superior color rendition, less graininess, and sharper definition with greater depth of focus. The greatest benefit, however, was in the area of lighting. "The new film," said cameraman Ray Rennahan, "is three times as fast as the old film under artificial light and four times as fast to daylight. This brings color lighting to levels practically identical to those used in monochrome. . . . In other words, this new film enables us to reduce our lighting levels by a good fifty per cent."

The news had immediate impact. Now far less light was needed. Smaller, handier units could be used and with greater flexibility, especially in lighting people. An added benefit was the lowering of production costs.

The turnabout had not come overnight. When it did, color cinematography took an impressive step forward.

9 Waiting for "Allah"

As 1936 neared its close, there were indications that the coming year would show a noticeable increase in Technicolor production. Warner Bros. had contracted for its largest volume of shorts which included its *Color Parade* package. The first filmed tour, a look at the Netherlands, was *Springtime in Holland*. Paramount followed with its series of *Color Cruises*. And Metro-Goldwyn-Mayer increased its color schedule of short subjects to about forty per cent. Included were the *James A. Fitzpatrick Traveltalks*, a popular, long-running series which began appearing in color with *Holland in Tulip Time*.

Searching for additional ways to expand the color market, Dr. Kalmus organized an affiliate office of Technicolor Motion Picture Corporation in Great Britain, Technicolor, Ltd. (later developed in association with Sir Adrian Baillie, Alexander Korda and the Prudential Assurance Company, Ltd.). The overseas subsidiary became active almost immediately with the production of the first Technicolor feature photographed in England, *Wings of the Morning*. Financed by New World Productions, the race track story starred Henry Fonda, in his second color role, and Annabella, a young French actress who had achieved considerable fame on the Continent. Shortly after completion of the production, which was processed in Technicolor's Hollywood plant, a laboratory was built on Bath Road in West Drayton, just outside of London. There, future British-made Technicolor films would be serviced, as well as prints for American productions to be distributed in the United Kingdom.

Feature filming in the United States continued at a slow pace, although several productions had been completed. The majority of studios were still hesitant to use color in full-length packages, and were content to bide their time to await public reaction. It was an anxious period for the people at Technicolor. They were concerned not only about overall reception to these new films but about areas of production that had previously been criticized and, hopefully, improved.

The first of the major new features to be released was *Ramona*, Twentieth Century-Fox's initial entry into color in a big way. The film, a remake of the classic Indian saga, starred the studio's only Technicolor veteran, Loretta Young (she had appeared briefly in the closing color sequence in *The House of Rothschild* two years earlier), Don Ameche, and Jane Darwell.

Of *Ramona*, released in late 1936, the *Hollywood Reporter* wrote: "This picture in color raises the artistic status of the screen by several degrees. It will be acclaimed the most beautiful motion picture ever filmed. . . . The color goes beyond anything previously achieved. Not only has the Technicolor process yielded truer values, more transparent shadows, closer uniformity, and sharper definition, but the use of color in costumes, properties, background, and make-up shows a vastly finer taste and artistry."

The *New York Times* stated:

Chromatically, the picture is superior to anything we have seen in the color line. Without striving for the splashing effects of *Becky Sharp*, but deepening the

On location for the "James A. Fitzpatrick Traveltalks," a long-running series of short subjects released by M-G-M. Here, at the San Francisco World's Fair.

Technicolor, Ltd. in West Drayton, England.

Director Henry King, Loretta Young, and Don Ameche, at far right, talk over scene for Twentieth Century-Fox's first all color picture, *Ramona*, 1936.

Publicity still of Loretta Young as *Ramona*.

'natural color' tones of *Trail of the Lonesome Pine*, it has achieved warmth and vigor without subjecting its beholders to a constant optic bombardment. Here and there, the cameramen have insisted upon showing off, inserting gaudy sunsets, sunrises . . . but generally they have been content with modest and harmonious tableaux, with tonal composition that is restful, pleasant and of definite relation to the

dramatic context. To that extent, color has added to, not detracted from, the simple story the producers set out to retell.

Variety commented: "Helen Hunt Jackson's haunting pastoral tragedy comes to the screen in its gorgeous Technicolor trappings as entertainment of high order. Technicolor tint plotting by Natalie Kalmus and Technicolor photography by William V. Skall are magnificent, standing with the best so far done in this medium. . . ."

Most heartening, perhaps, were the reactions to the color camera's treatment of the female lead. Wrote one critic: "Loretta Young, the most appealing of the screen's ladies, wears a black wig, photographs beautifully in natural colors."

Another noted: "Loretta Young . . . is graced by the Technicolor camera in a mood of idyllic beauty. . . . Color close-ups of Miss Young are breathtaking gems."

The color work on *Ramona* set studio heads thinking. But the real test was to come.

When Jock Whitney dissolved Pioneer Pictures and joined David O. Selznick in forming Selznick International, he took with him his continuing enthusiasm for color filming. Equally important, he brought along his contractual commitments with Technicolor.

The Selznick-Whitney team chose for its first subject Robert Hichens' *The Garden of Allah*. The property seemed to have all of the key elements necessary to make an outstanding motion picture: a compelling love story, an intriguing locale, glamorous settings, and a number of strong central characters.

Myron Selznick, David's brother, produced the picture with notable restraint, striving for understatement rather than the spectacular. He selected one of the industry's top talents as his director—Richard Boleslawsky—on the basis of his previous achievements, such films (all black-and-white) as *Clive of India* (1935), *Les Miserables* (1935) and *The Three Godfathers* (1936). The increasingly important area of art supervision was divided among three specialists: Sturges Carne, set designer; Ernest Dryden, costume designer; and Lansing C. Holden, a disciple of Robert Edmond Jones, color designer.

It was the casting, however, that started the film capital talking. The leading male role was given to the international favorite and matinee idol, Charles Boyer. Another popular import, the provocative Marlene Dietrich, was handed the starring female spot. In support were the highly respected actors, Basil Rathbone and Joseph Schildkraut.

The casting of Charles Boyer and, particularly, Marlene Dietrich, was not only a master stroke but a major accomplishment. Now, for the first time, a color

Ramona

in the new perfected Technicolor
with

LORETTA YOUNG
DON AMECHE

and a cast of thousands featuring

KENT TAYLOR · PAULINE FREDERICK · JANE DARWELL
KATHERINE DeMILLE · JOHN CARRADINE · VICTOR KILIAN
J. CARROL NAISH · CHARLES WALDRON · CLAIRE DuBREY
PEDRO De CORDOBA · RUSSELL SIMPSON · WILLIAM
BENEDICT · ROBERT SPINDOLA · CHIEF THUNDER CLOUD
Directed by HENRY KING · Executive Producer SOL M. WURTZEL
Screen play by Lamar Trotti · Based on the novel by Helen Hunt Jackson
Songs by William Kernell · Associate Producer John Stone
A 20th Century-Fox Picture   Darryl F. Zanuck in Charge of Production

20th CENTURY FOX

Ad, 1936.

New screening room at the Technicolor plant in Hollywood, mid-1930s. The mini-theater was completely equipped to handle projection of motion pictures with either film sound or disc recording. Its design and execution was considered an engineering achievement in its time and projection capabilities rivaled the most modern theaters.

Marlene Dietrich

movie could boast stars—and exploitation value. Hollywood knew that customers would find it difficult to ignore this dynamic pairing and, on that basis alone, felt the film would be immensely successful.

Ernest Hemingway once said of Miss Dietrich, "If she had nothing more than her voice, she could break your heart with it. But she also has that beautiful body and the timeless loveliness of her face."

The star, too, was not unaware of her assets. She had become intensely intrigued with the technique of color filming and prior to the start of the film worked seriously with the consultants on the best possible fabrics and tones to use in bringing the "Dietrich lure" to the new medium.

She voiced her opinions in other areas as well. Said Technicolor cameraman W. Howard Greene:

In this production, Hal Rosson and I had a rather peculiar problem. Much of the action was laid in the Sahara Desert and was filmed among the sand dunes near Yuma, Arizona. But our star, Marlene Dietrich, required a very definite style of lighting—one which Josef von Sternberg devised years ago to enhance the glamour for which Miss Dietrich is famous. And while this lighting is simplicity itself using artificial light, it is extremely difficult to achieve with less controllable natural sunlight. So it was decided to make only the longer shots on location, and to make all of the closer shots in the studio, by artificial light.

Miss Dietrich's close-ups were eminently satisfactory . . . more pleasing than we could possibly have made them with the less precise tools of natural lighting, yet they did not in the least look as though they were made in the studio.

As *The Garden of Allah* neared completion and its publicity increased, the black-and-white proponents stepped up their campaign. The priviledged few who had seen some of the film's footage boasted that it had "everything." The skeptics retorted that "even 'everything' is far from perfection" and renewed their questioning, "Is the picture as good a picture in color as it would have been in black-and-white?" The fringe group remained rather passive, noting, "The occasional color films—and may we always have them with us—are pleasant and interesting interludes in our production season."

The Garden of Allah was too important a picture, however, to be swept aside or even minimized. Wrote the *New York Times* on its opening in November, 1936:

The Selznick International production is a distinguished motion picture, rich in pictorial splendor yet unobtrusive, though accurate, in its color. (Director) Boleslawski's decision, despite the color medium, to emphasize the play and the players has placed the Music Hall's new presentation at the top of the Technicolor field. The choice, at long last of a story that permits of searching dramatic characterization made that possible for him, of course, but the realization that color, treated simply, will em-

Charles Boyer and Marlene Dietrich between scenes on *The Garden of Allah*, 1936.

Filming *The Garden of Allah*. Marlene Dietrich is seated directly in front of the camera (center).

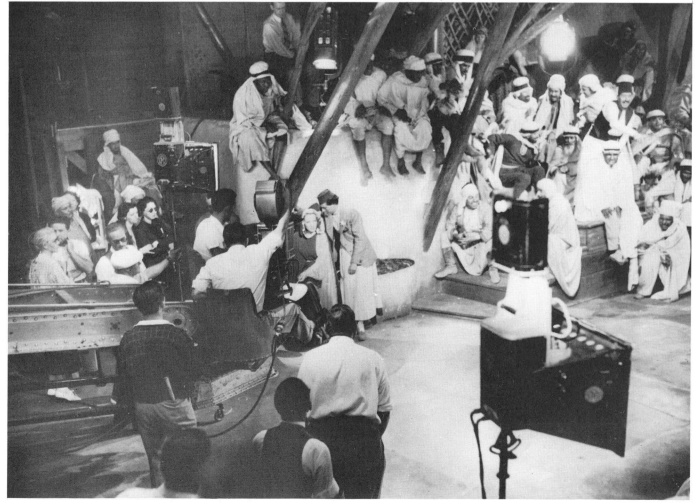

The Garden of Allah starring Charles Boyer and Marlene Dietrich.

phasize itself is Mr. Boleslawski's . . . Miss Dietrich and Mr. Boyer portray (the emotional turmoil) compellingly, and before a camera that is not too preoccupied with color to pay attention to them.

Other reviews cited ". . . the most discriminating use of Technicolor thus far . . ." and called the film a ". . . feast of Technicolor splendor," pointing out that "Technicolor goes into refinements and effects heretofore never achieved, especially the desert and sky scenes and the extraordinary night effects."

The picture was nominated for two Academy Awards (Assistant Director, Eric G. Stacey; Musical Score, Max Steiner) and on March 4, 1937, at the Biltmore Hotel in Los Angeles, the Academy of Motion Picture Arts and Sciences honored W. Howard Greene and Harold Rosson with special awards for their color cinematography. (Color cinematography did not become a separate classification until the 1939 awards.)

Prior to its release, many people in Hollywood felt that reaction to *The Garden of Allah* would be influential to the future of color in motion pictures. Their evaluation proved to be right. As studios firmed their production slates for the 1937 season, many stars were found to be more willing to give color a try. Among them, Carole Lombard. Selznick International had announced that she had been signed to co-star with Fredric March in Ben Hecht's satirical screenplay of *Nothing Sacred*. In Technicolor.

10 Hollywood Discovers Color

During the 1935-1936 production season, Technicolor's volume of release print footage had increased from over 22 million to slightly more than 37 million. Within the next two years that total would nearly double.

Hollywood was no longer saying color was simply "an artistic stunt" or "just too cute" or "nice but you get tired of it in large doses." Color had served its apprenticeship. Just as radio had helped prepare audiences for the acceptance of early artificial film sound tracks, short subjects and cartoons had helped prepare the public for full-length features. It had only been two years since the release of *Becky Sharp*. During that period, the people at Technicolor continued to move ahead, but not without some apprehension. Now that gap had been bridged. Producers were beginning to call again, much as they did during the early rush to two-color in the late 1920s.

The success of a handful of color films in 1936 had an effect not only at the Technicolor plant but elsewhere. Other systems began to make noise. Kodachrome and Cinecolor were being pushed in their development and the heads of Magnacolor, Vericolor and Fin-a-color were offering previews of their processes to any interested parties.

Out of all the names that vied for the industry's attention, Technicolor remained foremost in the minds of the studios and their policymakers—and for good reasons. Technicolor, with almost a quarter century of science and experience behind its cameras and

Marquee, Loew's State Theater, Los Angeles, 1937.

laboratories, offered the most proven product to date. The company's personnel included many of the finest technicians available. It was nearly impossible for an individual to qualify without a master's degree, or five years (at least) in a university of the M.I.T. calibre. And, despite its detractors, Technicolor also had, as Dr. Comstock pointed out many years before, "the rare wisdom of Dr. Kalmus."

In 1937 and 1938, Technicolor made its biggest splash to date. Audiences were treated to a variety of feature film fare, colorful productions that were no longer restricted mainly to musicals and period pieces. Cameras moved indoors and out to capture the excitement of the land, the sea, and the air. They recorded

81

Janet Gaynor clutches Oscar in a scene from *A Star Is Born*, 1937.

the jungle, the country, the big city, and the lands of fantasy. They discovered comedy and contemporary drama, and gave history a fresh, new look.

Film fans saw Janet Gaynor and Fredric March in David O. Selznick's modern classic, *A Star Is Born*; Ray Milland, Frances Farmer and Barry Fitzgerald in Paramount's exciting sea story, *Ebb Tide*; an all-star cast headed by Kenny Baker, Vera Zorina, Edgar Bergan and Charlie McCarthy in Samuel Goldwyn's lavish musical, *The Goldwyn Follies.*

With Walter Wanger's *Vogues of 1938*, the Joan Bennett-Warner Baxter feature, the reviews noted "Technicolor advances by a great stride toward the day when all important pictures will be prismatic" and applauded "Max Factor, with his new color harmony make-up . . . a great advance in the flesh tones, beautiful under the highlights and delicate in the shadows."

Men With Wings, an ambitious Paramount project

tracing the early days of flight, starred Fred MacMurray, Ray Milland, Donald O'Connor and Louise Campbell. The film was the third consecutive Technicolor production for producer-director William Wellman (preceded by *A Star Is Born* and *Nothing Sacred*). "At the drop of a hat," he stated at the conclusion of filming, "I'll talk for hours about color. There's nothing like it. Every night for years I used to get down on my knees and pray that I'd have the chance to make the first air picture in color. I did, and now I get down on my knees every night and offer thanks for it. When you see the picture, you'll know what I mean. The air was never like this before, unless you have flown yourself. The color gives depth, perspective, reality. It's wonderful! But I'll try to be calm."

Men With Wings was a cinematic achievement in its day. For several months, three planes flew over Southern California, from San Diego to Santa Barbara, chasing clouds and a score of other aircraft. Huge

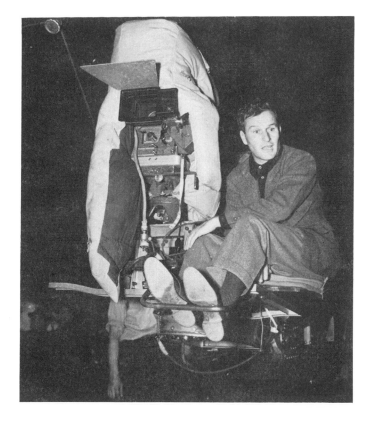

Technicolor cameras (measuring about three feet long, two feet high and a foot wide, and weighing up to three hundred and fifty pounds each) were specially mounted on fuselages, behind and in front of the pilots, on top and under wings, and from cockpits equipped with swivel mountings similar to those used for machine guns. Pilot Paul Mantz supervised the aerial acrobatics while W. Howard Greene, fresh from two special cinematic Academy Awards (*The Garden of Allah* and *A Star Is Born*) was responsible for the demanding camerawork.

Other feature films of note during the period included Alexander Korda's *Drums* with Valerie Hobson, Sabu, and Raymond Massey; Twentieth Century-Fox's *Kentucky* with Loretta Young, Richard Greene, and Walter Brennan; Paramount's *Her Jungle Love* with Dorothy Lamour and Ray Milland; and David O. Selznick's *The Adventures of Tom Sawyer* with Tommy Kelly and Anne Gillis.

Adolphe Menjou, Janet Gaynor and Andy Devine in *A Star Is Born*.

Ray Milland and Frances Farmer in *Ebb Tide*, 1937.

Character actor Mischa Auer on the salon set exterior of *Vogues of 1938*.

Vera Zorina in *The Goldwyn Follies*, 1938.

Two other motion pictures were particularly memorable but for different reasons. Ten years before, Jack Warner led the studio rush to two-color with a number of boxoffice hits. Aside from the short subjects of the mid-1930s, he was rather cautious in guiding his studio back into color. In 1937, however, he decided once again to splurge. His first three-color Technicolor feature production was *God's Country and the Woman*, starring George Brent and, in the role Bette Davis had rejected, Beverly Roberts. The second production, *Gold Is Where You Find It*, starred George Brent, again, and a relative newcomer named Olivia de Havilland. But it was Warner Bros.' third try that set a precedent.

One of the finest examples of the Technicolor process can be seen in *The Adventures of Robin Hood*, starring Errol Flynn and Olivia de Havilland, with Basil Rathbone and Claude Rains. Even today, color enthusiasts talk of the film's esthetically pleasing tones, the soft greens and russets of Sherwood Forest, and the

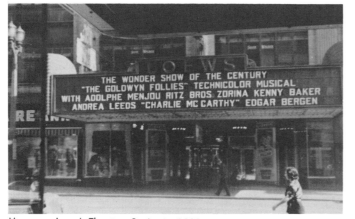

Marquee, Lowe's Theater, St. Louis, 1938.

Marquee, Chicago Theater, Chicago, 1938.

Director Irving Cummings rehearses Joan Bennett in a scene for *Vogues of 1938*. The film was billed as the screen's first fun-and-romantic fashion comedy in Technicolor.

To film the aerial acrobatics in *Men With Wings* (1938), Technicolor cameras were mounted in various positions on specially equipped camera planes (here, upsidedown between the wheels). The photography was supervised by 'Duke' Greene who flew alongside veteran stunt pilot Paul Mantz.

Director William Keighley (pointing to microphone), George Brent and Beverly Roberts on location with *God's Country and the Woman*, 1937. Of Miss Roberts, the *New York Times* noted, 'Her complexion flourishes and remains peaches and cream despite the rigors of north woods weather.'

Crew watches as Alan Hale and Errol Flynn rehearse scene from *The Adventures of Robin Hood*, filmed on location near Chico, California, 1938.

Ad, 1938.

cool grays of Nottingham Castle against which the more violent hues were used simply as accents. In 1938, undoubtedly aided by its Technicolor, *The Adventures of Robin Hood* won more Academy Awards (three) than any other picture of the year.

Another milestone was recorded on December 21, 1937, when Walt Disney's first full-length animated feature, *Snow White and the Seven Dwarfs*, premiered at the Carthay Circle Theater in Los Angeles. Prior to its release, it was generally conceded that the Disney cartoons, no matter how successful they had been in the short versions, could never compete on any level with live action feature films. *Snow White* took three years to reach the screen and, while it was eagerly awaited, most people felt that ninety minutes of drawings would only be tedious. But public opinion did an abrupt about-face after the first showing. *Snow White and the Seven Dwarfs* was an instant success and received rave reviews everywhere.

"Let your fears be quieted at once," wrote the *New York Times*. "Mr. Disney and his amazing technical crew have outdone themselves. It is a classic . . . Chromatically, it is far and away the best Technicolor to date, achieving effects possible only to the cartoon,

obtaining—through the multi-plane camera—an effortless third dimension. You'll not, most of the time, realize you are watching animated cartoons. And if you do, it will only be with a sense of amazement."

Snow White was, in a sense, not a cartoon at all—at least, not in the exaggerated style that audiences had come to expect. The latest Disney offering was a triumph of art, each step totally plotted and executed with precision. With his first feature film, Walt Disney brought a new sophistication to the field of animation. On "Oscar night," the production was recognized by the Academy as "a significant screen innovation which has charmed millions and pioneered a great new entertainment field for the motion picture cartoon." It was awarded a regulation-size statuette—and seven miniature versions.

Until now, Metro-Goldwyn-Mayer had been content to use Technicolor only for short subjects and cartoons. The studio had released a number of sepia-colored features during 1937 and 1938 but appeared hesitant to go full color. Two of the sepia productions, *Maytime* and *The Girl of the Golden West*, starred the enormously popular singing team of Nelson Eddy and Jeanette MacDonald. For their fifth picture together,

Snow White and the Seven Dwarfs, 1938.

Technicolor camera, high on a flying crane, films Jeanette MacDonald and chorus in *Sweethearts*, 1938.

M-G-M selected the romantic musical, *Sweethearts*, and planned to film it in black-and-white. At the last minute, because of a mix-up in scheduling, a decision was made to give audiences their first look at the duo in "living" color.

Jeanette MacDonald had appeared in the two-color version of *The Vagabond King* in 1930 with some success but she was recognized mainly for her physical appearance. "(She) is extremely beautiful in the clinging satins of the period," noted one reviewer. "Her performance supplies the requisite aroma of glamour." In the years following, she achieved star status, not only for her beauty but for her vocal abilities as well. She had become a valuable property and the studio used every means to protect its investment.

For her various roles, Miss MacDonald wore wigs and pieces to match her natural hair coloring, a rather nondescript shade of blonde. Color tests for *Sweethearts* showed that she needed a change. Her eyes, which were hazel, photographed slightly green

and it was felt that she should become a redhead. Many more tests were made until the right color was found and from then on audiences knew Jeanette MacDonald only with red hair.

By the end of 1938, Technicolor had twenty-five feature films in release. "Generally speaking," Dr. Kalmus said in December of that year, "these pictures have been extraordinarily well received, some of them having broken attendance records in many parts of the world." Technicolor was in the midst of its second great rush. The color process had turned into big business and the company was about to show a true profit for the very first time.

Despite the sunny outlook, the doctor was being cautious. He didn't want a repetition of the disaster that killed the color boom of 1929 and 1930. Expansion was rapid, but carefully paced. Over $1.5 million was appropriated for plant expansion to handle not only the commercial ventures but the new side line of non-theatrical films such as *Steel, Man's Servant* and *Men Make Steel* for the United States Steel Corporation. Additional cameras were built, plant capacity was

In 1938, Technicolor's facilities in Hollywood were nearly doubled by expanding plant capacity and adding a new office and research building.

Entrance to the newly completed headquarters building on Romaine Street in Hollywood. Dr. Kalmus' office was located on the second floor to the left of the entry.

doubled, a new office and research building was constructed, and a number of highly qualified technicians were hired.

The new Technicolor complex was a self-contained unit and nearly impregnable to outsiders. "It is the purpose of Technicolor, during the time that prints of any picture are being manufactured in its plant, to hold the laboratory open for, and at the disposal of, the customer as if it were his own," Dr. Kalmus explained. "His representative may inspect each of his prints and any changes suggested will be undertaken if practicable."

What the doctor didn't mention were the company's increasingly rigid security measures. With competitiors on the scene, the by-words were "top secrecy." Very few people were privy to the know-how and workings within the various departments, or to the methods and procedures that were discovered (and constantly being improved) solely by trial and error. Almost no one was allowed to roam at will, even insiders. It was impossible to gain admittance to the processing lab, for example, without a pass or the personal accompaniment of top-level management. Those employees who worked on an operational level were compartmentalized and stayed exclusively within the boundaries of their specialities. Rarely was anyone transferred to another department or division and only

A GREAT CLASSIC COMES TO LIFE
IN GLORIOUS TECHNICOLOR!

SHIRLEY TEMPLE
in THE
LITTLE PRINCESS

Shirley!...at last in
TECHNICOLOR

with
RICHARD GREENE
ANITA LOUISE
IAN HUNTER · CESAR ROMERO
ARTHUR TREACHER · MARY NASH
SYBIL JASON · MILES MANDER
MARCIA MAE JONES
Directed by Walter Lang · Associate Producer Gene
Markey · Screen Play by Ethel Hill and Walter Ferris
Based on the novel by Frances Hodgson Burnett
A 20th Century-Fox Picture
Darryl F. Zanuck in Charge of Production

Ad, 1939.

Pinocchio, 1940.

a small number had an overall view of the workings of the company. To some, such an atmosphere may sound totally restrictive. But each division was a world all its own, and the technicians took tremendous pride in their individual and group accomplishments as well as in their contributions to an increasingly prestigious wing of the growing motion picture industry.

As Technicolor entered 1939, newspapers traced the spreading war overseas. "The foreign situation is becoming more and more difficult," Dr. Kalmus reported to stockholders. "Sales to Germany, Spain, Japan and China have practically ceased, and in many other foreign countries they are below normal. The Italian government controls the entire distribution of films in Italy, which probably means that everything possible will be done to distribute Italian-made pictures at the expense of English and American-made pictures."

In spite of world news, the company was headed for its biggest year to date. Technicolor was proving itself at the ticket windows and any doubts the studios once had were quickly disappearing.

The London unit was involved with a screen version of Gilbert and Sullivan's *The Mikado*, featuring American-born Kenny Baker and an all-star cast, and Alexander Korda's *Four Feathers*, his follow-up to the previous year's *Drums*.

In Hollywood, Twentieth Century-Fox, one of the first studio's to give Technicolor a try, had firmed contracts for four features. Darryl F. Zanuck now had so much confidence in the process that he agreed to showcase Shirley Temple, the reigning box office champion for four straight years, in her first full-length color picture, *The Little Princess*.

Warner Bros. had scheduled the release of *Dodge City* with Errol Flynn, Olivia de Havilland and Ann Sheridan, and *The Private Lives of Elizabeth and Essex* with Bette Davis and Errol Flynn.

At the Disney studios, two long-term feature projects were in the works: *Fantasia* and *Pinocchio*.

In Culver City, two others were in production: Metro-Goldwyn-Mayer's *The Wizard of Oz* and David O. Selznick's *Gone With the Wind* (later released by M-G-M). For Metro, surprisingly, *The Wizard of Oz*

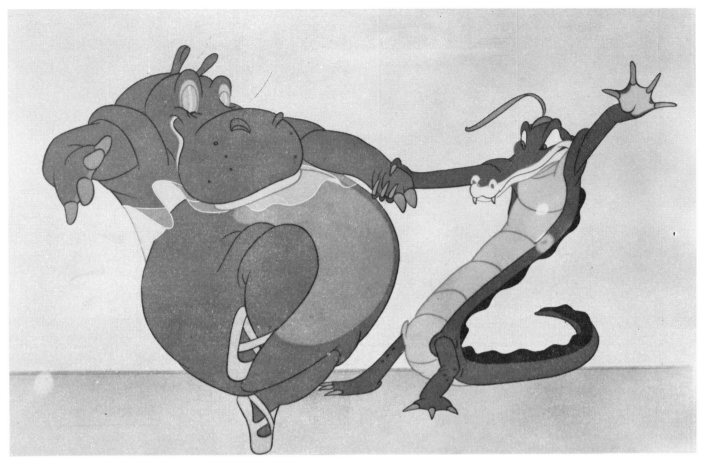

Fantasia, 1940.

Giant billboard outside the M-G-M studio in Culver City, 1939.

was only the second venture into feature-length Technicolor filming.

Technically, *The Wizard of Oz* was not a full-length color film. It opened and closed in sepia (actually black-and-white film washed in a brown bath). While the technique helped establish mood—from drab reality to a candy-colored dreamland and back—it put a stress on the make-up department, as make-up for the "black-and-white" scenes was not suitable for the color portions and vice versa.

The production was a masterpiece of imaginative design, the work of art director Cedric Gibbons and his assistant, William A. Horning. To create the total illusion of fantasy, they ingeniously had their artists combine painted backgrounds, on film, with the existing sets. The result was a stunning collage that helped bring the Frank Baum classic to life.

Throughout, color was an integral part of the picture—from the yellow brick road to the ruby slippers to the Emerald City and so on. It also caused a few problems, such as finding the right shade of yellow for the legendary brick road. Said producer Mervyn LeRoy, "We tried all kinds of exotic dyes and imported paints and photographed them, and none of them looked really right. Then one morning I suggested to Gibbons that he try some ordinary, cheap yellow fence

paint. He did and the yellow brick road finally looked like a yellow brick road should look."

The change from monochrome to color, in the early part of the film, had to be handled with extreme care. When Judy Garland, as young Dorothy, slowly opened the door of her home to go outside following the cyclone sequence, the exterior (Munchkinland), as seen through the door opening had to be revealed in color to keep the transition from being too abrupt. Each of the frames in the several-second scene required hand-tinting to show the visual richness of the outside fantasy world as it appeared through the opening door. From there, the screen went to full color.

More time was lost in preparing the "horse of a different color" scenes. In the story, Dorothy and her friends—the Straw Man, the Tin Woodman and the Cowardly Lion—follow the yellow brick road to Emerald City where the resident Wizard, with his magical powers, will grant their wishes. For Dorothy, it's a return to her home in Kansas; for the Straw Man, a brain; for the Tin Woodman, a heart; and for the Cowardly Lion, courage.

When the quartet arrives at the Emerald City, they are met by all the citizens and a carriage, which is pulled by a most unusual horse. On the way to the steps

10/31/38
original Dress —
own hair & fall
before darkening

Early wardrobe test for *The Wizard of Oz*. Judy Garland's long, dark stockings were later changed to short, light ones. Her hair was also trimmed and two small ribbons replaced the large bow.

Shooting the Munchkinland sequence for *The Wizard of Oz*. At right, Judy Garland and Billie Burke.

of the Wizard's secret chambers, it changes colors before everyones eyes.

At first, the film's creative team thought the horse could be painted to create the multi-hued illusion but the American Society for the Prevention of Cruelty to Animals said no. The trick was to find a substance that would not only pass the ASPCA test but would photograph clearly. Food coloring was tried, even liquid candy, and without success. The colors were too tame—and much too tasty. Finally, a paste of Jell-O powder was found acceptable. The horse continued to lick but, with frequent touch-ups, the problem was solved.

The role of the Tin Man was originally assigned to dancer Buddy Ebsen, but he became mysteriously ill and had to be rushed to a hospital where he was put in an iron lung for a time. It was later diagnosed that he had been poisoned from inhaling the silver-colored

Rehearsing the 'horse of a different color' scene.

Judy Garland relaxes with Toto during shooting of *The Wizard of Oz.*

Vivien Leigh in *Gone With the Wind*, 1939.

aluminum dust sprayed on his costume to give it a metallic look. The part was taken over by Broadway star Jack Haley.

The lands of Oz were constructed on the M-G-M back lot in one-fourth life size. Even so, the full set covered twenty-five acres and consisted of one hundred and twenty-two buildings. Over sixty different shades and colors were used in painting them.

The Wizard of Oz took over a year to prepare and shoot at a cost of $2.7 million. *Gone With the Wind*, an even more ambitious project, ran nearly $4 million.

The photoplay of Margaret Mitchell's Pulitzer Prize-winning novel went into production in late January, 1939, after a two year search for an actress to play the heroine, Scarlett O'Hara. Producer David O. Selznick talked to over 1,250 knowns and unknowns before he decided upon Vivien Leigh, a relatively obscure British actress who was in Hollywood only to be near her fiance, Laurence Olivier.

Gone With the Wind was one of the earliest motion pictures to be released with an intermission (it ran three hours and forty-two minutes) and was the first to be photographed using the new, faster Technicolor film, which revolutionized color lighting methods. Aside from cutting lighting requirements by at least fifty per cent, and allowing the use of smaller units such

as baby spots for precise facial lighting, the new film offered many other advantages. (Lighting costs for *The Wizard of Oz* amounted to $226,307—nearly $100,000 more than for *Gone With the Wind*.)

Cameraman Ray Rennahan noted at the time:

The new film has naturally increased the scope of projected-background cinematography tremendously (process shots). Heretofore . . . we were limited to relatively small background screens. We can now use screens as large as those generally employed in monochrome, and with equal flexibility.

Another important improvement . . . is improved color rendition, particularly in the greens. Every color process has found green one of the hardest colors to reproduce faithfully, and it is an especial problem here in California where the natural greens of the foliage, grass and the like seem to have a somewhat rusty shade unknown in moister climates . . .

Thomas Mitchell and Vivien Leigh, *Gone With the Wind.*

Clark Gable and Vivien Leigh, *Gone With the Wind*.

The beautiful greens of the finished film, particularly on exterior shots, were an asset in helping recreate the atmosphere of the Old South.

Ernest Haller, Mr. Rennahan's associate, had just completed the Bette Davis monochrome film, *Dark Victory*, when he landed the *Gone With the Wind* assignment. "I was amazed," he said, "to step into Technicolor production and find that instead of requiring immensely high light levels it now permitted me to light very much as I did for black-and-white . . .

"In the old days, shadows were strictly taboo in Technicolor; you had to crowd in 'filter light' from every angle to make sure that the shadows wouldn't vanish into inky blackness . . . Now that color has become more flexible technically, its artistic possibilities are so great one wants to keep on exploring them!"

When the Academy Awards were presented for 1939 productions, *Gone With the Wind* was named the best picture of the year (*The Wizard of Oz* was the only other color nominee). Ray Rennahan and Ernest Haller won the cinematography award and William Cameron Menzies was presented with a special plaque for his "outstanding achievement in the use of color for the enhancement of dramatic mood in the production of *Gone With the Wind*." Technicolor, too, received a coveted statuette "for its contributions in successfully bringing three-color feature production to the screen."

Dr. Kalmus was asked his reaction to this long deserved recognition after clinging "so tenaciously . . . through the 'dark ages' when color motion pictures were not so well appreciated."

His reply: "It was marvelously interesting, it was great fun. We couldn't let anybody down, neither customers, employees, stockholders nor directors. But there was something else too. There was always something just ahead, a plan for tomorrow, something exciting to be finished—yes, and something more to be finished after that. And I am willing to predict that it won't be finished for many years . . ."

Legendary lovers, Scarlett and Rhett.

Our *Congratulations*

to

ERNEST HALLER, A. S. C. *and* RAY RENNAHAN, A. S. C.

Winners of the

COLOR CINEMATOGRAPHY AWARD

of the

ACADEMY OF MOTION PICTURE ARTS AND SCIENCES

for their

TECHNICOLOR PHOTOGRAPHY

of

"GONE WITH THE WIND"

TECHNICOLOR

MOTION PICTURE CORPORATION

HERBERT T. KALMUS, *President*

Following the Oscar ceremonies, the Technicolor Corporation placed this
ad in film trade publications, 1940.

11 The Bright New Stars

With the release of each new picture, the studios and exhibitors felt the growing value of Technicolor. Public reaction to a Technicolor movie was extremely favorable and producers soon realized that a film in color meant extra profits, despite higher production costs.

As America moved into the war years of the early 1940s, the color process became a major draw. The words *In Technicolor* on a theater marquee created excitement—and usually a long line of customers. More and more, newspaper and magazine advertising socked out coined phrases designed to lure readers into the vibrantly hued world, catch words in big, bold type, often above the film title and leading players. They read of "Glorious Technicolor" and "Sizzling Technicolor" and "Gorgeous Technicolor." "Living Technicolor" and "Stirring Technicolor" and "Magnificent Technicolor." Suddenly, Technicolor had become a star in its own right.

During the filming of *Gone With the Wind*, cinematographer Ernest Haller remarked, "Whenever an established feminine star makes her first appearance in a color film the critics almost always exclaim at great length about the new personality color gives her.

"Now that we have this fast film, which enables a cinematographer to use all the little tricks of precision lighting he has used in monochrome to glamorize his stars, I am sure that color is going to be more flattering than ever to women."

It was wartime and there were millions of American G.I.'s around the world who wanted nothing more than to have lovely, talented ladies entertain them. Movies were a touch of home, and there were few things that pleased the men in the Armed Forces more than a Technicolor movie filled with attractive females.

The timing was perfect. Technicolor had managed to glorify the leading lady just when she was about to be in big demand. The combination of Technicolor *and* beautiful girls was hard to resist.

Hollywood searched for fresh, new personalities to use in its color creations. A hopeful didn't require an imposing list of credits—but she did have to be colorful in her own rights, either in looks or personality, or both.

Film fans wanted color and Technicolor gave it to them. Color became exaggerated, more colorful than life—extra rich, vibrant, and exciting. The performers, especially the females, reflected the palette that surrounded them. Nothing that could be dyed, tinted, toned, or painted remained the same. Honey blondes became butter blondes. Golden blondes became silver blondes. Brownettes turned strawberry or tangerine. Brunettes went henna or mahogany or jet. Complexions had to be peaches and cream. And lips, full and glistening, were brushed with one of any number of rose reds.

The studios, with their stables of stars, each had a number of performers who, with their looks and/or talent, seemed to be "born for Technicolor." Of those, only a few were true Technicolor stars. Technicolor helped take them to the top. In turn, they became the major contributing force in "selling" the Technicolor process to the vast motion picture public.

Ad, 1941.

Ad, 1943.

BETTY GRABLE was among the top ten boxoffice stars for ten consecutive years (1942-1951). During that period, she was the highest rated female seven times, and in 1948 the highest salaried woman in the United States. The G.I.'s favorite pin-up girl during World War II, she reportedly received over ten thousand fan letters a week and more than two million requests for a bathing suit photo that displayed her famous "gams." Of her legs, she often remarked that she thought Marlene Dietrich's were better. Of her talent, she noted, "There are a dozen girls I know who can sing better, dance better and act better. I can do a little of all three and I suppose that's why I get by." (Her mother took a slightly different view: "Betty's like any average American girl who makes a million a year.")

Born Elizabeth Ruth Grable on December 18, 1916, in St. Louis, Missouri, Betty was the daughter of Conn Grable, a wealthy stockbroker, and his wife, Lillian, who have given up her own dreams of show business only to later become a driving force in her daughter's career. At age five, Betty was dancing, studying tap, ballet and acrobatic, and playing the ukelele and saxophone. By the time she was seven, she was appearing on local talent shows.

During a 1929 visit to Southern California, twelve-year-old Betty talked her mother into staying in Hollywood. But Lillian Grable didn't have to be coaxed. She had toured the studios and seen the stars. She knew that this was the life she wanted for her daughter. And when she heard, the following year, that Fox Studio was looking for song-and-dance girls, she found her opening. Lying about her age, Betty won a spot in the chorus line of *Let's Go Places* (1930). Shortly thereafer, she became a Goldwyn Girl and appeared in Samuel Goldwyn's *Whoopee* (1930), *Palmy Days* (1931), and *The Kid From Spain* (1932), all with Eddie Cantor.

Betty Grable made her first big impression on movie audiences in the Fred Astaire-Ginger Rogers musical *The Gay Divorcee* (1934) when she was seen in a specialty number, *K-Knock Knees*, with Edward Everett Horton. She followed this with a series of co-ed parts in college-themed pictures at Paramount and Twentieth Century-Fox (*Collegiate, Pigskin Parade, College Swing, Campus Confessions*) until offers became scarce. In 1939, she accepted a supporting role in the Broadway production of *DuBarry Was A Lady*. Despite the presence of powerhouse stars Ethel Merman and Bert Lahr, Betty stole the show. Darryl F. Zanuck summoned her back to Hollywood and Twentieth Century-Fox when Alice Faye became ill and was unable to do his 1940 Technicolor musical, *Down Argentine Way*. Betty replaced her; it was Grable's

Down Argentine Way, 1941.

twenty-eighth film but, as far as audiences were concerned, they had never seen her until now. Technicolor made the difference.

Next came a black-and-white musical, *Tin Pan Alley*, opposite Alice Faye. Miss Faye had the bigger role, but Betty Grable further solidified her new reputation and was rewarded with a starring spot in another Technicolor production, *Moon Over Miami*.

In spite of her growing popularity, and her obvious forte in Technicolor films, Fox surprisingly cast Betty Grable in three distinctly different black-and-white productions: *A Yank in the R.A.F.*, *Footlight Serenade* and *I Wake Up Screaming*. While audiences were willing to pay to see her in anything, the studio now realized the best way to showcase its newest star was in color. Except for a guest appearance (as herself) in the 1944 *Four Jills In A Jeep*, she never again appeared in a black-and-white film.

Betty Grable was one of the most cooperative and unpretentious of the stars, and she knew best how to use her talents. She loved to dance and sing—and it showed. In 1945, after she had completed *The Dolly Sisters*, her biggest film to date (it broke every existing attendance record at New York's Roxy Theater), Darryl

Yes, boys and girls, it's **BETTY GRABLE**

...in love!
...in Miami!
...in a bathing suit!
...in Technicolor!
Join her holiday fling at romance...
in America's gay holiday town!

a Varga Esq.

MOON OVER MIAMI

IN TECHNICOLOR!

featuring

DON AMECHE
BETTY GRABLE
ROBERT CUMMINGS

and

Charlotte Greenwood • Jack Haley
Carole Landis • Cobina Wright, Jr.

Directed by Walter Lang • Produced by Harry Joe Brown
Screen Play by Vincent Lawrence and Brown Holmes
Adaptation by George Seaton and Lynn Starling • From a
Play by Stephen Powys • Lyrics and Music by Leo Robin
and Ralph Rainger • Dances Staged by Hermes Pan
A TWENTIETH CENTURY-FOX PICTURE

8 grand songs

"I'VE GOT YOU ALL TO MYSELF"
"HURRAH FOR TODAY"
"KINDERGARDEN CONGA"
"LOVELINESS and LOVE"
"YOU STARTED SOMETHING"
"SOLITARY SEMINOLE"
"IS THAT GOOD?"
"MIAMI"

Ad, 1941.

Ad, 1944.

Song Of The Islands, 1942.

Billy Rose's Diamond Horseshoe, 1945.

Zanuck offered her the role of the drunken Sophie in his black-and-white *The Razor's Edge*, promising that he could make her a great dramatic actress. "I'm strictly a song and dance girl," she told him good-naturedly. "If I play Sophie, my fans will expect me to rise from the ocean with seaweed in my hair and sing something." The role went to Anne Baxter and won her an Oscar.

After *The Dolly Sisters*, however, she did seek a change of pace. She had seen Judy Garland in *Meet Me In St. Louis* and was impressed with the look of the film. Her own musicals, she began to believe, were too garish and glossy. Now she wanted to do a musical that was more subdued in color. The studio cooperated and began to plan *The Shocking Miss Pilgrim*. George Seaton, who had written and directed her earlier *Billy Rose's Diamond Horseshoe*, was hired for similar duties. He tried to create a new image for her, that of a turn-of-the-century stenographer in very proper Boston. Although utilizing Technicolor, it was a role with less flash, darkened hair and unseen "gams"—and a musical without one big production number. The finished film, with its subdued color and a subdued Grable, disturbed her fans. With her next movie, *Mother Wore Tights* in 1947, the garish, glossy colors were back. It proved to be one of her most popular pictures.

Betty Grable made twenty-two Technicolor features during her career. For millions of movie-goers around the world, she was the darling of the Technicolor screen. (Her Technicolor credits also included *Song of the Islands*, 1942; *Springtime in the Rockies*, 1942; *Coney Island*, 1943; *Sweet Rosie O'Grady*, 1943; *Pin Up Girl*, 1944; *Do You Love Me?*, 1946; *That Lady In Ermine*, 1948; *When My Baby Smiles At Me*, 1948; *The Beautiful Blonde From Bashful Bend*, 1949; *Wabash Avenue*, 1950; *My Blue Heaven*, 1950; *Call Me Mister*, 1951; *Meet Me After The Show*, 1951; *The Farmer Takes A Wife*, 1953; *How To Marry A Millionaire*, 1953; and *Three For The Show*, 1955.)

RITA HAYWORTH was a blossoming star when she appeared in *Life* Magazine in 1941. The photo, a black-and-white pin-up shot, showed her kneeling on a bed, dressed in a white satin and black lace nightgown. Audiences had just seen her for the first time in a major role opposite Fred Astaire in a non-color musical, *You'll Never Get Rich*. Later that year, *Blood and Sand*—her first Technicolor film—was released. If Rita Hayworth was beautiful in black-and-white, she was magnificent in color. The girl with the flowing tresses and sensuous movements would soon become America's "love goddess"—and one of the most publicized women in the world.

Ad, 1944.

She was born Margarita Carmen Cansino in New York City, the daughter of Eduardo Cansino, a Spanish dancer, and Volga Haworth, an American who at one time had appeared on the English stage. Both parents wanted a theatrical career for Margarita, a talented youngster with deep black hair and dark eyes. She was taking dancing lessons almost as soon as she could walk; by the age of six, she was part of the family act.

By 1935, she and her father had become a team and were appearing at Agua Caliente, a multi-million dollar hotel and casino complex located in a flowery oasis just south of Tijuana in Baja California, where she was spotted by movieman Winfield Sheehan. "That girl is a great beauty," he reportedly told friends at the time. "She could be a movie star with the right training." The others laughed. They thought she was a good dancer and had a lovely face but that she was too shy and too plump. He signed her to a contract, nevertheless.

Margarita Cansino made her official film debut as a dancer in Fox Film's *Dante's Inferno*, although two later-made films were released first. Initially, she failed to impress audiences but she continued at Fox in a number of bit parts. The various studio press agents, at the time, were members of an organization called The Wampus, formed to promote promising young talent. They selected Miss Cansino to be one of their "Wampus Baby Stars" and, as Fox's representative, she received added recognition and was even announced to play the leading role in their Technicolor production of *Ramona*. Unfortunately, the studio was experiencing growing pains of its own. Fox Film Corporation merged with Twentieth Century Pictures to form Twentieth Century-Fox and Darryl F. Zanuck became head of production. With the change, Loretta Young (a favorite of Zanuck) got the part of Ramona and the newly named Rita Hayworth ("I do not like the name of Margarita Cansino," said one studio executive. "It's too long for billboards.") went to work in *Charlie Chan in Egypt* and other minor pictures.

At seventeen, she married Edward Judson, an

With Gene Kelly in Cover Girl, 1944.

With Lee Bowman in *Tonight And Every Night*, 1945.

Earth, 1947; *The Loves of Carmen*, 1948; *Salome*, 1953; *Miss Sadie Thompson*, 1953; *Fire Down Below*, 1957; *Pal Joey*, 1957; and *Circus World*, 1964.

MARIA MONTEZ was one of Universal's biggest money-makers throughout the war years. From *Arabian Nights* (1942) through *Sudan* (1945), she was seen adorning some of the most opulent and exotic sets Hollywood could create, gowned and jeweled in wondrous style. A fiery Latin beauty, she had reddish-brown hair, a magnificent complexion, and total confidence. She once noted, quite candidly, after viewing one of her performances, "When I look at myself I am so beautiful I scream with joy." Another time, after meeting Orson Welles, she commented, ". . . he is every bit as spectacular as I am."

Born on June 6, 1920, in the Dominican Republic, she was christened Maria Africa Gracis Vidal de Santos Silas. Her father, Ysidro Gracis, was the local Spanish council; her mother, Teresa Vidal de Santos Silas, the daughter of a political refugee. Unlike her nine brothers and sisters, she was educated at the Sacred Heart Convent in the Canary Islands where she learned to speak and read French and English as well as her native Spanish.

After her schooling, she traveled throughout Europe. In Ireland, she began her acting career with minor roles in a small theatrical group. It was in New

ambitious automobile salesman from Texas, who saw Rita Hayworth as a good investment. He became her agent, persuaded her to change her dark hair to titian red, introduced her to the right people, and saw to it that she was never out of the limelight. One of the people she met was Columbia Pictures' Harry Cohn, who put her under contract to his studio. She continued to be cast in mediocre parts and it wasn't until she did some "loan outs" to other studios that things began to happen. Metro-Goldwyn-Mayer borrowed her for *Susan and God* (1940). Warner Bros. got her as a last minute replacement for Ann Sheridan in *The Strawberry Blonde* (1941). Fox used her in *Blood and Sand* (1941) and, when Alice Faye became pregnant, in *My Gal Sal* (1942)—both in Technicolor. Her success in *My Gal Sal* told the Columbia chief, a shrewd showman, what the public wanted. With each picture her fan mail increased sharply and, before long, she was vying with Betty Grable for the affections of the servicemen. More photos of these two stars were sent to the war zones—the South Pacific, Africa and Europe—than of any others.

Although her great success, *Gilda*, was in black-and-white, Rita Hayworth's lingering impression is in Technicolor images—thanks to the memorable *Cover Girl*, 1944; *Tonight and Every Night*, 1945; *Down To*

With Don Ameche and Carmen Miranda in *That Night In Rio*, 1941.

With Sabu and Jon Hall (right) in *Arabian Nights,* 1942.

Maria Montez

York City, however, where she was working as a photographer's model, that she was spotted by a Hollywood agent. It took only one screen test for Universal to sign her, and soon she was appearing in several low budget films which were not to her liking. When she became temperamental, the studio arranged for her to play a small role in Twentieth Century-Fox's 1941 Technicolor musical, *That Night In Rio,* with Alice Faye, Don Ameche and Carmen Miranda. On her return to Universal, she was again relegated to relatively unimportant features—but not for long. Servicemen everywhere were starting to request publicity photos of her to pin up in their barracks. Universal executives took another look at their property and decided to cast her opposite Jon Hall in Walter Wanger's Technicolor production of *Arabian Nights.* It was the studio's first venture in full color filming. Her sultry beauty and rich accent were ideally suited to the role of Scheherazade. And Technicolor.

By the end of 1942, Maria Montez was a top star with

Wabash Avenue, 1950. "Betty Grable in Technicolor," wrote the New York Times, "is balm for the eyes."

Maria Montez: "I am so beautiful . . ."

Publicity still of Rita Hayworth for *The Loves of Carmen*, 1948.

Maureen O'Hara.

Lucille Ball.

Esther Williams in *Million Dollar Mermaid*, 1952.

Rhonda Fleming.

Carmen Miranda, the "Brazilian Bombshell."

Arlene Dahl in *Three Little Words*, 1950.

a string of exotic Technicolor costume fantasies to follow, including *White Savage*, 1942; *Ali Baba and the Forty Thieves*, 1944; *Cobra Woman*, 1944; *Gypsy Wildcat*, 1944; *Sudan*, 1945; and *Pirates of Monterey*, 1947.

MAUREEN O'HARA was crowned "Queen of Technicolor" after only a few appearances before the color camera. What sounds like a publicist's inspiration came instead from the Technicolor Corporation itself, which used test footage of her during the early 1940s to help sell their process to the studios. "In those days," she says, "we did not receive remuneration for such use of our name or likeness. I was proud of the honor."

Born in Dublin, Ireland, the oldest of six children, she inherited a love of the stage from her mother, Marguerita FitzSimons, who somehow found time while rearing her family to win a number of dramatic contests and become a member of the Abbey Players, Ireland's famed national theater group.

Young Maureen FitzSimons dramatized everything in her life. At five, she appeared in a church play; at twelve, she went on the radio and earned her first money as a professional entertainer. By the time she was fourteen, she too had joined the Abbey Players. Over the next few years she would win every award and medal bestowed in Ireland's play festivals and dramatic contests.

With John Payne in *To The Shores Of Tripoli*, 1942.

When she was eighteen, Harry Richman, the American singer, urged her mother to take her to London for screen tests. One was shot at Elstree Studios during the filming of the 1938 Richman film, *Kicking the Moon Around* (originally released in the U.S. as *The Playboy* and reissued in 1942 as *Millionaire Merry-Go-Round*). To her surprise, a portion of this test—showing her peeking around a door to announce a caller on the telephone—was used in the film.

If this brief exposure went unnoticed the full screen test did not. Actor Charles Laughton and producer-director Erich Pommer, who "discovered" Marlene Dietrich a decade earlier, saw it and signed her to a long-term contract with their company, Mayflower Pictures. Much against her will, they changed her name from FitzSimons to O'Hara then cast her in the 1939 production of *Jamaica Inn* opposite Mr. Laughton.

With her background limited to theater, the Mayflower group felt she needed camera experience prior to the start of their feature and, as Maureen FitzSimons, was loaned out for the title role in *My Irish Molly*. A modest film originally intended for viewing only in small English towns, *Molly* made it to the United States in 1940, undoubtedly prompted by the success of *Jamaica Inn*.

Maureen O'Hara appeared in a handful of dramatic black-and-white movies, among them, *The Hunchback of Notre Dame* (1939) and *How Green Was My Valley* (1941), before her statuesque Irish beauty and cascading auburn hair were first captured by the Technicolor cameras in Twentieth Century-Fox's *To the Shore of Tripoli* (1942). Because the harsh lights hurt her eyes, she felt she could never again make another Technicolor film. Today, with thirty-three color films on record, she credits the combination of Technicolor and great cameramen (specifically Edward Cronjager and Leon Shamroy) for escalating her productive screen career.

She was a film favorite in Technicolor and at Technicolor. Prior to the start of each picture she made, whether in color or not, the company sent her an enormous basket of roses in every color of the spectrum. They came to be known as her "Technicolor roses."

Maureen O'Hara's lengthy list of Technicolor features spans nearly thirty years, from *To the Shores of Tripoli* and *The Black Swan*, 1942; *Buffalo Bill*, 1944; *The Spanish Main*, 1945; *Sinbad the Sailor*, 1947; and *The Quiet Man*, 1952, to the more recent *The Parent Trap*, 1961; *Mr. Hobbs Takes A Vacation*, 1962; *Spencer's Mountain*, 1963; *McLintock!*, 1963; *The Rare Breed*, 1966; and *Big Jake*, 1971.

With Paul Henreid in *The Spanish Main*, 1945.

Ad, 1945.

With Barry Fitzgerald and John Wayne in *The Quiet Man*, 1952.

CARMEN MIRANDA, the lady who wore fruit baskets on her head, was a Technicolor extravaganza in her own right, on and off the screen. The exhuberant entertainer had a tremendous influence on fashion as well as on the music of the day.

She was a creature of contradictions. Known as "the Brazilian Bombshell," she was actually born in Portugal, on February 9, 1914. As a so-called product of the world's leading coffee producing country, she let it be known she detested the drink.

Her real name was Maria da Carmo da Cunha and she was educated in a convent in Rio de Janeiro. When she was fifteen, she knew that she wanted to be a singer but her well-to-do parents thought it would be improper for a girl to appear on the stage. She turned to radio and found a job at a local station. Within a short time, she was making phonograph records of her most popular radio numbers. Her success on records led to engagements in casinos, night clubs and theaters, and parts in South American films.

Week-End in Havana, 1941.

116

Ad, 1944.

It was only a matter of time until the United States discovered her. Lee Shubert, of the Broadway Shuberts, was on a South American cruise in 1938 when he was invited to see Miss Miranda perform at the Casino Urqua in Rio. He placed her, and her six singing accompanists, under contract at once.

In New York, her unique talent and style created a sensation and, within months, she had been spotted (and signed) by a Twentieth Century-Fox scout. She was first cast in *Down Argentine Way* with Betty Grable and Don Ameche, but getting her to Hollywood proved difficult, as commitments prevented her from leaving New York. Instead, the studio sent the director, Irving Cummings, and the entire Technicolor crew to New York and filmed her scenes at the Movietone Studio on Tenth Avenue. It was not until the following year, 1941, when the studio decided to do a film set in her adopted country (*That Night In Rio*) that she was able to head west. Even then, the start of production had to be postponed to permit her to fulfill a long-standing engagement at Chicago's Chez Paris.

When Carmen Miranda arrived in California, her vocabulary consisted of less than two dozen words. But it was the way she handled dialog—or mishandled it—and her flashy interpretations of catchy tunes (*I'Yi, Yi, Yi, Yi, Yi I Like You Very Much; Chica, Chica, Boom, Chic; Cuanta La Gusta; Mamae Eu Quero*) that captivated Americans. For a time, she was the rage of the fashion world. New York debutantes started it by "borrowing" her look, the Bahiana costume she originated for a Rio carnival, distinguished by an abundance of chunky junk jewelry, colorful bandannas, and high platform wedgies.

Carmen Miranda's Technicolor features also included *Week-End In Havana*, 1941; *Springtime in the Rockies*, 1942; *The Gang's All Here*, 1943; *Greenwich Village*, 1944, *A Date With Judy*, 1948; and *Nancy Goes to Rio*, 1950. It is not surprising that this colorful performer failed to be at her best when cast in several non-Technicolor musicals. Such black-and-white films as *Doll Face* (1946), *If I'm Lucky* (1946), and *Copacabana* (1947) undoubtedly helped speed the decline of her meteoric screen career.

ESTHER WILLIAMS brought a special talent to motion pictures. Swimming. Over ten spectacular years, she appeared in sixteen Technicolor extravaganzas, more than any other Metro-Goldwyn-Mayer star—and earned the distinction of being the studio's all-time female money-maker.

She was born in Los Angeles in the shadows of M-G-M. Even as a child, she was obsessed with swimming to such an extent that she spent part of every

With Keenan Wynn and Betty Garrett in *Neptune's Daughter*, 1949.

day at the local municipal pool in Inglewood where she paid her admission by counting towels.

As a teenager, Esther Jane Williams won sixteen titles and held the world's breast stroke record. In 1940, she qualified for the American Olympic team, winning three berths, but the games were canceled because of the war.

Ad, 1951.

119

Million Dollar Mermaid, 1952.

The long-legged, freckle-face girl was working as a stock girl at I. Magnin & Co., with her sights set on being a buyer, when she was contacted by showman Billy Rose who wanted to star her in his glittering aquacade at the San Francisco World's Fair. The result was a measure of fame and a call from one of Louis B. Mayer's aides at M-G-M. Surprisingly, she did not jump at the opportunity to appear in pictures. The biggest obstacle, she felt, was that she couldn't act. (Years later, after her stardom was long established, she commented, "If they ever teach a duck to act, I'm in trouble.") Mr. Mayer, who was known to be persuasive at times, signed her to a seven year contract at $250 a week.

The studio groomed Esther Williams for stardom, giving her lessons in everything from "how to walk" to "how to sit." After a few minor roles in black-and-white films, she was cast in her first Technicolor movie, *Mr. Co-ed*, starring Red Skelton. Technicolor heightened her natural assets to such an extent that the studio built up her part, changed the title of the film to *Bathing Beauty*, and gave her co-star billing. An average picture with an average plot, *Bathing Beauty* became a bigger draw than anticipated. In South America, it broke many attendance records, even those of *Gone With the Wind*. The first three Technicolor pictures in which she starred (*Bathing Beauty*, 1944; *Thrill of a Romance*, 1945; *Easy To Wed*, 1946) grossed over $15 million in the United States alone. Except for a minor black-and-white melodrama with William Powell called *The Hoodlum Saint* (1946), her future films were exclusively color.

By the early 1950s, Esther Williams had been showcased in every conceivable water setting and dreaming up new ways to display her skills became a real problem. Twentieth Century-Fox had encountered similar problems with its Olympic ice skating champion, Sonja Henie, a few years earlier. Miss Henie normally had three skating sequences in each picture and finding new ways to get her on the ice, logically or otherwise, was not easy. Too, the Norwegian-born star was less versatile, making the situation even more difficult. Esther Williams had learned to dance and sing. Still, in an effort to please her public, production numbers became more astonishing and colorful with each outing. (Miss Henie, incidentally, only once had the advantage of color during her ten-picture career: RKO's *It's A Pleasure* in 1945.)

In 1952, Busby Berkeley was hired to create the water sequences for *Million Dollar Mermaid*, the dramatic, true story of swimmer Annette Kellerman. Of all her films, it is Miss Williams' favorite. For her

millions of fans, it marked a high point in a glamorous career that included such other Technicolor features as *Fiesta*, 1947; *This Time For Keeps*, 1947; *On An Island With You*, 1948; *Take Me Out To The Ball Game*, 1949; *Neptune's Daughter*, 1949; *Duchess of Idaho*, 1950; *Pagan Love Song*, 1950; *Texas Carnival*, 1951; *Skirts Ahoy!*, 1952; *Dangerous When Wet*, 1953; and *Easy To Love*, 1953.

LUCILLE BALL, the self-made redhead with the big blue eyes, was once called "Technicolor Tessie" by *Life* Magazine. That tag was a long time coming, however. For several years, prior to 1943, she played brittle, smart-girl roles in nearly thirty colorless productions where "I'd say one fresh line and exit . . . I hated it." Then came *DuBarry Was A Lady*. The filmed version of the Broadway success, in Technicolor, was a turning point in Lucille Ball's career.

Her ambition to become an actress surfaced in Jamestown, New York. As a young girl she would play "show business" in the attic of her home, dressing in her mother's costumes and acting out little plays. When she graduated from high school, she persuaded her mother to let her go to New York City to enroll in John Murray Anderson's dramatic school. "No talent," was Mr. Anderson's appraisal of her ability.

With director Roy Del Ruth on the set of *DuBarry Was a Lady*, 1943.

121

Ziegfeld Follies, 1946.

Disillusioned but not discouraged, she turned to bread-and-butter jobs, working as office help, waitress, soda jerk and wholesale garment model. In between, she managed to land chorus jobs with various Broadway musical productions, but never got beyond the rehearsal stage. An agent finally got her a spot as a showgirl in Samuel Goldwyn's movie, *Roman Scandals,* which led to a contract with Columbia Pictures and a series of featured roles in "B" films. Unhappy, she went to RKO Radio Pictures and did small parts in *Roberta, Top Hat,* and *Follow the Fleet.* She felt she found her big chance when she was hired for the lead in an out-of-town musical called *Hey, Diddle Diddle.* But it never reached Broadway, and she returned to Hollywood for more minor parts. Then Metro-Goldwyn-Mayer discovered her.

Lucille Ball had reddish-brown hair when she arrived at M-G-M. The color was serviceable enough for black-and-white pictures, but lacked the proper punch for the Technicolor cameras. Sidney Guilaroff, the famed M-G-M hair stylist, decided to make her a definite redhead, and in *DuBarry Was A Lady* she appeared for the first time with flaming tresses. They became her trademark throughout an active career that also includes such Technicolor films as *Best Foot Forward,* 1943; *Thousands Cheer,* 1943; *Ziegfeld Fol-*

lies, 1946; *Easy To Wed,* 1946; *Fancy Pants,* 1950; and *Critic's Choice,* 1963.

ARLENE DAHL was called "the girl for whom Technicolor was invented." She had red-gold hair, bright blue eyes, a flawless complexion, and two heart-shaped beauty marks—one above the corner of her mouth, the other on her shoulder. Her publicity releases were peppered with irresistible phrases, such as "Oh, you beautiful Dahl," "Dahl face" and "Hollywood's Dahl-ling."

She was born in Minneapolis, Minnesota, descended from a line of Scandinavian ancestors. At seven, she was named "Queen of the May" by her grammar school classmates. In high school, she was doubly honored as "the prettiest girl ever graduated from Washburn High" and "the most likely to succeed."

Because she had received some acclaim as an art student, she was offered a job in interior display for a Minneapolis department store. Her good looks and height (nearly five-foot-seven) also led to modeling assignments. By 1945, she was the leading model at Marshall Field & Company in Chicago.

Arlene Dahl

During a vacation in New York, she was seen at a party by Broadway producer Felix Brentano. She was soon in show business with a contract to appear in the musical comedy revue, *Mr. Strauss Goes to Boston*. This was followed with the ingenue lead in the pre-Broadway disaster, *Questionable Ladies*. Warner Bros. director Curtis Bernhardt had spotted her, however, and it wasn't long before she was heading for Hollywood.

Her first film assignment was in Technicolor, opposite Dennis Morgan in Warner Bros.' 1947 musical, *My Wild Irish Rose*. It led to an M-G-M contract and an appearance in another important Technicolor production, *Three Little Words*, with Fred Astaire, Red Skelton and Vera-Ellen.

Arlene Dahl's Technicolor credits also include *Desert Legion*, 1953; *Sangaree*, 1953; *Woman's World*, 1954; *Bengal Brigade*, 1954; and *Slightly Scarlet*, 1956.

RHONDA FLEMING was an accomplished singer and an excellent actress. With her lustrous auburn hair, gray-green eyes and classic beauty, she was a natural for color films. Of all the "Technicolor stars," her talent was perhaps the most misused.

She was born Marilyn Louis in Los Angeles. Her mother, Effie Graham Louis, had once gained national fame on the Broadway stage where she starred as Al Jolson's leading lady in the 1916 production of *Dancing Around*. Her grandfather, John C. Graham, was a famous actor and producer at the old Salt Lake City Theater.

Her career really began when she entered Jesse Lasky's "Gateway to Hollywood" radio contest while in high school. She didn't win, but her picture appeared on the cover of the high school magazine. A Hollywood talent scout saw it and she won a spot in Ken Murray's *Blackouts Revue*. She left the show after only six weeks when she was offered a contract with Twentieth Century-Fox.

Rhonda Fleming found herself sitting around at Fox and asked for her release. She was soon signed by David O. Selznick and in 1945 she made her screen debut in *Spellbound*, the Ingrid Bergman-Gregory Peck classic. For her portrayal of a neurotic patient in a sanitarium, she was hailed as the finest dramatic newcomer of the year. Had her role figured more importantly in the story, one critic commented, she would have won an Oscar as best supporting actress.

Appearing with Bing Crosby, she achieved stardom in the 1949 Paramount musical, *A Connecticut Yankee in King Arthur's Court*. It was her first film in Technicolor, and audiences and producers were highly impressed with her beauty. At that point, however,

Miss Fleming's career took a turn. Too quickly forgetting the dramatic promise shown in *Spellbound*, she was cast in stock "siren" roles that provided little opportunity for her potential. In rapid succession, she starred in a series of colorful, high-adventure films, among them: *The Eagle and the Hawk*, 1950; *Little Egypt*, 1951; *Crosswinds*, 1951; *Those Redheads From Seattle*, 1953; *Yankee Pasha*, 1954; *Slightly Scarlet*, 1956; *Gunfight at the OK Corral*, 1957; *The Big Circus*, 1959; and *The Crowded Sky*, 1961.

LASSIE was a major boxoffice attraction all during the 1940s when "she" (actually a female impersonator) appeared exclusively in Technicolor productions.

Lassie, the collie, was created in 1938 when Eric Knight wrote a short dog story for his young daughter. The manuscript was later expanded into a children's book and published as *Lassie Come Home*. Metro-Goldwyn-Mayer purchased the film rights from the author in 1941 for a flat fee, less than ten thousand dollars. That same year, Lassie, the star, was born.

M-G-M planned to film *Lassie Come Home* as a low-budget production with a cast of English character actors and two youngsters named Roddy McDowell and Elizabeth Taylor. The casting had been completed with the exception of the canine lead. Auditions were held at a baseball park in Los Angeles but not one of the three hundred dogs, mostly mongrels, was acceptable—including the one brought by trainer Rudd Weatherwax.

Mr. Weatherwax's collie, Pal, was a two-year-old that he had been given as a pup in exchange for an unpaid kennel bill. The dog was mild mannered and well-trained but lacked the look of "the perfect collie" that everyone thought would endear him to the hearts of movie fans. Pal was summoned, however, in desperation when the studio had a chance to film some rare footage for one of the scenes in the picture.

The San Joaquin River in northern California was overflowing its banks and, as producer Sam Marx put it, "We needed a collie fast. As a last resort we signed with Weatherwax for one scene, using Pal to swim the flooded river. All wet collies look alike anyway. We figured we could match long shots of Pal with close-ups of the dog we eventually picked."

According to studio sources, the dog was phenomenal. "Pal jumped into that river but it was Lassie who climbed out."

Lassie Come Home was one of M-G-M's biggest hits of the year. Others followed, including *Son of Lassie*, 1945; *Courage of Lassie*, 1946; *Hills of Home*, 1948; *The Sun Comes Up*, 1949; and *Challenge to Lassie*, 1950.

Just a boy and his dog...

From the pages of Eric Knight's great best-seller (he wrote "This Above All" too, remember?) comes a great drama. No roar of guns, no bombs, no tanks, no planes here . . . but emotion deep, human and intense in a story you'll live and love. The kind of story real people like to pass along to their friends.

M-G-M PRESENTS THE TECHNICOLOR PRODUCTION **LASSIE COME HOME**

A Metro-Goldwyn-Mayer Picture

with RODDY McDOWALL · DONALD CRISP
DAME MAY WHITTY · EDMUND GWENN
NIGEL BRUCE · ELSA LANCHESTER · LASSIE
Directed by FRED M. WILCOX · Produced by SAMUEL MARX

Screen Play by Hugo Butler
Based Upon the Novel by Eric Knight

Ad, 1943.

Ad, 1944.

There were others, too, who were well known for their Technicolor appearances—but to a lesser degree and for varied reasons. Danny Kaye and Vera-Ellen, for example, appeared almost exclusively in lush Technicolor productions, as did Jane Powell and Kathryn Grayson, but they were performers whose talents, incidentally, happened to be filmed in color. Virginia Mayo's blonde beauty reached the screen in over twenty color productions. Her best role, however, was in the black-and-white *The Best Years of Our Lives* (1946). June Haver danced and sang her way through thirteen Technicolor Fox musicals (aside from Lassie, she was the only star never to face a black-and-white camera), but she was always overpowered—by Betty Grable in the 1940s and by Marilyn Monroe in the 1950s. Sabu, in the early days of his career, appeared in a number of magnificently produced Technicolor pictures, notably Korda's *Drums* (1938), *The Thief of Bagdad* (1940) and *Jungle Book* (1942), only to be upstaged by the colorful effects and surroundings. Judy Garland, Gene Kelly, Betty Hutton, Jeanne Crain, Paulette Goddard, Olivia de Havilland, Dorothy Lamour, and others appeared in

Danny Kaye and Vera-Ellen in *Wonder Man*, 1945.

Technicolor productions but with less consistency.

As time went on and Technicolor increased in popularity, appearances in color became the rule. Today, it would be difficult to name five established stars who, at one time or another, have not had a Technicolor credit.

12 Color Grows Up

As long as color was denied the cinematographer, his art was necessarily incomplete. But once Technicolor features had been produced in sufficient numbers to be regarded as a staple commodity, the motion picture reached its maturity and became, for the first time, a true art form.

When Rouben Mamoulian accepted Darryl F. Zanuck's offer to direct *Blood and Sand* in 1941, it had been six years since he'd worked on the first full-length full-color picture, *Becky Sharp*. Looking back, he stated, "The story was, I am convinced, none too happily chosen as a vehicle for launching the color medium . . . nevertheless, in that first pioneering effort we all learned valuable lessons about color and its use."

During the intervening years, the Technicolor process had been greatly improved, particularly in efficiency and technical smoothness. Like many others within the industry, Mr. Mamoulian tried to advance with the process in his understanding of color in all its uses. Hoping for another opportunity to direct a Technicolor feature, he noted, "I have tried to study color from every angle—the history of color, the psychology of color, the artistic application of color as four thousand years of painters have taught it to us, and something, at least, of the scientific aspect of color as regards color in pigments and light values."

That Mr. Mamoulian was extremely well prepared to handle the new assignment on *Blood and Sand* was evident from the start. Working with co-cameramen Ernest Palmer and Ray Rennahan, he developed a color plan which would coordinate the emotional aspects of action and dialog with the physical production—keying the coloration of the settings and costumes for each scene and sequence to the emotional mood of that particular action in exactly the same way a cinematographer keys his lighting to match the mood of the action.

Blood and Sand was not only a story of Spain, it was a story of Spanish people. The aim of the creative team in preparing the film was to capture the authentic atmosphere of the country, in its literal, everyday reality as well as in its poetic essence, an atmosphere that had been best expressed pictorially by the great Spanish painters. It was only fitting then that they should become the basis of inspiration. As Mr. Mamoulian stated:

After all, in making a motion picture, and especially a motion picture in color, we are essentially making a series of paintings. What does it matter if we are not painting our picture with water color or oil paint, but with colored light projected on a white screen? What does it matter if our picture moves and speaks? It is still fundamentally a picture. To what better source of inspiration could we turn than the greatest masters of painting?

Not that any of us made a slavish attempt to imitate them! That would have been fatal. We were working in a different medium, expressing different thoughts. But we could—and did—turn to them as fellow artists who knew the country and its emotions, for guidance in expressing similar emotions in our

On the set of *Blood and Sand* with Tyrone Power, Rita Hayworth and crew, 1941.

Ad, 1941.

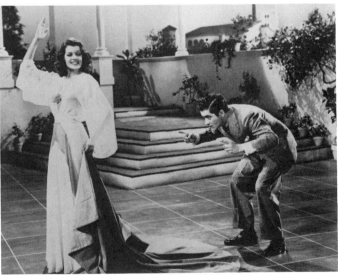

Rita Hayworth and Tyrone Power, *Blood and Sand.*

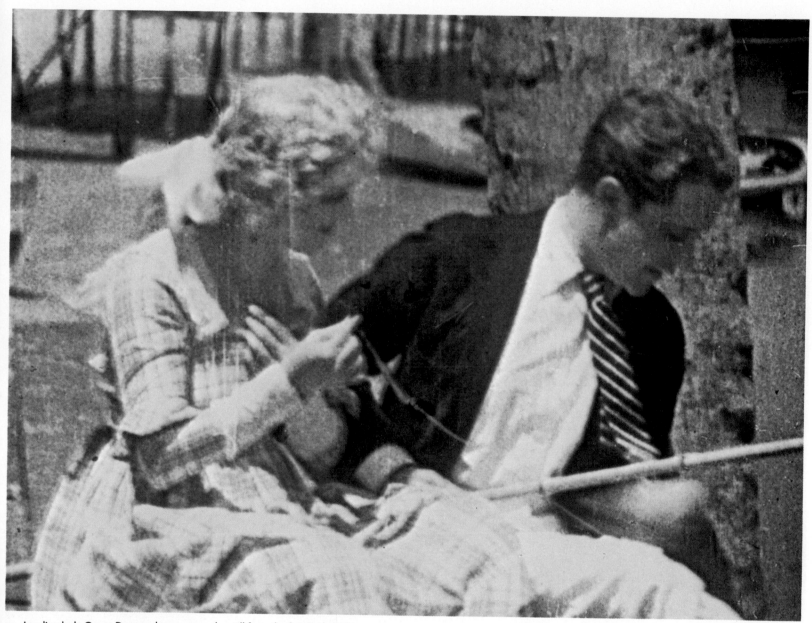

Leading lady Grace Darmond on a rare color still from the first Technicolor film, *The Gulf Between*. "Fringing" was a major problem in early color cinematography.

Leading lady Grace Darmond in a rare color still from the first Technicolor film, *The Gulf Between*. "Fringing" was a major problem in early
color cinematography.

Jack Holt in *Wanderer of the Wasteland*, 1924.

The Black Pirate, 1926.

Cecil B. DeMille's *King of Kings*, 1927.

Whoopee, 1930.

own medium. Their use of color, proven by centuries of approval, could guide us in choosing the color we used in expressing similar emotions, painting comparable scenes.

For the early sequences showing Juan's (Tyrone Power) poverty-ridden childhood, they turned to the painting of Murillo and borrowed the bronze-browns and blacks of his *Young Spanish Beggar*. For the bullring scenes, and those of violent action, they followed the style of Goya, using dramatic and vivid colorings. The paintings of Spain's foremost religious painter, El Greco, supplied the color mood for sequences in the chapel, and those of Sorolla were used as guides for the street and market scenes. Finally, they turned to the Venetian painters, particularly Titian and Veronese, for help in capturing the luxuriousness of color and strong suggestions of bustling movement.

In selecting colors for the costuming, they tried to express the essential qualities of each character. For Juan's childhood sweetheart and wife, played by Linda Darnell, they selected white, the color of purity. Later, when she was in danger of losing her husband, she wore either blue or black. Dona Sol, performed by Rita Hayworth, was an aristocratic seductress. In her introductory scene, she was seen wearing royal purple and, during a passionate love sequence, a hot orange.

To achieve a look of total realism with the props and backgrounds, a number of unrealistic steps had to be

Leon Shamroy describes Technicolor camera to Carmen Miranda on the set of *That Night In Rio*, 1941.

taken. According to the director, "On the set, they looked incredibly artificial. But on the screen, they gave the effect we desired. Often they proved more realistic than reality its literal self." Those steps included the coloring of selected white objects, a practice introduced by Natalie Kalmus years earlier. In *Blood and Sand*, however, it was carried to the extreme.

For one scene, a white shirt was sprayed with traces of greens and blues. For another, a death-bed scene, hospital accessories (white sheets and enameled surgical cases) were sprayed a dull gray-green. Throughout the film, wherever necessary, various white objects were either falsified or subdued for effect. Left alone they would have been too stark and jarring within the setting. Though toned down, they still appeared to be white on film.

Blood and Sand, nominated by members of the Academy of Motion Picture Arts and Sciences for best Interior Decoration (color) and winner of the Academy Award for the year's best Color Cinematography, ranks as one of the first truly artistic cinematic achievements in Technicolor. In many respects, it was the forerunner of another visually magnificent film from Twentieth Century-Fox, 1947's *Forever Amber*. Highly acclaimed for its camera work, though controversial in regard to its dramatic values, the lusty Kathleen Windsor novel of Restoration England was said to have been "brought to the screen in a burst of Technicolor glory."

As one critic exclaimed, ". . . *Amber* is distinguished (and the word is used literally) by color photography that probably comes as close to perfection as any blending of art and mechanics can come. Leon Shamroy (cinematographer) has infused the production

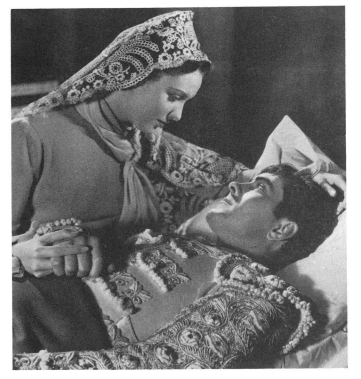

Linda Darnell and Tyrone Power, *Blood and Sand*.

Forever Amber (1947), starring Linda Darnell and Cornel Wilde.

with jewel-like color that seems to sparkle and glow at the same time. His camera treatment, combined with art direction and costume design of superlative quality, results in a screen pageant that is like nothing so much as a Gobelin tapestry brought to life."

Leon Shamroy, whose work on *Forever Amber*, starring Linda Darnell and Cornel Wilde, followed his previous award-winning efforts (*The Black Swan*, 1942; *Wilson*, 1944; *Leave Her To Heaven*, 1945), was a master of the color camera and highly acclaimed for his highly individualistic style of "painting with light." Unlike many other cinematographers of the day who believed that only white light should be used for Technicolor, Mr. Shamroy employed colored light to great effect, infusing a warm tone here, a cooler tone there, until he achieved the correct emotional pattern of the scene. Like Rouben Mamoulian, he admitted to being inspired by the works of famous painters: Rembrandt, Ruben, and others.

The photography of *Forever Amber* was enhanced by the use of "the ultimate lamp," the Type 450 "Brute" Molarc introduced in 1946, which offered a hard, clean streak of light (at double the intensity) that could be employed from a relatively long distance to produce a "single shadow" impression. It enabled cinematographers to turn their attention, more than ever, toward lighting for mood and dramatic effect.

As Technicolor pictures grew in stature during the 1940s, the cinematographer gained new respect within the industry. Now officially titled Director of Photography, his select group included a number of newcomers to the color field—though hardly new to motion picture cinematography. Ray Rennahan, W. Howard Greene, William V. Skall and Allen M. Davey were among the most respected veterans of their craft. To this group was added such names as Shamroy, Jack Cardiff, Charles Rosher, George Barnes, Robert L. Surtees, Winton Hoch, Robert Burks and Harry Stradling.

For the years 1927 and 1928, Charles Rosher was

Jane Wyman and Gregory Peck in *The Yearling*, 1946.

Sabu and Jean Simmons in *Black Narcissus*, 1947.

nominated for his black-and-white cinematography on three films. One of them, *Sunrise*, won the Academy Award at the first Oscar ceremony. In 1945, Mr. Rosher, in tandem with Arthur Arling and Leonard Smith, began filming the picture that would win him another "best" trophy. The film was Metro-Goldwyn-Mayer's Technicolor production of Marjorie Kinnan Rawling's *The Yearling*, the story of a family's fight for survival in the Florida wilderness.

"As a Director of Photography," Mr. Rosher recalled, "my main concern was achieving on film the complete realism envisioned by director Clarence Brown. In my first discussion with Mr. Brown, I learned of his decision to dispense with all artificial make-up. It was a bold step and a photographic challenge. It meant that the normal control over flesh tones possible with make-up, a very important factor in color, would be removed. Although I had more than an inkling of

the difficulty involved, it was something I had long wanted to do . . . to show skin color and texture as they really are."

Maintaining constant color values in the faces of the principal players was not easy. Claude Jarman, Jr., who played the character of young Jody, was made to wear a large straw hat when away from the cameras to keep his delicate complexion from tanning (Florida was in the midst of a drought and heat spell during much of the company's stay). As Pa Baxter, Gregoy Peck's naturally ruddy complexion had to be treated frequently with iced chamois skin to hold the redness down. The situation was reversed for Jane Wyman. Her role as the drab Ma Baxter was a complete departure for the star who had, until then, made a career of playing snappy, modern career girls. Miss Wyman spent fifteen minutes a day under a sunlamp to achieve the outdoorsy look associated with backwoods life.

If *The Yearling* was a milestone in the filming of naturalism in color, *Black Narcissus*, a British production released the following year, was a masterpiece of visual splendor.

Black Narcissus (1948) was the work of Jack Cardiff, who directed the photography. Known as Britain's leading Technicolor cameraman, Mr. Cardiff was the son of a music hall comedian and a one-time child actor. When he moved to the other side of the lens, as assistant cameraman at the Elstree Studios near London, he served under such notable directors as Rene Clair, Alfred Hitchcock, and Fred Niblo. He had worked with the camera crew on *Wings of the Morning*, Alexander Korda's *Four Feathers* and, in France, the first French Technicolor film, *Main Streets of Paris*. The latter project was never completed, however, because of the war. Later, he established himself with the acclaimed British productions of *Caesar and Cleopatra* and *A Matter of Life and Death* (released in the United States as *Stairway To Heaven*).

Black Narcissus was heralded as "a cameraman's picture" and contained what many enthusiasts called "the most beautiful Technicolor photography ever to appear on the screen." The locale of the picture was the Himalayan mountains, the story centering around five Anglican nuns who were sent into the rugged terrain to take over a remote palace and convert it into a convent. The film, starring Deborah Kerr, Jean Simmons, David Farrar, Flora Robson and Sabu, was particularly distinguished for its use of low-key lighting, dramatic framing of individual scenes, and spectacular atmospheric shots. The magnificent backgrounds were especially impressive in that they were all filmed at Pinewood Studios in England using backdrops—huge canvasses skillfully painted in rich,

131

Moira Shearer in *The Red Shoes*, 1948.

glowing colors to capture the mood and authenticity of the Indian setting.

During the mid-to-late 1940s, high-quality imports from England, both in color and in black-and-white, began to make entertainment news in America. Aside from *Caesar and Cleopatra* and *Black Narcissus*, England had sent over such fine Technicolor films as *Henry V*, awarded a special Oscar in 1946, and *The Red Shoes*, a four-Oscar nominee and two-time winner in 1948. At the time, Natalie Kalmus stated that the ballet-themed film was, of all the Technicolor movies, her own personal choice, as it demonstrated the best use of the process.

By the early 1950s, Technicolor had again advanced the speed of its film, offering film-makers even more flexibility in production. One of the first motion pictures that saw its use was Metro-Goldwyn-Mayer's ambitious musical, *An American In Paris*. Produced by Arthur Freed and directed by Vicente Minnelli, the picture had choreography by Gene Kelly and art direction by Preston Ames. Although the Director of Photography, Alfred Gilks, was not assigned to the film until a few days before shooting began, the top command (Freed, Minnelli, Kelly and Ames) had all been in on the pre-production work and assisted him in speedily understanding the spirit of the project.

"Because the picture was to be produced entirely in Hollywood," Mr. Gilks recalled, "it became a formidable and challenging assignment in art direction and photography. Without the pictorial impact of authentic Parisian scenes and locales, the picture—as conceived—would lose much of its punch. And so Paris was recreated in the M-G-M studio.

"There are many advantages in building sets for a picture like this instead of shooting in the original locales—especially for the cameraman. When the sets are designed and built at the studio, the full require-ments of the camera can be considered in the planning and the sets constructed to permit widest utilization of the camera. Also, color more suitable to Technicolor photography can be used. . . ."

According to Mr. Gilks, one of the most interesting sequences in the film was perhaps the most difficult to light and shoot: the Beaux Arts Ball, a vast, elegant set crowded with scores of dancers. The costumes and decor were either in jet black or stark white, yet had to be filmed in color. Creating and retaining the mood envisioned by the designers was, said Mr. Gilks, "a real challenge for Technicolor."

A similar problem was faced several years later with *The Nun's Story* (1959). The screenplay detailed a young woman's experiences in becoming, and being, a nursing nun in the Belgian Congo. To delineate the theme of the story, director Fred Zinnemann felt it was absolutely essential to present a harsh visual contrast between the stark cloistered life of the convent and that of the more colorful outside world. Mr. Zinnemann, at first, considered shooting the entire production in black-and-white. That idea was abandoned on the basis that a monochrome treatment would present the secular world as too drab and, therefore, destroy the aimed-for contrast.

The problem, that of achieving a black-and-white look with color film, was left to Director of Photography Franz Planer. He emphasized:

Color is a double-edged sword. In many ways it is much more difficult to be creative with color than with black-and-white. In black-and-white you have black and you have white, plus a range of intermediate gray tones which make it relatively easy to create certain moods and sustain them. For example, if you need a sunrise in black-and-white, you can shoot a sunset and get away with it. But a sunrise is entirely different in color from a sunset.

In color you may have an exterior sequence that runs six pages in the script and will cut down to about a minute on the screen. Yet it may require three or four days to shoot the sequence. Shooting throughout the day you run into vast changes in color and lighting. On the screen, that sequence must appear to be the same moment with the same light.

In *The Nun's Story*, Franz Planer had to contend not only with the problems of shooting a film in full color but those akin to shooting in black-and-white as well. His big challenge, however, was in subduing, even destroying, color for the important sequences in and around the convent. To accomplish this he arranged for

Gene Kelly dances with Mary Young in *An American In Paris*, 1951.

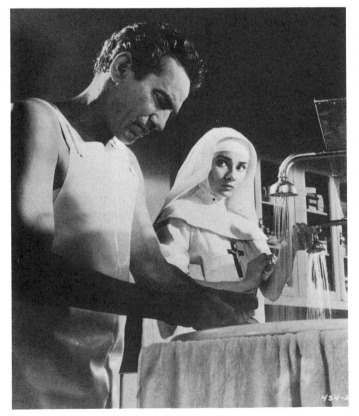

all interior sets to be sprayed with a toning-down gray paint. The word *interior* included everything that would be caught by the eye of the camera—from the rich red velvet hangings of the chapel to a red-bound Bible with gilt-edged pages. No item was left untouched. Outside the convent walls, scenes were shot only on gray, overcast days.

This attention to detail also extended to the make-up worn by the cast members. White greasepaint was used to subdue eyebrows and lips, taking special care to avoid a mask-like look. Even the delicate structuring of Audrey Hepburn's face was lightened to perpetuate the desired mood.

As Franz Planer had indicated, it is often difficult to achieve a consistency in color and lighting during the shooting of a sequence, particularly if the sequence has to be shot over a period of time. The position of the sun creates problems; it casts different shadows at noon than it does at three in the afternoon. A slightly hazy

Peter Finch and Audrey Hepburn in *The Nun's Story*, 1959.

Gregory Peck, as Captain Ahab, harpoons white whale in *Moby Dick*, 1956.

do something that somebody else doesn't know quite how to do has been a godsend to us many times."

A clear example of Technicolor's technological know-how was evident in John Huston's daring experimentation for *Moby Dick* (1956), a film in which the subtle color effect was achieved by desaturation. The process, developed in the laboratory of Technicolor Italiana in Rome, was unique in that it rendered all colors in a sepia-like monochrome, except for shades of red which were translated into varying tones of scarlet. Red, therefore, became the only color to reach the screen in its true form or, at least, semi-realistically.

In 1967, eleven years after the release of *Moby Dick*, Mr. Huston was again anxious to try a new technique for his *Reflections In A Golden Eye*. By now, even though less than half of his films had been shot in color, he had come to be known as a color innovator. His *Moulin Rouge*, in 1952, was an excellent example of the esthetic use of color, achieved by the use of filters on the camera lenses to simulate the tonal effects of Toulouse-Lautrec paintings. Said his Director of Photography, Oswald Morris, "Houston and I did so many odd things with filters on *Moulin Rouge* that the laboratory people disclaimed all responsibility."

As a rule, Mr. Huston filmed in black-and-white when the plotline was basically concerned with human emotions. *Reflections In A Golden Eye* was such a story. But because of the unusual nature of the theme,

sky presents conditions unlike those of a clear day. And so on.

Much of the stabilizing of color can be handled in the filming but often it is left for the laboratory in processing. For example, according to a Technicolor spokesman,

We processed a picture that was shot in Texas and the sky was very blue. Then the studio added some "Texas" scenes that were shot in California. The skies wouldn't match so we had to "desaturate" the film to take out some of the blue in the original footage.

There were problems, too, in matching the outdoor photography for *Jaws* (1975). Waters in the west don't always match those of Martha's Vineyard on the east coast. And, occasionally, you have to take a shot that was made in the day and make it look like night. It isn't just making it darker. To a great extent, you have to make it bluer and darker.

Over the years, Technicolor technicians have been exposed to a number of situations that were not routine. But as their spokesman put it, "Our ability to

Elizabeth Taylor and Marlon Brando in *Reflections In a Golden Eye*, 1967.

135

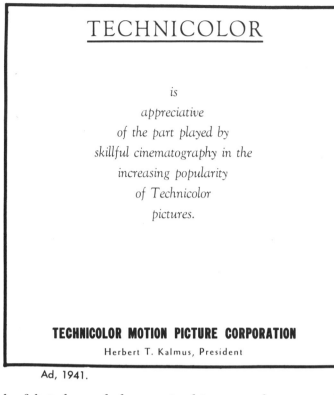

Ad, 1941.

he felt it demanded more. In this case, color was used sparingly. Said Mr. Huston:

Color in nature is very different from color on the screen. When you sit in a darkened theater your attention is so concentrated on the screen that the images seem more fully saturated with color than they are in reality. Thus color effects are unnaturally heightened. This kind of color has been fine for extravaganzas and spectacular films. But when we are dealing with material of psychological content it becomes invariably distracting as it gets between the viewer and the mind he is trying to search into. Until now, the film-maker had a single choice, the use of black and white or of color. This is as though all painters were limited to either pure pigment or black india ink washes. This day and night difference is no longer the only choice. . . .

When *Reflections In A Golden Eye* was released, critics and ticket buyers were divided in their feelings toward color desaturation. Successful or not, it marked another advance in technology. Dr. Frank P. Brackett, Director of Research at Technicolor, stated at the time:

It opens a whole avenue of new color combinations which can be obtained in varying degrees of saturation from extremely vivid color to black and white. John Huston chose to work in an overtone of sepia with the pinks and reds accentuated. Someone else might prefer a shift to accentuate another color of the spectrum with a totally different overtone. For example, in a night sequence, a producer might want an overall cold tone—or he might prefer a shift to the green, with perhaps a warm tone accented. Moreover, alterations of the color mood can be made from sequence to sequence or even from scene to scene. There is an almost unlimited range of effects available.

That range, however, would be controlled to some degree by a factor that has influenced color guidelines from the very beginning, that of maintaining a certain fidelity to the complexions of the cast members.

Technicolor, as projected on the screen, has undergone many changes since audiences first saw the original three-color process in the mid-1930s—from the then self-conscious use of color to the garish, candy-coated look of the 1940s to the more natural, sometimes experimental tonings that followed. Of all the techniques, however, Technicolor is perhaps best remembered by film fans for the lush, highly stylized color renditions that came into vogue about the time of World War II. The acceptance of the Technicolor process during that period was phenomenal. By 1946, the company had reached a twelve-month peak of output with over thirty feature productions. Before another ten years would pass, that figure would more than triple. But events taking place within the industry over those same years would ultimately change the course of the company's future. Soon, Technicolor's three-color camera, the most revolutionary advance in commercial color cinematography, would become a thing of the past.

13 Technicolor Today

In 1941, Technicolor introduced its new multi-layer single film process, Monopack, originally developed by Dr. Leonard Troland in the 1920s. The aerial shots in *Dive Bomber* (1941) and *Captains of the Clouds* (1942) took advantage of the more compact camera. It was used again for the spectacular fire sequence in *The Forest Rangers* (1942) as well as for all the exterior scenes in *Lassie Come Home* (1943). By 1944, Monopack was improved to the point that it was used entirely for both exteriors and interiors on *Thunderhead, Son of Flicka*.

Dr. Kalmus believed that Monopack would one day replace the bulky three-color Technicolor camera. He also believed that, had it not been for World War II, Monopack would have accomplished that feat before the end of the decade. But with the Navy and the Air Force converting much of the Technicolor laboratory into a top top-secret plant during the early 1940s, its development was interrupted. Because of Dr. Kalmus's faith in the future of Monopack, coupled with his feeling that the present system would eventually, if not soon, be obsolete, he decided not to add any more expensive three-color cameras to the company's existing stock of thirty-six.

Following the war, box office attendance zoomed. Producers were anxious to get their productions before audiences as quickly as possible. But the Technicolor process was much in demand and a number of films had to be rescheduled according to the availability of cameras. The smaller studios found it impossible to obtain cameras, because the majors had them reserved months in advance.

Too, the processing of prints was considerably slowed by the industry labor strikes of 1945 and 1946. With a skeleton crew and a demand for "rush" jobs—which the company tended to ignore, preferring instead to maintain the quality of its product—Technicolor found itself with a growing reputation for

Russell Arms (in cockpit) with James Cagney during filming of *Captains Of the Clouds*, 1942.

A PICTURE WITH A HEART AS *Big* AS TODAY'S GOLDEN WEST!

Heed the call to adventure great and thrilling! All the sweep and power of "My Friend Flicka"...more rousing ... more compelling!

Mary O'Hara's Best-Loved Best-Seller

THUNDERHEAD
SON OF FLICKA
in Technicolor!

with

RODDY McDOWALL
PRESTON FOSTER RITA JOHNSON

A 20th CENTURY-FOX PICTURE

Directed by LOUIS KING • Produced by ROBERT BASSLER
Screen Play by Dwight Cummins & Dorothy Yost • Based on the Novel by Mary O'Hara

Ad, 1945.

Lynne Overman, Robert Preston and Dorothy Lamour in *Typhoon*, 1940.

Greer Garson in *Blossoms In The Dust*, 1941.

Technicolor camera dollies back to film Randolph Scott (right, on horse) as he rides into town for scene in *Western Union*, 1941.

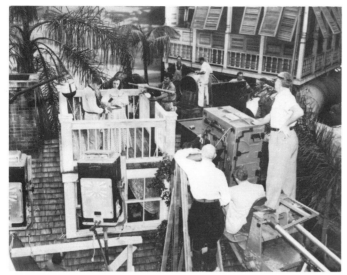

As Cecil B. DeMille watches from ladder, Paulette Goddard readies for scene in *Reap The Wild Wind,* 1942.

Fred Astaire and Lucille Bremer in *Yolanda And The Thief,* 1945.

Claude Rains in *Phantom Of The Opera,* 1943.

Barry Fitzgerald and Betty Hutton in *Incendiary Blonde,* 1945.

Judy Garland with Henry Daniels, Jr. in *Meet Me In St. Louis,* 1944.

140

The "Saga of Jenny" dream sequence in *Lady In The Dark* (1944), starring
Ginger Rogers and Ray Milland.

Benay Venuta, Howard Keel, Betty Hutton, Louis Calhern and Keenan
Wynn in *Annie Get Your Gun*, 1950.

Ad, 1946.

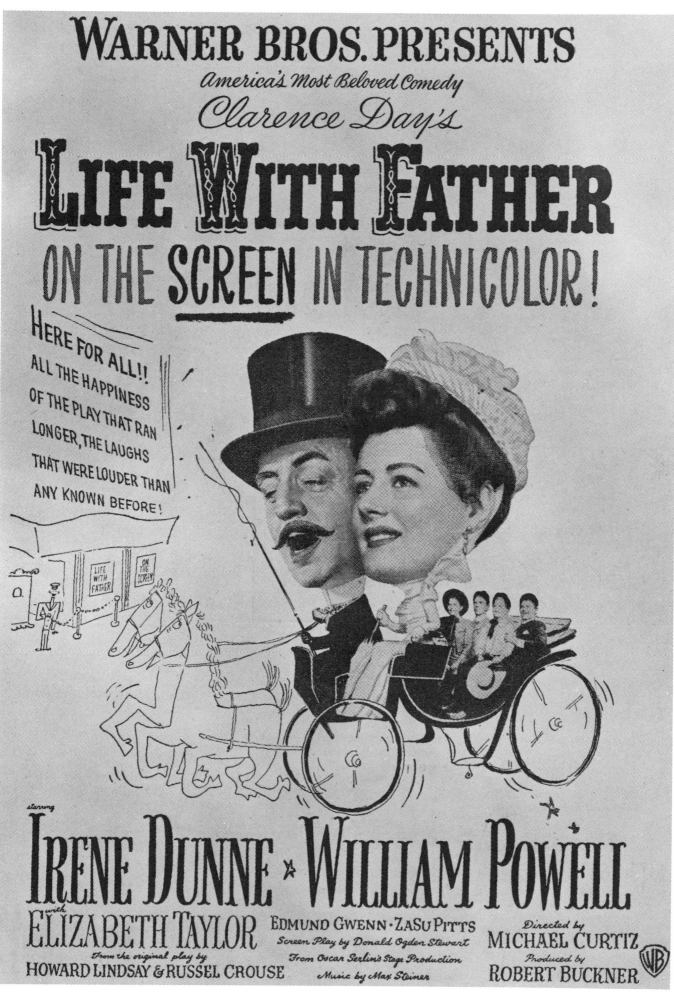

Ad, 1947.

IT SPEAKS OF LOVE! IT SINGS IN
COLOR BY
Technicolor!
Worlds apart... yet their hearts are as close together as the hands of a clock at midnight!
M-G-M... producer of the screen's finest Technicolor musicals... presents another wonderful entertainment!
That Midnight Kiss
STARRING
KATHRYN GRAYSON
JOSE ITURBI
WITH
ETHEL BARRYMORE
KEENAN WYNN
J. CARROL NAISH • JULES MUNSHIN
THOMAS GOMEZ • MARJORIE REYNOLDS
and introducing
MARIO LANZA
Screen Play by Bruce Manning and Tamara Hovey
Directed by NORMAN TAUROG
Produced by JOE PASTERNAK
A Metro-Goldwyn-Mayer Picture
MEET A NEW STAR! He's the rugged, romantic type and the singing discovery of a lifetime!

Ad, 1948.

LADD'S IN THE WEST...
IN TWO-GUN TECHNICOLOR!

Here's a LADD you've always dreamed about—quiet, gentle-like—but the most feared man on the wild frontier! Afraid of nothing but the woman who loved him!

Filmed on a scale to rival the never-to-be-forgotten "Union Pacific"!

ALAN LADD
ROBERT PRESTON · BRENDA MARSHALL
DONALD CRISP
in
"Whispering SMITH"

Color by TECHNICOLOR

A Paramount Picture with
WILLIAM DEMAREST
Fay Holden · Murvyn Vye · Frank Faylen
Associate Producer Mel Epstein · Directed by Leslie Fenton
Screenplay by Frank Butler and Karl Kamb · Based on the Novel by Frank H. Spearman

Ad, 1949

Dr. Kalmus (left) and M-G-M's Louis B. Mayer, circa 1950.

being uncooperative and "difficult." The company soon became the target of a number of nuisance suits.

In 1947, the United States Department of Justice filed an anti-trust suit against Technicolor (and Eastman Kodak, supplier of Technicolor's film) charging restraint of trade and monopolization of professional color cinematography. The court wanted to know, among other things, why the Technicolor company didn't have enough color cameras available for everybody that wanted one.

The suit against Technicolor dragged on for three years. During that time, Dr. Kalmus contended that his organization did not have a monopoly on color, pointing out that while Technicolor was being used in over fifty feature productions in 1948, rival processes (such as Cinecolor and Trucolor) were being used almost in equal number. Nevertheless, the court proceedings ended with a consent decree ordering Technicolor to set aside a certain number of cameras—on a first-come, first-served basis—for film-makers other than the major studios. The decision was to have little bearing on Technicolor's future operations. Another event, much more encompassing in effect, had taken place a year earlier.

From the beginning, it had been Technicolor's goal, indeed that of all color enthusiasts, to perfect a method of commercial color cinematography using a single rather than a multiple record. In 1949, news of such a breakthrough hit the industry with the introduction of Eastman Kodak single-strip color negative and printing film stock. With the news, came the realization that Technicolor had finally lost its edge in the color field. Soon smaller (and more accessible) black-and-white cameras, loaded with the new color negative film, began appearing on Hollywood sound stages. Before too long, the public was seeing, in addition to Technicolor, new commercial trade names— WarnerColor, Ansco Color, DeLuxe, Eastman and more—in ads and on movie credits acknowledging the studio and/or the processing plant that handled the developing and printing of the film.

The sudden appearance of these new entries into color (and so many, at that) confused many patrons of the cinema. Technicolor had become a household word. Everyone knew what to expect when they saw *Technicolor* advertised in print. But few people knew what to expect from the new processes. Were they as intense and glorious as Technicolor or simply pale imitations like Trucolor? It didn't take long for the public to discover that Technicolor had some serious rivals.

It seemed that the days of Technicolor's three-color camera and process were numbered. But the expected "revolution" was slow in coming. For five more years, the Technicolor name appeared on the vast majority of feature motion pictures produced in color: over seventy-five in 1951; nearly one hundred in 1952; over one hundred and twenty-five in 1953. In 1954, Technicolor commemorated the manufacture of four billion feet of 35mm color motion picture release prints. That same year, Technicolor cameras were used for the last time on an American-made film. The production was Universal's *Foxfire*, starring Jane Russel and Jeff Chandler.

While many advances were being made in motion picture color, that phase of operation was not unique to change. The entire motion picture industry was in a state of evolution. Television, an amusing novelty just a few years earlier, had suddenly brought fear to the hearts of the studios. Box office receipts had dropped sharply as many filmgoers began changing their entertainment habits, now often preferring to stay home and watch the little box rather than attend a theater. To counteract the trend, Hollywood developed its own novelties: wide-screen and three-dimensional presentations.

In 1955, Dr. Kalmus wrote, "The fourth Technicolor process which took care of a very substantial part of the motion picture requirements from 1934 to 1953 was

Spectacle in Rome: *Quo Vadis*, 1951.

Donald O'Connor, Gene Kelly and Debbie Reynolds in *Singin' In The Rain*, 1952.

Gregory Peck and Susan Hayward in *David and Bathsheba*, 1951.

Van Heflin, Alan Ladd, Jean Arthur and Brandon de Wilde in *Shane*, 1953.

Cyd Charisse and Fred Astaire in *The Band Wagon*, 1953.

Grace Kelly and Ava Gardner in *Mogambo*, 1953.

Lana Turner and producer-director Mervyn LeRoy on the set of *Latin Lovers*, 1953.

tailored to make prints in the laboratory from Technicolor special three-strip negative and to be projected on screens not larger than thirty or thirty-five feet in width. Both of these conditions have changed and again Technicolor research and development departments have had to do something to meet the new demands." (With the introduction of the single-strip negative, Technicolor had rather successfully adapted its three-strip processing techniques to the new product. While the resultant prints were satisfactory in tonal quality and color rendering, they lacked in definition. This became increasingly apparent when the images had to be projected upon the wider and larger screens.)

When the first signs of change swept through the industry, Technicolor began to modify its procedures, devise new ones, and install new equipment to serve the large screen requirements. According to Dr. Kalmus:

This work progressed on an emergency basis through a period of about two years until in May, 1955, I saw on a fifty-foot screen in Hollywood a demonstration of an improved new Technicolor process. The 35mm print used for this demonstration embodied all the changes in its imbibition (dye-transfer) process that Technicolor has been striving for since the advent of Eastman and Ansco color type negative and the advent of large screens in the theaters. The result was the most wonderful picture in color made by any process that I have ever seen on the screen from all technical points of view, including sharpness or definition and especially color rendition.

The Technicolor camera may have become obsolete but the company's heralded method of processing prints had been reborn.

Early wide-screen releases featuring Color by Technicolor were Twentieth Century-Fox's *The Robe*, the first CinemaScope picture; Paramount's *White Christmas*, the first VistaVision feature; and Cinerama's *This Is Cinerama*, for which Technicolor manufactured the prints. Three-dimensional Technicolor productions included Columbia's *Miss Sadie Thompson* and *Fort Ti*, and Fox's *Inferno*. Technicolor also introduced such wide-screen developments as Technirama and Technirama-70.

Color by Technicolor, a term that was commonly used in movie ads of the 1950s, meant that Technicolor handled all stages of the laboratory work. *Print by Technicolor* indicated that Technicolor was responsible only for the final release prints, not for any of the steps that preceeded in the laboratory. Today, a distinction between the two is not often made and the word *Technicolor* generally appears alone.

On January 1, 1960, at the age of seventy-eight, Dr. Herbert T. Kalmus retired. During his forty-five years with Technicolor, he had guided the company he founded through four severe depressions, each one resulting in the invention and development of a new and separate process. Following the original plan of progressive step development, his scientists and technicians proved, working in an early atmosphere of "it can't be done," that commercial color cinematography not only was possible but practical. Technicolor had become Hollywood's most famous name in color. Dr. Kalmus, though virtually unknown by the general public, found himself being honored world-wide as "the man who threw color on the silver screen."

As a new era began, Technicolor moved in many directions. Diversification became the rule and the company expanded its operations to include not only motion pictures (commercial and non-theatrical) but

Jane Wyman and Rock Hudson in *Magnificent Obsession,* 1954.

Dana Andrews and Elizabeth Taylor in *Elephant Walk,* 1954.

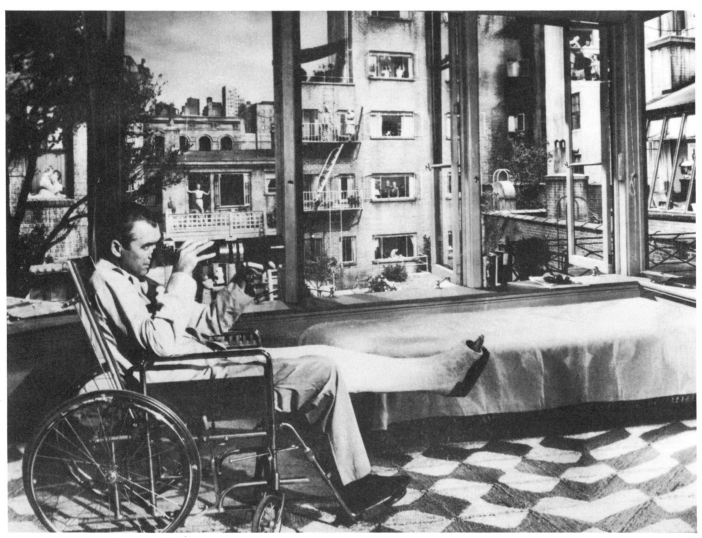

James Stewart in *Rear Window,* 1954.

Rosemary Clooney, Danny Kaye, Bing Crosby and Vera-Ellen in *White Christmas*, 1954.

Fred MacMurray, Robert Francis, Van Johnson and Humphrey Bogart in *The Caine Mutiny*, 1954.

Cary Grant in *To Catch a Thief,* 1955.

The last American-made production filmed with the revolutionary Technicolor camera, *Foxfire* (1955), starring Jeff Chandler and Jane Russell.

Technicolor Italiana in Rome, launched in 1955 to service foreign producers shooting in continental Europe, Asia and Africa. (Reduction in personnel due to changes in printing methods stirred union problems and forced Technicolor to threaten closure of the facility in 1978.)

Kim Novak and Tyrone Power in *The Eddy Duchin Story*, 1956.

Frank Sinatra, Hugh O'Brian and Betty White at the Hollywood opening of *Pal Joey*, 1957.

Rosalind Russell, director Morton DaCosta and cinematographer Harry Stradling on the set of *Auntie Mame*, 1958.

Tab Hunter and Tuesday Weld at the premiere of *Porgy and Bess*, 1959.

Composer-conductor Johnny Green interviews Natalie Wood and Robert Wagner at the *Porgy and Bess* premiere in Hollywood.

Pearl Bailey leads strutting Sammy Davis, Jr. and picnickers along riverfront set in Samuel Goldwyn's *Porgy and Bess*, 1959.

John Wayne and son, Michael, take a break during shooting of *The Alamo*, 1960.

Charlton Heston in *El Cid*, 1961.

television, photographic services and film processing for government and industry, audio-visual systems for schools and industry, and consumer photoprocessing.

Motion pictures had been the foundation of the company since its earliest days. As Technicolor neared its Fiftieth Anniversary in the mid-1960s, they continued to play the dominant role in company operations. With its silenced three-strip cameras on display at the Smithsonian Institute in Washington, D.C. and Eastman House in Rochester, New York, Technicolor had now become almost exclusively a laboratory, in

Shortly after his retirement, Dr. Kalmus became one of the few non-performers to be honored in the Walk of Fame on Hollywood Boulevard.

direct competition with other processing plants. Even so, the name was still associated with much of the finest in filmed entertainment, prestigious features such as *Spartacus* (1960), *West Side Story* (1961), *Lawrence of Arabia* (1962), *My Fair Lady* (1964), *A Man For All Seasons* (1966), *Funny Girl* (1968) and more. Year after year, scores of films traveled through the Technicolor laboratories, in California and overseas. But Technicolor had broadened its scope and was no longer limited only to color work. Black-and-white films printed by Technicolor included 1965's *The Spy Who Came In From The Cold* and 1966's *Who's Afraid of Virginia Woolf?* and *Is Paris Burning?*, among others.

The swing, however, was to color. Monochromatic filming, once the overwhelming choice of the industry, was now being pushed aside. The ratio of color to black-and-white took a pronounced leap in 1965 when practically all film exposed for television was multi-hued. And, beginning in 1967, with so few black-and-white films being made, the Academy of Motion Picture Arts and Sciences no longer felt it was neces-

sary to continue the two separate classifications in their awards structure.

Technicolor's decision to enter the television field was influenced by its major customers and independent producers, as well as by the move of the three major networks to increase broadcasting of programs filmed in color. The company's reputation was enhanced almost immediately by the disclosure, in late 1966, of a revolutionary technical breakthrough developed by its subsidiary division, Vidtronics. The new technique made possible production of full color television prints from television color tapes of both feature shows and commercials. Previously, shows and commercials on color video tape could not be used overseas because of incompatibility with foreign telecasting equipment. Transferring such color taped shows to color film by the Technicolor Vidtronics systems made taped color shows economically available for telecasting anywhere in the world.

Over the years, Technicolor has also processed a number of popular television shows. Among them: *The*

Rita Moreno and dancers in *West Side Story,* 1961.

Rosalind Russell as Rose in *Gypsy*, 1962.

Faye Dunaway and Warren Beatty in *Bonnie and Clyde*, 1967.

Tippi Hedren and Rod Taylor in *The Birds*, 1963.

Elvis Presley in *Paradise, Hawaiian Style*, 1966.

Virginian, Marcus Welby, M.D., Ironside, Columbo, Hawaii Five-O, The Six-Million Dollar Man, Emergency, Kojak, The Wonderful World of Disney, Baretta, Rich Man, Poor Man and *Battlestar Galactica*.

During 1975, the company completed its move from the processing plant in Hollywood, built in the 1930s, to a sprawling modern complex in Universal City (North Hollywood). With the move, came the end, at least in America, of Technicolor's heralded three-strip method of processing films and howls of protests from motion picture preservationists. The shift in operations was hardly responsible. Rather, it stemmed from a change in distribution procedures that began in the 1960s. In late 1977, Technicolor moved its executive offices from the historic Hollywood site to Century Plaza Towers in Century City, Los Angeles.

Technicolor's labs were geared for large print orders of the "old Hollywood." Latter-day film-makers, however, were cautious of the softening market and began ordering only small numbers of prints to test the strength of their productions. Handling of these projects became tailor-made and distribution patterns began to reflect the new awareness of audiences to specialized attractions. For Technicolor and its clients,

Barbra Streisand in *Funny Girl*, 1968.

The Technicolor plant at Cole and Romaine in Hollywood, late 1960s.

Flowers and Trees, 1932.

Three Little Pigs, 1933.

Snow White And The Seven Dwarfs, 1938.

Steffi Duna in *La Cucaracha*, 1934.

Marlene Dietrich with Basil Rathbone (left) in *Garden of Allah*, 1936.

Carole Lombard and Fredric March in *Nothing Sacred*, 1937.

Vivien Leigh and Clark Gable in *Gone With the Wind*, 1939.

Nigel Bruce and Miriam Hopkins in *Becky Sharp*, 1935.

Mickey Mouse as a neophyte magician in "The Sorcerer's Apprentice"
sequence, *Fantasia*, 1940.

Gale Sondergaard, Shirley Temple, Laura Hope Crews and Nigel Bruce in
The Blue Bird, 1940.

Betty Grable and John Payne in *Springtime In The Rockies*, 1942.

Merle Oberon as George Sand in *A Song To Remember*, 1945.

Fred Astaire and Ginger Rogers in *The Barkleys Of Broadway*, 1949.

Alice Faye and Carmen Miranda in *Week-End In Havana*, 1941.

Ingrid Bergman and Gary Cooper in *For Whom The Bell Tolls*, 1943.

Hedy Lamarr, Henry Wilcoxon (center) and Victor Mature in *Samson and Delilah*, 1949.

Watusi dancers in *King Solomon's Mines*, 1950.

Gregory Peck and Jennifer Jones in *Duel In The Sun*, 1946.

ZaSu Pitts, William Powell, Elizabeth Taylor, Irene Dunne and Jimmy Lydon
in *Life With Father*, 1947.

Edward Arnold and Ronald Colman (seated, left) in *Kismet*, 1944.

Bob Hope and Lucille Ball in *Fancy Pants*, 1950.

Ingrid Bergman in *Joan Of Arc*, 1948.

Humphrey Bogart and Katharine Hepburn in *The African Queen*, 1951.

Jane Wyman, Claude Jarman, Jr. and Gregory Peck in *The Yearling*, 1946.

Richard Burton and Jean Simmons in *The Robe*, 1953.

Dorothy Lamour leads dancers to center ring in *The Greatest Show On Earth*, 1952.

Marilyn Monroe strikes it rich in *How To Marry A Millionaire*, 1953.

Betty Field, Cliff Robertson, Verna Felton, Kim Novak, William Holden, Rosalind Russell, Arthur O'Connell and Susan Strasberg in *Picnic,* 1955.

The chariots bearing Rameses (Yul Brynner) and his army sweep forward along the Avenue of Sphinxes in *The Ten Commandments,* 1956.

Judy Garland and James Mason in *A Star Is Born,* 195

John Wayne and Janet Leigh in *Jet Pilot*, 1957.

Rosalind Russell as *Auntie Mame*, 1958.

The great chariot race—with Charlton Heston—in *Ben-Hur*, 1959.

Kirk Douglas spars with Woody Strode in *Spartacus*, 1960.

Nancy Kwan and dancers in *Flower Drum Song*, 1961.

Julie Andrews as *Mary Poppins*, 1964.

Peter O'Toole as *Lawrence of Arabia*, 1962.

George Peppard leads the cavalry in *How The West Was Won*, 1963.

Robert Shaw and Paul Scofield in *A Man for all Seasons*, 1966.

David Niven and Ava Gardner in *55 Days At Peking*, 1963.

Audrey Hepburn in *My Fair Lady*, 1964.

Olivia Hussey and Leonard Whiting in Ziffirelli's *Romeo And Juliet*, 1968.

Chita Rivera, Shirley MacLaine and Paula Kelly in *Sweet Charity*, 1969.

Mary Tyler Moore, James Fox and Julie Andrews in *Thoroughly Modern Millie*, 1967.

Peter Falk, Jack Lemmon, Natalie Wood and Tony Curtis in *The Great Race*, 1965.

Lucille Ball as *Mame*, 1974.

Jon Voight and Ned Beatty in *Deliverance*, 1972.

Richard Harris as *A Man Called Horse*, 1970.

Jane Fonda in *Klute*, 1971.

Jesus Christ, Superstar, 1973.

Paul Newman and Robert Redford in *The Sting,* 1973.

Roy Scheider in *Jaws*, 1975.

John Cassavetes in *Two-Minute Warning*, 1976.

Warren Beatty and Julie Christie in *Shampoo*, 1975.

Sally Field, Burt Reynolds and Jerry Reed in *Smokey And The Bandit*, 1977.

Nipsey Russell, Diana Ross and Michael Jackson in *The Wiz*, 1978.

Elvis Presley and Mary Tyler Moore listen to offstage directions just before starting a scene for *Change of Habit*, 1969.

Gary Grimes and Jennifer O'Neill in *Summer of '42*, 1971.

Liza Minnelli in *Cabaret*, 1972.

Cindy Williams and Ronny Howard in *American Graffiti*, 1973 (re-released in 1978).

Life-like scale model of Los Angeles, constructed for disaster sequences in
Earthquake, 1974.

Ryan O'Neal and Barbra Streisand in *What's Up, Doc?*, 1972.

Gateway to the new Technicolor complex in Universal City, 1975.

Technicolor revival in Los Angeles, handbill, 1976. Reverse side urged the public to "take this opportunity—possibly the only one you will ever have—to see Technicolor at its most beautiful and as it will never be again since the process which produced these pictures was permanently discontinued last year."

Richard Pryor and the Pointer Sisters in *Car Wash*, 1976.

Robert Redford in *All The President's Men*, 1976.

The Bee Gees and George Burns in *Sgt. Pepper's Lonely Hearts Club Band,* 1978.

the dye transfer process was competitive only with orders of approximately one hundred or more prints. Anything less was custom and expensive.

Dr. Kalmus once said that "until a story is filmed in Technicolor it hasn't been told in color." His words, obviously aimed at the decision-makers of the day, were also prophetic. Films made less than a decade ago, processed by other methods than dye transfer Technicolor, are beginning to fade, slowly turning red in the studio vaults.

Despite modern technology, scientists have yet to discover how to create dyes for color positive prints that will remain stable when exposed to sunlight and air. Purists, in their concern, say that the most fool-proof way to preserve color films is to isolate the three basic colors—as in the old Technicolor process—and make dye transfer prints. The dyes in these prints are so stable that the life of the prints is not yet known. The oldest available samples, prior to 1930, show no visible signs of fading.

Film fanciers and historians are fearful that the quality color motion pictures of today will, within a few years, be lost forever. Their apprehension extends to old films as well, motion pictures originally made in the dye transfer process and subsequently re-released via quicker, cheaper processing methods. *Gone With the Wind* is a good example. The beauty and often thrilling color of the original prints, now closeted in archives and private collections, may never again be seen by the general public.

Because of the growing concern over vintage color films, a number of institutions have initiated programs to preserve them. The American Film Institute, the Library of Congress, George Eastman House in Rochester, New York, and the Museum of Modern Art in New York City are all currently involved. But the task is time consuming, costly, and complicated by the fact that most movies of the past exist on nitrate film, which is notorious for decomposing or igniting spontaneously.

Color in motion pictures very probably reached its height with Technicolor's exclusive dye transfer process. It may not have been perfect but it certainly came close to perfection. During his tenure as president of the Academy of Motion Picture Arts and Sciences, writer-producer Charles Brackett was quoted as saying to Dr. Kalmus, "I well remember when *La Cucaracha* broke like a sunrise on the drab gray screens of the world. It dazzled us all by its beauty and its novelty. The beauty of the process remains. Its novelty is certainly gone.

"The only complaint about Technicolor I ever heard from anybody is that, after seeing a picture in your process, the world outside looks a little drab. The same thing can be said about an exhibition of van Goghs."

If not van Gogh, surely a rainbow.

Frank Langella as *Dracula,* 1979.

Part II

The World of Technicolor

Appendices

1

Technicolor Filmography

The following filmography of Technicolor productions includes feature films, features that contained Technicolor sequences, and a sampling of the more historic Technicolor short subjects and cartoons (i.e., 1932s *Flowers and Trees*, the first animated short subject produced in Technicolor's three-color process). Films are listed (a) by title or titles if more than one was used during release (b) alphabetically within their initial release year. Major producers and/or distributors in the United States are also noted. A dot (•) preceding the title indicates the production was done by the Technicolor company in one of its basic two-color processes rather than the full three-color process developed in the early 1930s.

1917

• *The Gulf Between*—Technicolor

1920

• *Way Down East* (sequences)—United Artists

1922

• *The Toll of the Sea*—Metro

1923

• *The Ten Commandments* (sequences)—DeMille/ Paramount

1924

• *Cytherea**—First National
• *The Uninvited Guest* (sequences)—Metro-Goldwyn-Mayer

• *Wanderer of the Wasteland*—Famous Players-Lasky/ Paramount

*First Technicolor footage to show artificially lit interiors.

1925

• *The Big Parade* (sequences)—Metro-Goldwyn-Mayer
• *The King on Main Street* (sequences)—Paramount
• *Marionettes*—Independent
• *The Merry Widow* (sequences)—Metro-Goldwyn-Mayer
• *The Phantom of the Opera* (sequences)—Universal
• *Pretty Ladies* (sequences)—Metro-Goldwyn-Mayer
• *Stage Struck* (sequences)—Paramount

1926

• *An American Venus* (sequences)—Paramount
• *Beau Geste* (sequences)—Paramount
• *Ben-Hur* (sequences)—Metro-Goldwyn-Mayer
• *The Black Pirate*—Fairbanks/United Artists
• *Irene* (sequences)—Fox
• *Michael Strogoff* (sequences)—United Artists

1927

• *The Fire Brigade* (sequences)—Metro-Goldwyn-Mayer
• *The Flag* (short)—Technicolor/Metro-Goldwyn-Mayer
• *The King of Kings* (sequences)—Pathe
• *The Joy Girl*—Fox

1928

• *Casanova* (sequences)—Metro-Goldwyn-Mayer
• *Court Martial*—Columbia

- *None But the Brave*—Fox
- *Red Hair* (sequence)—Paramount
- *The Viking**Technicolor/Metro-Goldwyn-Mayer
- *The Water Hole*—Paramount
- *The Wedding March* (sequences)—Paramount

*First Technicolor film with synchronized music and sound effects

1929

- *Broadway* (sequences)—Universal
- *Broadway Melody* (sequences)—Metro-Goldwyn-Mayer
- *The Cuckoos* (sequence)—RKO Radio
- *Dance of Life* (sequences)—Paramount
- *Devil May Care*—Metro-Goldwyn-Mayer
- *The Desert Song* (sequences)—Warner Bros.
- *Footlights and Fools* (sequence)—First National
- *Glorifying the American Girl* (sequences)—Paramount
- *Gold Diggers of Broadway*—Warner Bros.
- *Good News* (sequences)—Metro-Goldwyn-Mayer
- *His First Command* (sequences)—Pathe
- *The Hollywood Revue of 1929* (sequences)—Metro-Goldwyn-Mayer
- *Loves of Casanova*—Metro-Goldwyn-Mayer
- *Mamba*—Tiffany
- *The Mysterious Island*—Metro-Goldwyn-Mayer
- *On With the Show**—Warner Bros.
- *Paris* (sequences)—First National
- *Peacock Alley* (sequences)—Tiffany
- *Pointed Heels* (sequences)—Paramount
- *Red Hot Rhythm* (sequence)—Pathe
- *Redskin*—Paramount
- *Rio Rita* (sequences)—RKO Radio
- *The Show of Shows*—Warner Bros.

1930

- *Bride of the Regiment*—First National
- *Bright Lights*—First National
- *Chasing Rainbows* (sequences)—Metro-Goldwyn-Mayer
- *Dixiana* (sequences)—RKO Radio
- *The Floradora Girl* (sequences)—Metro-Goldwyn-Mayer
- *Follow Thru*—Paramount
- *General Crack* (sequences)—Warner Bros.
- *Golden Dawn*—Warner Bros.
- *Hell's Angels* (sequences)—Hughes/United Artists
- *Hit the Deck* (sequences)—Metro-Goldwyn-Mayer
- *Hold Everything*—Warner Bros.
- *It's a Great Life* (sequences)—Metro-Goldwyn-Mayer
- *King of Jazz**—Universal
- *Leathernecking*—RKO Radio
- *The Life of the Party*—Warner Bros.
- *Lord Byron of Broadway* (sequences)—Metro-Goldwyn-Mayer
- *The Lottery Bride* (sequences)—United Artists
- *Mammy* (sequences)—Warner Bros.
- *The March of Time*—Metro-Goldwyn-Mayer (unreleased)
- *The Melody Man*—Columbia
- *No, No Nanette* (sequences)—First National
- *Paramount on Parade* (sequences)—Paramount

*First all-talking, all-color picture

- *Puttin' on the Ritz* (sequences)—United Artists
- *The Rogue Song*—Metro-Goldwyn-Mayer
- *Sally*—First National
- *Showgirl in Hollywood* (sequences)—First National
- *Son of the Gods* (sequences)—First National
- *Song of the Flame* (sequences)—First National
- *Song of the West*—Warner Bros.
- *Sweet Kitty Bellairs*—Warner Bros.
- *They Learned About Women* (sequences)—Metro-Goldwyn-Mayer
- *Toast of the Legion* (sequences)—First National
- *Under a Texas Moon*—Warner Bros.
- *The Vagabond King*—Paramount
- *Whoopee*—Goldwyn/United Artists

*First Technicolor film to win an Academy Award—for best Set Decoration (by Herman Rosse)

1931

- *Fanny Foley Herself* (sequences)—RKO Radio
- *Fifty Million Frenchmen*—Warner Bros.
- *Kiss Me Again*—First National
- *The Runaround (Lovable and Sweet)* (sequences)—RKO Radio
- *Viennese Nights*—Warner Bros.
- *Waiting at the Church* (sequences)—RKO Radio
- *Woman Hungry*—First National

1932

- *Doctor X*—First National
  *Flowers and Trees** (animated short)—Disney/United Artists
- *Manhattan Parade* (sequences)—Warner Bros.

*First three-color animation—and the first Disney production to win an Academy Award

1933

- *Below the Sea* (sequences)—Columbia
- *The Mystery of the Wax Museum*—Warner Bros.

1934

The Cat and the Fiddle (sequences)—Metro-Goldwyn-Mayer
La Cucaracha (short)*—Pioneer/RKO Radio
Hollywood Party (sequences)—Metro-Goldwyn-Mayer
*House of Rothschild** (sequences)—Twentieth Century/United Artists
Kid Millions (sequences)—Goldwyn/United Artists
- *Kliou*—Independent

*First three-color live-action production
**First three-color live-action sequence in a feature

1935

*Becky Sharp**—Pioneer/RKO Radio
- *Le Gong: The Dance of the Virgins*—Independent
The Little Colonel (sequences)—Twentieth Century-Fox

*First three-color feature-length production

1936

The Dancing Pirate—Pioneer/RKO Radio
The Garden of Allah—Selznick/United Artists

Ramona*—Twentieth Century-Fox
Trail of the Lonesome Pine**—Wanger/Paramount

*Twentieth's initial full color feature
**First outdoor drama filmed in full color—and Paramount's first feature in the new Technicolor

1937

Coronation Film—British—Independent
Ebb Tide—Paramount
God's Country and the Woman*—Warner Bros.
Nothing Sacred—Selznick/United Artists
A Star Is Born—Selznick/United Artists
Victoria the Great (sequences)—British—RKO Radio
Vogues of 1938—Wanger/United Artists
When's Your Birthday? (sequences)—RKO Radio
Wings of the Morning**—British—Twentieth Century-Fox

*Warner's first full color film
**First Technicolor feature filmed in England

1938

Adventures of Robin Hood—Warner Bros.
Adventures of Tom Sawyer—Selznick/United Artists
The Divorce of Lady X—British—Korda/United Artists
Drums—British—Korda/United Artists
The Goldwyn Follies—Goldwyn/United Artists
Gold is Where You Find It—Warner Bros.
Heart of the North—Warner Bros.
Her Jungle Love—Paramount
Jezebel (sequences)—Warner Bros.
Kentucky—Twentieth Century-Fox
Men With Wings—Paramount
Sixty Glorious Years—British—RKO Radio
Snow White and the Seven Dwarfs (animated)—Disney/RKO Radio
Sweethearts*—Metro-Goldwyn-Mayer
Valley of the Giants—Warner Bros.

*M-G-M's first three-color feature

1939

Dodge City—Warner Bros.
Drums Along the Mohawk—Twentieth Century-Fox
Four Feathers—British—Korda/United Artists
Gone With the Wind*—Selznick/Metro-Goldwyn-Mayer
Gulliver's Travels (animated)—Paramount
Hollywood Cavalcade—Twentieth Century-Fox
Ice Follies of 1939 (sequences)—Metro-Goldwyn-Mayer
Jesse James—Twentieth Century-Fox
Land of Liberty (sequences)—Metro-Goldwyn-Mayer
The Little Princess—Twentieth Century-Fox
The Mikado—British—Universal
The Private Lives of Elizabeth and Essex—Warner Bros.
The Wizard of Oz (sequences)—Metro-Goldwyn-Mayer
The Women (sequences)—Metro-Goldwyn-Mayer

*First film to win an Academy Award in the newly created Color Cinematography classification

1940

Bittersweet—Metro-Goldwyn-Mayer

The Blue Bird—Twentieth Century-Fox
Chad Hanna—Twentieth Century-Fox
Doctor Cyclops—Paramount
Down Argentine Way—Twentieth Century-Fox
Fantasia (animated)—Disney/RKO Radio
Irene (sequence)—RKO Radio
Maryland—Twentieth Century-Fox
Northwest Mounted Police—DeMille/Paramount
Northwest Passage—Metro-Goldwyn-Mayer
Over the Moon—British—Korda/United Artists
Pinocchio (animated)—Disney/RKO Radio
The Return of Frank James—Twentieth Century-Fox
Swanee River—Twentieth Century-Fox
The Thief of Bagdad*—British—Korda/United Artists
Typhoon—Paramount
Untamed—Paramount

*Academy Award winner for best Color Cinematography

1941

Aloma of the South Seas—Paramount
Belle Starr—Twentieth Century-Fox
Billy the Kid—Metro-Goldwyn-Mayer
Blood and Sand*—Twentieth Century-Fox
Blossoms in the Dust—Metro-Goldwyn-Mayer
Dive Bomber—Warner Bros.
Dumbo (animated)—Disney/RKO Radio
Fiesta—Roach/United Artists
Louisiana Purchase—Paramount
Mr. Bug Goes to Town (animated)—Paramount
Moon Over Miami—Twentieth Century-Fox
The Reluctant Dragon (part animation)—Disney/RKO Radio
Shepherd of the Hills—Paramount
Smilin' Through—Metro-Goldwyn-Mayer
That Night in Rio—Twentieth Century-Fox
Virginia—Paramount
Week-End in Havana—Twentieth Century-Fox
Western Union—Twentieth Century-Fox

*Academy Award winner for best Color Cinematography

1942

Arabian Nights*—Wanger/Universal
Bahama Passage—Paramount
Bambi (animated)—Disney/RKO Radio
Beyond the Blue Horizon—Paramount
The Black Swan**—Twentieth Century-Fox
Captains of the Clouds—Warner Bros.
The Forest Rangers—Paramount
Jungle Book—Korda/United Artists
The Moon and Sixpence (sequence)—United Artists
My Gal Sal—Twentieth Century-Fox
Reap the Wild Wind—DeMille/Paramount
Song of the Islands—Twentieth Century-Fox
Springtime in the Rockies—Twentieth Century-Fox
Thunder Birds—Twentieth Century-Fox
To the Shores of Tripoli—Twentieth Century-Fox

*Universal's first American-made film in full color Technicolor—the studio's first Technicolor film since *King of Jazz*, 1930
**Academy Award winner for best Color Cinematography

1943

Best Foot Forward—Metro-Goldwyn-Mayer
Cobra Woman—Universal
Coney Island—Twentieth Century-Fox
Crash Drive—Twentieth Century-Fox
The Desperados—Columbia
Dixie—Paramount
DuBarry Was A Lady—Metro-Goldwyn-Mayer
For Whom the Bell Tolls—Paramount
The Gang's All Here—Twentieth Century-Fox
The Great Mr. Handel—British—Independent
Happy Go Lucky—Paramount
Heaven Can Wait—Twentieth Century-Fox
Hello, Frisco, Hello—Twentieth Century-Fox
Lassie Come Home—Metro-Goldwyn-Mayer
My Friend Flicka—Twentieth Century-Fox
*Phantom of the Opera**—Universal
Report from the Aleutians—Independent
Riding High—Paramount
Saludos Amigos (animated)—Disney/RKO Radio
Salute to the Marines—Metro-Goldwyn-Mayer
Sweet Rosie O'Grady—Twentieth Century-Fox
This Is the Army—Warner Bros.
Thousands Cheer—Metro-Goldwyn-Mayer
Victory Through Air Power (animated)—Disney/United
   Artists
White Savage—Universal

*Academy Award winner for best Color Cinematography

1944

Ali Baba and the Forty Thieves—Universal
An American Romance—Vidor/Metro-Goldwyn-Mayer
Bathing Beauty—Metro-Goldwyn-Mayer
Broadway Rhythm—Metro-Goldwyn-Mayer
Buffalo Bill—Twentieth Century-Fox
Can't Help Singing—Universal
The Climax—Universal
Cover Girl—Columbia
The Desert Song—Warner Bros.
Greenwich Village—Twentieth Century-Fox
Gypsy Wildcat—Universal
Home in Indiana—Twentieth Century-Fox
Irish Eyes Are Smiling—Twentieth Century-Fox
Kisenga, Man of Africa—British—Independent
Kismet—Metro-Goldwyn-Mayer
Lady in the Dark—Paramount
Meet Me in St. Louis—Metro-Goldwyn-Mayer
Pin Up Girl—Twentieth Century-Fox
The Princess and the Pirate—Goldwyn/RKO Radio
Rainbow Island—Paramount
Shine on Harvest Moon (sequence)—Warner Bros.
Something for the Boys—Twentieth Century-Fox
The Story of Dr. Wassell—DeMille/Paramount
Up in Arms—Goldwyn/RKO Radio
*Wilson**—Twentieth Century-Fox

*Academy Award winner for best Color Cinematography

1945

Anchors Aweigh—Metro-Goldwyn-Mayer
Belle of the Yukon—International/RKO Radio
Billy Rose's Diamond Horseshoe—Twentieth Century-Fox

Blithe Spirit—British—Two Cities/United Artists
Bring on the Girls—Paramount
Colonel Blimp—British—Powell-Pressburger/United Art-
   ists
The Dolly Sisters—Twentieth Century-Fox
The Fighting Lady—Twentieth Century-Fox
Frenchman's Creek—Paramount
Frontier Gal—Universal
Incendiary Blonde—Paramount
It's a Pleasure—International/RKO Radio
*Leave Her to Heaven**—Twentieth Century-Fox
National Velvet—Metro-Goldwyn-Mayer
Nob Hill—Twentieth Century-Fox
The Picture of Dorian Gray (sequences)—Metro-
   Goldwyn-Mayer
Salome, Where She Danced—Wanger/Universal
San Antonio—Warner Bros.
Son of Lassie—Metro-Goldwyn-Mayer
A Song to Remember—Columbia
The Spanish Main—RKO Radio
State Fair—Twentieth Century-Fox
Sudan—Universal
The Three Caballeros (part animation)—Disney/RKO
   Radio
A Thousand and One Nights—Columbia
Thrill of a Romance—Metro-Goldwyn-Mayer
Thunderhead, Son of Flicka—Twentieth Century-Fox
Tonight and Every Night—Columbia
Where Do We Go from Here?—Twentieth Century-Fox
Wonder Man—Goldwyn/RKO Radio
Yolanda and the Thief—Metro-Goldwyn-Mayer

*Academy Award winner for best Color Cinematography

1946

The Bandit of Sherwood Forest—Columbia
Blue Skies—Paramount
Caesar and Cleopatra—British—Pascal/United Artists
Canyon Passage—Wanger/Universal
Centennial Summer—Twentieth Century-Fox
Courage of Lassie—Metro-Goldwyn-Mayer
Do You Love Me?—Twentieth Century-Fox
Easy to Wed—Metro-Goldwyn-Mayer
The Harvey Girls—Metro-Goldwyn-Mayer
Henry V—British—Olivier/United Artists
Holiday in Mexico—Metro-Goldwyn-Mayer
I've Always Loved You—Republic
The Jolson Story—Columbia
The Kid from Brooklyn—Goldwyn/RKO Radio
Laughing Lady—British—Independent
Make Mine Music (animation)—Disney/RKO Radio
Margie—Twentieth Century-Fox
Night and Day—Warner Bros.
Night in Paradise—Wanger/Universal
The Raider—British—Independent
Renegades—Columbia
Smoky—Twentieth Century-Fox
Song of the South (part animation)—Disney/RKO Radio
Stairway to Heaven—British—Universal-International
Three Little Girls in Blue—Twentieth Century-Fox
Till the Clouds Roll By—Metro-Goldwyn-Mayer

The Time, the Place and the Girl—Warner Bros./First National
The Virginian—Paramount
Wake Up and Dream—Twentieth Century-Fox
The Yearling*—Metro-Goldwyn-Mayer
Ziegfeld Follies—Metro-Goldwyn-Mayer

*Academy Award winner for best Color Cinematography

1947

Black Narcissus*—British—Universal-International
California—Paramount
Captain from Castile—Twentieth Century-Fox
Carnival in Costa Rica—Twentieth Century-Fox
Desert Fury—Wallis/Paramount
Down to Earth—Columbia
Duel in the Sun—Selznick Releasing Organization
Fiesta—Metro-Goldwyn-Mayer
Forever Amber—Twentieth Century-Fox
Fun and Fancy Free (part animation)—Disney/RKO Radio
Good News—Metro-Goldwyn-Mayer
Gunfighters—Columbia
The Homestretch—Twentieth Century-Fox
I Wonder Who's Kissing Her Now?—Twentieth Century-Fox
Life With Father—Warner Bros.
Mother Wore Tights—Twentieth Century-Fox
My Heart Goes Crazy (London Town)—British—Independent
My Wild Irish Rose—Warner Bros.
The Perils of Pauline—Paramount
Pirates of Monterey—Universal-International
The Private Affairs of Bel Ami (sequences)—United Artists
The Secret Life of Walter Mitty—Goldwyn/RKO Radio
The Shocking Miss Pilgrim—Twentieth Century-Fox
Sinbad the Sailor—RKO Radio
Slave Girl—Universal-International
Song of Scheherazade—Universal-International
The Swordsman—Columbia
This Happy Breed—British—Universal-International
This Time For Keeps—Metro-Goldwyn-Mayer
Thunder in the Valley (Bob, Son of Battle)—Twentieth Century-Fox
Tycoon—RKO Radio
Unconquered—DeMille/Paramount
The Unfinished Dance—Metro-Goldwyn-Mayer

*Academy Award winner for best Color Cinematography

1948

Apartment For Peggy—Twentieth Century-Fox
Black Bart—Universal-International
Blanche Fury—British—Eagle-Lion
The Boy With Green Hair—RKO Radio
A Date With Judy—Metro-Goldwyn-Mayer
Easter Parade—Metro-Goldwyn-Mayer
The Emperor Waltz—Paramount
Fighter Squadron—Warner Bros.
The Gallant Blade—Columbia
Give My Regards to Broadway—Twentieth Century-Fox
Green Grass of Wyoming—Twentieth Century-Fox
Hills of Home—Metro-Goldwyn-Mayer

An Ideal Husband—British—Korda/Twentieth Century-Fox
Jassy—British—Universal-International
Joan of Arc*—Wanger/RKO Radio
The Kissing Bandit—Metro-Goldwyn-Mayer
The Loves of Carmen—Columbia
Luxury Liner—Metro-Goldwyn-Mayer
The Man from Colorado—Columbia
Melody Time (animated)—Disney/RKO Radio
On An Island With You—Metro-Goldwyn-Mayer
One Sunday Afternoon—Warner Bros.
The Paleface—Paramount
The Pirate—Metro-Goldwyn-Mayer
The Red Shoes—British—Powell-Pressburger/Eagle-Lion
Relentless—Columbia
The Return of October—Columbia
River Lady—Universal-International
Romance on the High Seas—Warner Bros.
Rope—Hitchcock/Warner Bros.
Scudda Hoo, Scudda Hay—Twentieth Century-Fox
The Secret Land—Metro-Goldwyn-Mayer
The Smugglers—British—Eagle-Lion
A Song Is Born—Goldwyn/RKO Radio
Summer Holiday—Metro-Goldwyn-Mayer
Tale of the Navajos—Metro-Goldwyn-Mayer
Tap Roots—Wanger/Universal-International
Task Force (sequences)—Warner Bros.
That Lady in Ermine—Twentieth Century-Fox
Three Daring Daughters—Metro-Goldwyn-Mayer
Three Godfathers—Argosy/Metro-Goldwyn-Mayer
The Three Musketeers—Metro-Goldwyn-Mayer
Two Guys from Texas—Warner Bros.
The Untamed Breed—Columbia
When My Baby Smiles at Me—Twentieth Century-Fox
Words and Music—Metro-Goldwyn-Mayer

*Academy Award winner for best Color Cinematography and the first film to win an Oscar for Color Costume Design (motion picture costume design was not honored by the Academy until 1948)

1949

Adventures of Don Juan—Warner Bros.
The Adventures of Ichabod and Mr. Toad (animated)—Disney/RKO Radio
Bagdad—Universal-International
The Barkleys of Broadway—Metro-Goldwyn-Mayer
The Beautiful Blonde from Bashful Bend—Twentieth Cenutry-Fox
The Big Cat—Eagle-Lion
The Blue Lagoon—British—Universal-International
Calamity Jane and Sam Bass—Universal-International
Christopher Columbus—British—Universal-International
Cinderella (animated)—Disney/RKO Radio
A Connecticut Yankee in King Arthur's Court—Paramount
Dancing in the Dark—Twentieth Cenutry-Fox
The Gal Who Took the West—Metro-Goldwyn-Mayer
The Inspector General—Warner Bros.
It's a Great Feeling—Warner Bros.
Jolson Sings Again—Columbia
Little Women—Metro-Goldwyn-Mayer
Look for the Silver Lining—Warner Bros.

Mother is a Freshman—Twentieth Cenutry-Fox
The Mutineers—Columbia
My Dream is Yours—Curtiz/Warner Bros.
Neptune's Daughter—Metro-Goldwyn-Mayer
Oh, You Beautiful Doll—Twentieth Cenutry-Fox
On the Town—Metro-Goldwyn-Mayer
Red Canyon—Universal-International
The Red Pony—Republic
Samson and Delilah—DeMille/Paramount
Sand—Twentieth Cenutry-Fox
Saraband—British—Eagle-Lion
Scott of the Antarctic—British—Eagle-Lion
The Secret Garden (sequences)—Metro-Goldwyn-Mayer
She Wore a Yellow Ribbon*—Argosy/RKO Radio
So Dear to My Heart (part animation)—Disney/RKO
  Radio
Some of the Best (sequences)—Metro-Goldwyn-Mayer
South of St. Louis—Warner Bros.
The Story of Seabiscuit—Warner Bros.
Streets of Laredo—Paramount
The Sun Comes Up—Metro-Goldwyn-Mayer
Take Me Out to the Ball Game—Metro-Goldwyn-Mayer
That Forsyte Woman—Metro-Goldwyn-Mayer
That Midnight Kiss—Metro-Goldwyn-Mayer
Tulsa—Wanger/Eagle-Lion
Under Capricorn—British—Hitchcock/Warner Bros.
Yes, Sir, That's My Baby—Universal-International
The Younger Brothers—Warner Bros.
You're My Everything—Twentieth Cenutry-Fox
*Academy Award winner for best Color Cinematography

Beginning in the early 1950s, an increasing number of new color processes came into wide use—Ansco Color, Eastmancolor, WarnerColor, Deluxe, Metrocolor, among others—many of which were aided by the Technicolor laboratories in certain phases of processing which the other labs were not equipped to handle at the time. For instance, 1954s *There's No Business Like Show Business* had most of its original release prints done at the Technicolor laboratories but earlier post-production lab work was handled at the DeLuxe Color plant. The film was officially credited as having "Color by DeLuxe." Combination lab work continues today for a variety of reasons (more recently, Technicolor did the up-front work for Twentieth Century-Fox's 1977 *Star Wars* with DeLuxe handling the release prints). Such duo-processed color features are listed only when domestic release prints have been credited to Technicolor.

1950

An American Guerrilla in the Philippines—Twentieth
  Century-Fox
Annie Get Your Gun—Metro-Goldwyn-Mayer
Barricade—Warner Bros.
The Black Rose—Twentieth Century-Fox
The Blue Lamp—British—Eagle-Lion
Broken Arrow—Twentieth Century-Fox
Buccaneer's Girl—Universal-International
Challenge to Lassie—Metro-Goldwyn-Mayer
Cheaper by the Dozen—Twentieth Century-Fox
Colt .45—Warner Bros.
Comanche Territory—Universal-International

Copper Canyon—Paramount
Curtain Call at Cactus Creek—Universal-International
The Daughter of Rosie O'Grady—Warner Bros.
The Desert Hawk—Universal-International
Destination Moon—Pal/Eagle-Lion
Duchess of Idaho—Metro-Goldwyn-Mayer
The Eagle and the Hawk—Paramount
Fancy Pants—Paramount
The Fighting Pimpernell—British—Independent
The Flame and the Arrow—Warner Bros.
The Happy Years—Metro-Goldwyn-Mayer
High Lonesome—Eagle-Lion
I'll Get By—Twentieth Century-Fox
The Kid from Texas—Universal-International
Kim—Metro-Goldwyn-Mayer
King Solomon's Mines*—Metro-Goldwyn-Mayer
Let's Dance—Paramount
Montana—Warner Bros.
My Blue Heaven—Twentieth Century-Fox
Nancy Goes to Rio—Metro-Goldwyn-Mayer
The Outriders—Metro-Goldwyn-Mayer
Pagan Love Song—Metro-Goldwyn-Mayer
The Palomino—Columbia
Peggy—Universal-International
The Petty Girl—Columbia
Return of the Frontiersman—Warner Bros.
Rogues of Sherwood Forest—Columbia
Saddle Tramp—Universal-International
Sierra—Universal-International
Summer Stock—Metro-Goldwyn-Mayer
The Sundowners—Eagle-Lion
Tea For Two—Warner Bros.
Three Little Words—Metro-Goldwyn-Mayer
A Ticket to Tomahawk—Twentieth Century-Fox
The Toast of New Orleans—Metro-Goldwyn-Mayer
Treasure Island—Disney/RKO Radio
Tripoli—Paramount
Two Weeks With Love—Metro-Goldwyn-Mayer
Wabash Avenue—Twentieth Century-Fox
The White Tower—RKO Radio
Wyoming Mail—Universal-International
*Academy Award winner for best Color Cinematography

1951

Across the Wide Missouri—Metro-Goldwyn-Mayer
The African Queen—Horizon/United Artists
Alice in Wonderland (animation)—Disney/RKO Radio
Al Jennings of Oklahoma—Columbia
An American in Paris*—Metro-Goldwyn-Mayer
Anne of the Indies—Twentieth Century-Fox
Apache Drums—Universal-International
Best of the Badmen—RKO Radio
Bird of Paradise—Twentieth Century-Fox
Branded—Paramount
Call Me Mister—Twentieth Century-Fox
Captain Horatio Hornblower—British—Warner Bros.
Cattle Drive—Universal-International
Cave of Outlaws—Universal-International
Cimarron Kid—Universal-International
Crosswinds—Paramount

Dallas—Warner Bros.
David and Bathsheba—Twentieth Century-Fox
Distant Drums—Warner Bros.
Double Crossbones—Universal-International
Excuse My Dust—Metro-Goldwyn-Mayer
Flame of Araby—Universal-International
Flaming Feather—Paramount
Flying Leathernecks—RKO Radio
Fort Worth—Warner Bros.
Frenchie—Universal-International
Golden Girl—Twentieth Century-Fox
The Golden Horde—Universal-International
The Great Caruso—Metro-Goldwyn-Mayer
The Great Missouri Raid—Paramount
Half Angel—Twentieth Century-Fox
The Halls of Montezuma—Twentieth Century-Fox
Happy Go Lovely—British—RKO Radio
I'd Climb the Highest Mountain—Twentieth Century-Fox
I'll Never Forget You—Twentieth Century-Fox
Kansas Raiders—Universal-International
The Lady from Texas—Universal-International
The Last Outpost—Paramount
Little Egypt—Universal-International
Lorna Doone—Columbia
Lullaby of Broadway—Warner Bros.
Man in the Saddle—Columbia
Mark of the Renegade—Universal-International
Mark of the Avenger—Columbia
Meet Me After the Show—Twentieth Century-Fox
Mr. Imperium—Metro-Goldwyn-Mayer
On Moonlight Bay—Warner Bros.
On the Riviera—Twentieth Century-Fox
The Painted Hills—Metro-Goldwyn-Mayer
Painting the Clouds With Sunshine—Warner Bros.
Pandora and the Flying Dutchman—Metro-Goldwyn-Mayer
Passage West—Paramount
The Prince Who Was a Thief—Universal-International
Quebec—Paramount
Quo Vadis—Metro-Goldwyn-Mayer
Red Mountain—Wallis/Paramount
Rich, Young and Pretty—Metro-Goldwyn-Mayer
The River—British—United Artists
Royal Wedding—Metro-Goldwyn-Mayer
Santa Fe—Columbia
Show Boat—Metro-Goldwyn-Mayer
Silver City—Paramount
Smuggler's Island—Universal-International
Stage to Tucson—Columbia
Sugarfoot—Warner Bros.
Take Care of My Little Girl—Twentieth Century-Fox
Tales of Hoffman—British—Powell-Pressburger/Lopert
Ten Tall Men—Columbia
Texas Carnival—Metro-Goldwyn-Mayer
Tomahawk—Universal-International
Two Tickets to Broadway—RKO Radio
Valentino—Columbia
Vengeance Valley—Metro-Goldwyn-Mayer
Warpath—Paramount
When Worlds Collide—Pal/Paramount

*Academy Award winner for best Color Cinematography

1952

Aaron Slick from Punkin Crick—Paramount
About Face—Warner Bros.
Against All Flags—Universal-International
All Ashore—Columbia
Ambush at Tomahawk Gap—Columbia
At Sword's Point—RKO Radio
Battle of Apache Pass—Universal-International
Because You're Mine—Metro-Goldwyn-Mayer
Belle of New York—Metro-Goldwyn-Mayer
Belles on Their Toes—Twentieth Century-Fox
Bend of the River—Universal-International
La Bergere et le Ramoneur—French—Independent
The Big Trees—Warner Bros.
Blackbeard the Pirate—RKO Radio
Blazing Forest—Paramount
Bloodhounds of Broadway—Twentieth Century-Fox
Bonnie Prince Charlie—British—Korda/United Artists
Brave Warrier—Columbia
The Brigand—Columbia
Bronco Buster—Universal-International
Bugles in the Afternoon—Warner Bros.
California Conquest—Columbia
Captain Pirate—Columbia
Caribbean—Paramount
Crimson Pirate—British—Warner Bros.
Cripple Creek—Columbia
Denver and the Rio Grande—Paramount
Duel At Silver Creek—Universal-International
The Dupont Story—Independent
Everything I Have is Yours—Metro-Goldwyn-Mayer
The Firebird—United Artists
Golden Hawk—Columbia
The Greatest Show on Earth—DeMille/Paramount
Half Breed—RKO Radio
Hangman's Knot—Columbia
Hans Christian Anderson—Goldwyn/RKO Radio
Has Anybody Seen My Gal?—Universal-International
Hong Kong—Paramount
Horizons West—Universal-International
Hurricane Smith—Paramount
The Importance of Being Earnest—British—Universal-International
The Iron Mistress—Warner Bros.
Island of Desire—United Artists
Ivanhoe—Metro-Goldwyn-Mayer
Ivory Hunter (Where No Vultures Fly)—British—Universal-International
Just For You—Paramount
Kangaroo—Twentieth Century-Fox
Latuko—Independent
Lovely to Look At—Metro-Goldwyn-Mayer
Lure of the Wilderness—Twentieth Century-Fox
Lydia Bailey—Twentieth Century-Fox
The Magic Box—British—Independent
Maytime in Mayfair—British—Independent
The Merry Widow—Metro-Goldwyn-Mayer
Million Dollar Mermaid—Metro-Goldwyn-Mayer
Montana Territory—Columbia
Montemarte—French—Independent
Moulin Rouge—Horizon/United Artists
Mutiny—United Artists

Naked Spur—Metro-Goldwyn-Mayer
Girls of Pleasure Island—Paramount
Plymouth Adventure—Metro-Goldwyn-Mayer
Pony Soldier—Twentieth Century-Fox
Powder River—Twentieth Century-Fox
Prisoner of Zenda—Metro-Goldwyn-Mayer
The Quiet Man*—Argosy/Republic
The Raiders—Universal-International
Rainbow Round My Shoulder—Columbia
Ramble in Erin—Irish—Independent
Rancho Notorious—RKO Radio
Red Skies of Montana (Smoke Jumpers)—Twentieth
   Century-Fox
The Savage—Paramount
Scaramouche—Metro-Goldwyn-Mayer
Scarlet Angel—Universal-International
She's Working Her Way Through College—Warner Bros.
Singin' in the Rain—Metro-Goldwyn-Mayer
Skirts Ahoy—Metro-Goldwyn-Mayer
The Snows of Kilimanjaro—Twentieth Century-Fox
Somebody Loves Me—Paramount
Son of Paleface—Paramount
Stars and Stripes Forever—Twentieth Century-Fox
Steel Town—Universal-International
The Story of Robin Hood—Disney/RKO Radio
The Story of Will Rogers—Warner Bros.
Thief of Damascus—Columbia
This Is Cinerama—Cinerama Releasing Corp.
Treasure of Lost Canyon—Universal-International
Tropic Zone—Paramount
Untamed Frontier—Universal-International
Wait Till the Sun Shines Nellie—Twentieth Century-Fox
Way of a Gaucho—Twentieth Century-Fox
What Price Glory—Twentieth Century-Fox
Where's Charley?—Warner Bros.
The Wild Heart—Selznick/RKO Radio
With a Song in My Heart—Twentieth Century-Fox
The World in His Arms—Universal-International
Yankee Buccaneer—Universal-International
*Academy Award winner for best Color Cinematography

1953

Aan—United Artists
Affair in Monte Carlo—British—Allied Artists
All Ashore—Columbia
All the Brothers Were Valiant—Metro-Goldwyn-Mayer
Ambush at Tomahawk Gap—Columbia
April in Paris—Warner Bros.
Appointment in Honduras—RKO Radio
Arrowhead—Paramount
Back to God's Country—Universal-International
The Band Wagon—Metro-Goldwyn-Mayer
The Beggar's Opera—British—Warner Bros.
Below the Sahara—RKO Radio
Beneath the Twelve Mile Reef—Twentieth Century-Fox
Bonjour Paris—French—Independent
Botany Bay—Paramount
By the Light of the Silvery Moon—Warner Bros.
Calamity Jane—Warner Bros.
Call Me Madam—Twentieth Century-Fox

Captain Scarlet—United Artists
Caroline Cherie—French—Independent
City Beneath the Sea—Universal-International
City of Bad Men—Twentieth Century-Fox
Column South—Universal-International
Conquest of Cochise—Columbia
Conquest of Everest—British—United Artists
Cruisin' Down the River—Columbia
Dangerous When Wet—Metro-Goldwyn-Mayer
Decameron Nights—British—RKO Radio
Desert Legion—Universal-International
Desert Song—Warner Bros.
Destination Gobi—Twentieth Century-Fox
Devil's Canyon—RKO Radio
Down Among the Sheltering Palms—Twentieth Century-
   Fox
East of Sumatra—Universal-International
Easy to Love—Metro-Goldwyn-Mayer
The Eddie Cantor Story—Warner Bros.
The Farmer Takes a Wife—Twentieth Century-Fox
Father's Doing Fine—British—Independent
The 5,000 Fingers of Dr. T—Kramer/Columbia
Flame of Calcutta—Columbia
Flight to Tangier—Paramount
Fort Ti—Columbia
Gentlemen Prefer Blondes—Twentieth Century-Fox
Gilbert and Sullivan—British—United Artists
The Girl Next Door—Twentieth Century-Fox
Give a Girl a Break—Metro-Goldwyn-Mayer
The Golden Blade—Universal-International
The Great Sioux Uprising—Universal-International
Gun Belt—United Artists
Gun Fury—Columbia
Gunsmoke—Universal-International
Here Come the Girls—Paramount
Houdini—Pal/Paramount
How to Marry a Millionaire—Twentieth Century-Fox
The 'I Don't Care' Girl—Twentieth Century-Fox
I Love Melvin—Metro-Goldwyn-Mayer
Inferno—Twentieth Century-Fox
It Started in Paradise—British—Independent
Jack McCall, Desperado—Columbia
Jamaica Run—Paramount
The Jazz Singer—Warner Bros.
Johnny, the Giant Killer—Lippert
Kiss Me Kate—Metro-Goldwyn-Mayer
Last of the Comanches—Columbia
Latin Lovers—Metro-Goldwyn-Mayer
Law and Order—Universal-International
Let's Do It Again—Columbia
Lili—Metro-Goldwyn-Mayer
A Lion is in the Streets—Warner Bros.
Lone Hand—Universal-International
Lucretia Borgia—Italian—Independent
Man Behind the Gun—Warner Bros.
Man from the Alamo—Universal-International
Master of Ballentrae—British—Warner Bros.
Meet Me at the Fair—Universal-International
Melba—Horizon/United Artists
Miss Sadie Thompson—Columbia
Mississippi Gambler—Universal-International
Mogambo—Metro-Goldwyn-Mayer
Monsoon—British—United Artists

Naked Spur—Metro-Goldwyn-Mayer
The Nebraskan—Columbia
Niagra—Twentieth Century-Fox
Paris Express—British—Independent
The Pathfinder—Columbia
Peter Pan (animated)—Disney/RKO Radio
Pony Express—Paramount
Powder River—Twentieth Century-Fox
Prince of Pirates—Columbia
Prisoners of the Casbah—Columbia
Puccini—Italian—Independent
A Queen is Crowned—British—Universal-International
Raiders of the Seven Seas—United Artists
Redhead from Wyoming—Universal-International
Return to Paradise—United Artists
Road to Bali—Paramount
The Robe—Twentieth Century-Fox
Saadia—Metro-Goldwyn-Mayer
Salome—Columbia
Sangaree—Paramount
Scandal at Scourie—Metro-Goldwyn-Mayer
The Sea Around Us—RKO Radio
Sea Devils—RKO Radio
Second Chance—RKO Radio
Seminole—Universal-International
Serpent of the Nile—Columbia
Shane*—Paramount
Siren of Bagdad—Columbia
Slaves of Babylon—Columbia
Small Town Girl—Metro-Goldwyn-Mayer
So This Is Love—Warner Bros.
Sombrero—Metro-Goldwyn-Mayer
Stand at Apache River—Universal-International
The Stars are Singing—Paramount
The Story of Three Loves—Metro-Goldwyn-Mayer
The Stranger Wore a Gun—Columbia
The Sword and the Rose—Disney/RKO Radio
Take Me to Town—Universal-International
Those Redheads from Seattle—Paramount
Three Sailors and a Girl—Warner Bros.
Thunder Bay—Universal-International
Titfield Thunderbolt—British—Universal-International
Tonight at 8:30—British—Independent
Tonight We Sing—Twentieth Century-Fox
Torch Song—Metro-Goldwyn-Mayer
Treasure of the Golden Condor—Twentieth Century-Fox
Tropic Zone—Paramount
Tumbleweed—Universal-International
The Vanquished—Paramount
Veils of Bagdad—Universal-International
Walking My Baby Back Home—Universal-International
War Arrow—Universal-International
War of the Worlds—Pal/Paramount
White Witch Doctor—Twentieth Century-Fox
Wings of the Hawk—Universal-International
Young Bess—Metro-Goldwyn-Mayer
*Academy Award winner for best Color Cinematography

1954

Animal Farm—British—Independent
Annapurna—Independent
Apache—United Artists

Arrow in the Dust—Allied Artists
The Barefoot Contessa—Figaro/United Artists
Battle of Rogue River—Columbia
The Beachcomber—British—United Artists
Beachhead—United Artists
Beau Brummel—Metro-Goldwyn-Mayer
Bengal Brigade—Universal-International
The Black Dakotas—Columbia
Black Horse Canyon—Universal-International
The Black Knight—Columbia
Black Shield of Falworth—Universal-International
Border River—Universal-International
A Bullet is Waiting—Columbia
The Caine Mutiny—Kramer/Columbia
Casanova's Big Night—Paramount
Charge of the Lancers—Columbia
Conquest of Everest—British—Independent
Dangerous Mission—RKO Radio
Dawn at Socorro—Universal-International
Demitrius and the Gladiators—Twentieth Century-Fox
Destry—Universal-International

Drums Across the River—Universal-International
Drums of Tahiti—Columbia
Duel in the Jungle—British—Moulin/Warner Bros.
Elephant Walk—Paramount
Fire Over Africa—Columbia
Flame and the Flesh—Metro-Goldwyn-Mayer
Four Guns to the Border—Universal-International
The French Line—RKO Radio
The Gambler from Natchez—Twentieth Century-Fox
Garden of Evil—Twentieth Century-Fox
Genevieve—British—Universal-International
The Glenn Miller Story—Universal-International
The Golden Coach—Italian—Independent
The Golden Mask—United Artists
The Golden Mistress—United Artists
Gorilla at Large—Twentieth Century-Fox
Hansel and Gretel—Independent
Hell and High Water—Twentieth Century-Fox
Hell Below Zero—Columbia
His Majesty O'Keefe—Warner Bros.
The Iron Glove—Columbia
Jesse James vs. the Daltons—Columbia
Jesse James' Women—United Artists
Jivaro—Paramount
Johnny Dark—Universal-International
King of the Khyber Rifles—Twentieth Century-Fox
Knock on Wood—Paramount
The Last Time I Saw Paris—Metro-Goldwyn-Mayer
Laughing Anne—Republic
The Law vs. Billy the Kid—Columbia
The Living Desert—Disney/Buena Vista
Living It Up—Paramount
Mad About Men—British—Independent
Magnificent Obsession—Universal-International
Man With a Million—United Artists
Masterson of Kansas—Columbia
Men of the Fighting Lady—Metro-Goldwyn-Mayer
Money from Home—Paramount
The Naked Jungle—Pal/Paramount
Night People—Twentieth Century-Fox
Out of This World—Independent
Outlaw Stallion—Columbia

Passion—RKO Radio
Prince Valiant—Twentieth Century-Fox
Puccini—Italian—Independent
The Purple Plain—United Artists
The Raid—Twentieth Century-Fox
Rails Into Laramie—United Artists
The Rainbow Jacket—British—Independent
Rear Window—Hitchcock/Paramount
The Red and the Black—French/Italian—Independent
Red Garters—Paramount
Rhapsody—Metro-Goldwyn-Mayer
Ride Clear of Diablo—Universal-International
River of No Return—Twentieth Century-Fox
Rob Roy, the Highland Rogue—Disney/RKO Radio
Romeo and Juliet—British—United Artists
The Saracen Blade—Columbia
Saskatchewan—Universal-International
Scarlet Spear—United Artists
Secret of the Incas—Paramount
The Siege at Red River—Twentieth Century-Fox
Silver Lode—RKO Radio
Sixth Continent—Italian—Independent
Son of Sinbad—RKO Radio
A Star Is Born—Warner Bros.
Stormy, the Thoroughbred—Disney/Buena Vista
Susan Slept Here—RKO Radio
Tanganyika—Universal-International
Taza, Son of Cochise—Universal-International
They Rode West—Columbia
This Is Your Army—Independent
Three Hours to Kill—Columbia
Three Ring Circus—Wallis/Paramount
Three Young Texans—Twentieth Century-Fox
Tonight's the Night—British—Allied Artists
20,000 Leagues Under the Sea—Disney/Buena Vista
The Vanishing Prairie—Disney/Buena Vista
Vera Cruz—United Artists
War Arrow—Universal-International
White Christmas—Paramount
Woman's World—Twentieth Century-Fox
Yankee Pasha—Universal-International
Yellow Mountain—Universal-International

NOTE: 1954 was the first year since 1939, when the Academy established its Color Cinematography award, that a Technicolor film did not get the top honor. Twentieth Century-Fox's *Three Coins in the Fountain* in DeLuxe color won the Oscar.

1955

The African Lion—Disney/Buena Vista
Ain't Misbehavin'—Universal-International
The Americano—RKO Radio
The Annapolis Story—Allied Artists
Artists and Models—Wallis/Paramount
Attila—French/Italian—Independent
The Bridges at Toko-Ri—Paramount
Bring Your Smile Along—Columbia
Cattle Queen of Montana—RKO Radio
Chief Crazy Horse—Universal-International
Cinerama Holiday—Cinerama Releasing Corp.
Conquest of Space—Pal/Paramount
Countraband Spain—British—Independent

Count Three and Pray—Columbia
Davy Crockett, King of the Wild Frontier—Disney/Buena Vista
Desert Sands—United Artists
Doctor at Sea—British—Republic
Doctor in the House—British—Republic
Duel on the Mississippi—Columbia
Escape to Burma—RKO Radio
Fabulous India—Indian—Independent
The Far Country—Universal-International
The Far Horizons—Paramount
Footsteps in the Fog—Columbia
Fort Yuma—United Artists
*Foxfire**—Universal-International
Gentlemen Marry Brunettes—United Artists
The Girl Rush—Paramount
The Gun That Won the West—Columbia
Hell's Island—Paramount
House of Ricordi—French/Italian—Independent
The Indian Fighter—Bryna/United Artists
The Kentuckian—United Artists
Kiss of Fire—Universal-International
Lady and the Tramp (animation)—Disney/Buena Vista
Lady Godiva—Universal-International
The Last Frontier—Columbia
A Lawless Street—Columbia
The Littlest Outlaw—Disney/Buena Vista
The Long Gray Line—Columbia
Lucy Gallant—Paramount
Ludwig II—German—Independent
Madame Butterfly—Japanese—Independent
Maddalena—Italian—Independent
The Man from Laramie—Columbia
Man Without A Star—Universal-International
My Sister Eileen—Columbia
The Naked Dawn—Universal-International
Oklahoma! (roadshow prints)—Independent
One Desire—Universal-International
Only the French Can (French Can-Can)—French—Independent
Pearl of the South Pacific—RKO Radio
Picnic—Columbia
Pirates of Tripoli—Columbia
A Prize of Gold—Columbia
The Purple Mask—Universal-International
Raising a Riot—British—Independent
Run for Cover—Paramount
Sabaka—United Artists
Seminole Uprising—Columbia
Seven Little Foys—Paramount
Shotgun—Allied Artists
Sign of the Pagan—Universal-International
Simon and Laura—British—Universal-International
Smoke Signal—Universal-International
So This Is Paris—Universal-International
Son of Sinbad—RKO Radio
The Spoilers—Universal-International
Strategic Air Command—Paramount
Tam Tam Mayumbre—African—Independent
Ten Wanted Men—Columbia
Tennessee's Partner—RKO Radio
Texas Lady—RKO Radio
This Island Earth—Universal-International

Three for the Show—Columbia
The Tiger and the Flame—Indian—Independent
To Catch A Thief**—Hitchcock/Paramount
To Hell and Back—Universal-International
To Paris With Love—British—Independent
Touch and Go—British—Universal-International
The Treasure of Pancho Villa—RKO Radio
The Trouble With Harry—Hitchcock/Paramount
Ulysses—Paramount
Underwater!—RKO Radio
Value for Money—British—Independent
The Violent Men—Columbia
Wakumba!—RKO Radio
The Warriors—Allied Artists
Wee Geordie—British—Independent
We're No Angels—Paramount
White Feather—Twentieth Century-Fox
Wichita—Allied Artists
The Woman for Joe—British—Independent
Wyoming Renegades—Columbia
You Know What Sailors Are—British—Independent
You're Never Too Young—Paramount

*Last American-made film shot with Technicolor's three-color camera
**Academy Award winner for best Color Cinematography

1956

Abdulla the Great—Twentieth Century-Fox
Alexander the Great—United Artists
All for Mary—British—Independent
All That Heaven Allows—Universal-International
An Alligator Named Daisy—British—Independent
The Ambassador's Daughter—United Artists
The Animal World—Warner Bros.
Anything Goes—Paramount
Around the World in 80 Days*—Todd/United Artists
At Gunpoint—Allied Artists
Away All Boats—Universal-International
Backlash—Universal-International
The Benny Goodman Story—Universal-International
The Birds and the Bees—Paramount
The Black Tent—British—Rank
The Brave One—RKO Radio/Universal-International
Bundle of Joy—RKO Radio
Cockleshell Heroes—Columbia
Congo Crossing—Universal-International
The Conqueror—RKO Radio
The Court Jester—Paramount
Davy Crocket and the River Pirates—Disney/Buena Vista
A Day of Fury—Universal-International
Don Juan—German—Independent
The Eddy Duchin Story—Columbia
The Feminine Touch—British—Independent
The First Texan—Allied Artists
The First Traveling Saleslady—RKO Radio
Glory—RKO Radio
Great Day in the Morning—RKO Radio
The Great Locomotive Chase—Disney/Buena Vista
He Laughed Last—Columbia
High Society—Metro-Goldwyn-Mayer
Hollywood or Bust—Wallis/Paramount

Hot Blood—Columbia
House of Secrets—British—Independent
Invitation to the Dance—Metro-Goldwyn-Mayer
It's a Wonderful World—British—Independent
It's a Great Life—British—Independent
Jubal—Columbia
The Ladykillers—British—Independent
Madame Butterfly—Italian—Independent
The Man Who Knew Too Much—Hitchcock/Paramount
Marie Antoinette—French/Italian—Independent
Moby Dick**—Moulin/Warner Bros.
The Mountain—Paramount
Odongo—Columbia
Oh, Rosalinda!—British—Independent
Pardners—Paramount
Pillars of the Sky—Universal-International
Point Afrique—Columbia
The Rainmaker—Wallis/Paramount
Raw Edge—Universal-International
The Rawhide Years—Universal-International
The Red Balloon—French—Independent
Red Sundown—Universal-International
Reprisal—Columbia
Richard III—British—Lopert
Run for the Sun—Universal-International
Safari—Columbia
The Searchers—Warner Bros.
The Second Greatest Sex—Universal-International
Secrets of Life—Disney/Buena Vista
Seven Wonders of the World—Cinerama Releasing Corp.
7th Cavalry—Columbia
The Sharkfighters—United Artists
Showdown at Abilene—Universal-International
Slightly Scarlet—RKO Radio
Smiley—Twentieth Century-Fox
The Solid Gold Cadillac (sequence)—Columbia
Star in the Dust—Universal-International
Star of India—United Artists
Storm Over the Nile—British—Columbia
The Ten Commandments—DeMille/Paramount
Tension at Table Rock—RKO Radio
That Certain Feeling—Paramount
Thrillarama Adventure—Independent
Toy Tiger—Universal-International
The Vagabond King—Paramount
Walk the Proud Land—Universal-International
War and Peace—Paramount
World Without End—Allied Artists
You Can't Run Away from It—Columbia
Zarak—Columbia

*Academy Award winner for best Color Cinematography
**First film to use desaturated color process

1957

The Admirable Crichton—Columbia
The Adventures of Arsene Lupin—French/Italian—
    Independent
Les Adventures de Till L'Espiegle—French/German—
    Independent
All Mine to Give—RKO Radio/Universal-International

Battle Hymn—Universal-International
Beau James—Paramount
Beyond Mombasa—British—Columbia
Bridge on the River Kwai*—Horizon/Columbia
Casino de Paris—German/French—Independent
Decision at Sundown—Columbia
The Devil's Hairpin—Paramount
Doctor at Large—British—Universal-International
Escape in Japan—RKO Radio/Universal-International
Fire Down Below—Columbia
Folies-Bergere—French—Independent
Four Girls in Town—Universal-International
Funny Face—Paramount
The Girl Most Likely—RKO Radio
The Good Companions—British—Independent
Gunfight at the OK Corral—Wallis/Paramount
The Guns of Fort Petticoat—Columbia
The Hard Man—Columbia
Immortal Garrison—Universal-International
Interlude—Universal-International
The Iron Petticoat—Metro-Goldwyn-Mayer
Istanbul—Universal-International
It Happened in Rome—Italian—Independent
Jet Pilot—Hughes/Universal-International
Joe Butterfly—Universal-International
Johnny Tremain—Disney/Buena Vista
Kelly and Me—Universal-International
Legend of the Lost—United Artists
Loving You—Wallis/Paramount
The Miller's Beautiful Wife—Italian—Independent
Monte Carlo Story—United Artists
Night Passage**—Universal-International
The Oklahoman—Allied Artists
Old Yeller—Disney/Buena Vista
Omar Khayyam—Paramount
Pal Joey—Columbia
Paris Does Strange Things—French—Warner Bros.
Parson and the Outlaw—Columbia
Le Pays D'ou Je Viens—French—Independent
Perri—Disney/Buena Vista
The Pride and the Passion—Kramer/United Artists
The Prince and the Showgirl—British—Warner Bros.
Public Pigeon No. 1—RKO Radio/Universal-International
Pursuit of the Graf Spee (Battle of the River Plate)—
    British—Rank
Raintree County—Metro-Goldwyn-Mayer
Run of the Arrow—RKO Radio
Sayonara—Warner Bros.
Search for Paradise—Cinerama Releasing Corp.
The Spanish Gardner—British—Rank
The Story of Mankind—Warner Bros.
The Tall 'T'—Columbia
Tammy and the Bachelor—Universal-International
Tarzan and the Lost Safari—Metro-Goldwyn-Mayer
Three Violent People—Paramount
Triple Deception—British—Rank
Typhon a Nagazaki—French/Japanese—Independent
Westward Ho, the Wagons—Disney/Buena Vista
Woman of the River—Columbia
Written on the Wind—Universal-International

*Academy Award winner for best Color Cinematography
**First feature in Technicolor/Technirama, multi-purpose photography and print system

1958

Auntie Mame—Warner Bros.
Bell, Book and Candle—Columbia
The Big Country—Wyler/United Artists
The Big Money—British—Independent
Bonjour Tristesse (sequences)—Preminger/Columbia
The Buccaneer—DeMille/Paramount
Cowboy—Columbia
Damn Yankees—Warner Bros.
Davy—British—Independent
Enchanted Island—Warner Bros.
The Flute and the Arrow—Swedish—Independent
From the Earth to the Moon—Warner Bros.
Gideon of Scotland Yard—British—Columbia
Gunman's Walk—Columbia
The Geisha Boy—Paramount
Horror of Dracula—British—Universal-International
The Horse's Mouth—British—Lopert
Houseboat—Paramount
Indiscreet—Warner Bros.
The Light in the Forest—Disney/Buena Vista
Mark of the Hawk—Universal-International
Les Miserables—French—Independent
The Missouri Traveler—Buena Vista
The Moonraker—British—Independent
Mother India—Indian—Independent
The Naked and the Dead—RKO/Warner Bros.
Night Ambush (Ill Met By Moonlight)—British—
    Independent
No Time to Die—Columbia
Paris Holiday—United Artists
The Proud Rebel—Goldwyn, Jr./Buena Vista
La Ragazza del Palio—Italian—Independent
Return to Warbow—Columbia
Revenge of Frankenstein—British—Columbia
Rock-A-Bye Baby—Paramount
Seven Hills of Rome—Metro-Goldwyn-Mayer
Seventh Voyage of Sinbad—Columbia
South Pacific (roadshow prints)—Twentieth Century-Fox
South Seas Adventure—Independent
A Spanish Affair—Paramount
Stage Struck—Buena Vista
The Story of Vickie—Buena Vista
Tempest—Italian/Yugoslavian/French—Paramount
This Angry Age—Columbia
Tonka—Disney/Buena Vista
Le Triporteur—French—Independent
Une le Parisienne—French—United Artists
The Unholy Wife—RKO Radio/Universal-International
Vertigo—Hitchcock/Paramount
The Vikings—United Artists
Wind Across the Everglade—Warner Bros.

1959

The Big Circus—Allied Artists
Ben-Hur*—Metro-Goldwyn-Mayer
The Big Fisherman—Buena Vista
The Bridal Path—British—Independent
The F.B.I. Story—LeRoy/Warner Bros.
The Five Pennies—Paramount
For the First Time—Metro-Goldwyn-Mayer
A Handful of Grain—Indian—Independent

The Hanging Tree—Warner Bros.
The Hound of the Baskervilles—British—United Artists
Invitation to Monte Carlo—British—Independent
The Jayhawkers—Paramount
John Paul Jones—Bronston/Warner Bros.
Last Train from Gun Hill—Wallis/Paramount
Li'l Abner—Paramount
The Man Who Could Cheat Death—Paramount
The Miracle—Warner Bros.
The Mummy—Universal-International
The Naked Maja—United Artists
North By Northwest—Hitchcock/Metro-Goldwyn-Mayer
The Nun's Story—Warner Bros.
1001 Arabian Nights—Columbia
Porgy and Bess—Goldwyn/Columbia
Rio Bravo—Warner Bros.
Serenade of a Great Love—German—Independent
Sleeping Beauty—Disney/Buena Vista
Solomon and Sheba—United Artists
A Summer Place—Warner Bros.
The Sword and the Dragon—Russian—Independent
Tank Force (No Time to Die)—British—Independent
Third Man on the Mountain—Disney/Buena Vista
This Earth Is Mine—Universal-International
Thunder in the Sun—Paramount
The Trap—Paramount
Watusi—Metro-Goldwyn-Mayer
The Wonderful Country—United Artists
The Young Land—Columbia

*Academy Award winner for best Color Cinematography

1960

The Alamo—United Artists
Blood and Roses—French/Italian—Paramount
The Bramble Bush—Warner Bros.
The Brides of Dracula—British—Universal-International
Can-Can—Twentieth Century-Fox
Cash McCall—Warner Bros.
Cinderfella—Paramount
The Cossacks—Italian—Universal-International
The Crowded Sky—Warner Bros.
The Crowning Experience—Independent
The Dark at the Top of the Stairs—Warner Bros.
Doctor in Love—British—Independent
Elmer Gantry—United Artists
Exodus—Preminger/United Artists
G.I. Blues—Wallis/Paramount
The Grass Is Greener—Universal-International
Guns of the Timberland—Warner Bros.
Hannibal—Italian—Warner Bros.
Heller in Pink Tights—Paramount
Hercules Unchained—Italian—Warner Bros.
The Hound That Thought He Was A Racoon—Disney/Buena Vista
Ice Palace—Warner Bros.
It Started in Naples—Paramount
Jungle Cat—Disney/Buena Vista
Kidnapped—Disney/Buena Vista
Man With the Green Carnation (Trials of Oscar Wilde)—British—Independent

Once More With Feeling—Columbia
Ocean's Eleven—Warner Bros.
One, Two, Three, Four—French—Independent
Pepe—Columbia
Pollyanna—Disney/Buena Vista
The Rat Race—Paramount
The Savage Innocents—Italian/French/British/U.S.—Paramount
Scent of Mystery (Holiday in Spain)—Todd, Jr./Independent
Sergeant Rutledge—Warner Bros.
Spartacus*—Bryna/Universal-International
The Sundowners—Warner Bros.
Sunrise at Campobello—Warner Bros.
Swiss Family Robinson**—Disney/Buena Vista
Ten Who Dared—Disney/Buena Vista
Tunes of Glory—British—Lopert
Toby Tyler or: 10 Weeks With A Circus—Disney/Buena Vista
The Two Faces of Dr. Jekyll—British—Columbia
The Unforgiven—United Artists
The World at Night—Warner Bros.
The World of Susie Wong—Paramount

*Academy Award winner for best Color Cinematography
**A reprint order of this film in 1975 was the last made in the three-strip process in Technicolor's Hollywood plant, ironic in that the very first film processed was also a Disney product (*Flowers and Trees*, 1932)

1961

All in a Night's Work—Wallis/Paramount
Babes in Toyland—Disney/Buena Vista
Blue Hawaii—Wallis/Paramount
Breakfast at Tiffany's—Paramount
Call Me Genius—British—Independent
Carthage in Flames—French/Italian—Columbia
El Cid—Bronston/Allied Artists
Come September—Universal-International
Fanny—Warner Bros.
Flower Drum Song—Universal-International
Ghosts in Rome—Italian—Independent
Gorgo—Metro-Goldwyn-Mayer
Greyfriar's Bobby—Disney/Buena Vista
The Hellion's—British—Columbia
The Honeymoon Machine—Metro-Goldwyn-Mayer
I Bombed Pearl Harbor—Japanese—Independent
King of Kings—Bronston/Metro-Goldwyn-Mayer
The Ladies Man—Paramount
Love in a Goldfish Bowl—Paramount
The Minotaur (The Wild Beast of Crete)—Italian—United Artists
Nikki, Wild Dog of the North—Disney/Buena Vista
On the Double—Paramount
One-Eyed Jacks—Paramount
One Hundred and One Dalmations—Disney/Buena Vista
The Parent Trap—Disney/Buena Vista
Parrish—Warner Bros.
The Pleasure of His Company—Paramount
The Queen's Guards—British—Twentieth Century-Fox
Raising the Wind—British—Independent
The Roman Spring of Mrs. Stone—Warner Bros./7 Arts
Romanoff and Juliet—Universal-International
Rommel's Treasure—Italian—Independent

The Sins of Rachel Cade—Warner Bros.
Splendor in the Grass—Warner Bros.
The Steel Claw—Warner Bros.
Summer and Smoke—Wallis/Paramount
Susan Slade—Warner Bros.
Vanina Vanini—French/Italian—Independent
West Side Story*—Mirisch/United Artists
The White Warrior—Warner Bros.
The World By Night—Warner Bros.
X-15—United Artists

*Academy Award winner for best Color Cinematography

1962

Almost Angels—Buena Vista
Barabbas—Columbia
Big Red—Disney/Buena Vista
Boccaccio '70—Italian—Levine/Embassy
Bon Voyage—Disney/Buena Vista
The Chapman Report—Zanuck/Warner Bros.
The Counterfeit Traitor—Paramount
Damn the Defiant!—British—Columbia
Dangerous Charter—Independent
Dr. No—British—United Artists
Escape from Zahrain—Paramount
A Family Diary—Italian—Metro-Goldwyn-Mayer
The First Spaceship on Venus—Independent
Forever My Love—Austrian—Paramount
Gay Purr-ee (animated)—UPA/Warner Bros.
Geronimo—United Artists
A Girl Named Tamiko—Wallis/Paramount
Girls! Girls! Girls!—Wallis/Paramount
Gypsy—Warner Bros.
Hatari!—Paramount
Hero's Island—United Artists
In Search of the Castaways—Disney/Buena Vista
Jessica—U.S./Italian/French—United Artists
Lad: A Dog—Warner Bros.
Lafayette—French/Italian—Independent
Lawrence of Arabia*—Columbia
The Legend of Lobo—Disney/Buena Vista
Madam Sans-Gene—Italian/French/Spanish—Independent
A Majority of One—Warner Bros.
Merrill's Marauders—Warner Bros.
Mondo Cane—Italian—Independent
Moon Pilot—Disney/Buena Vista
The Music Man—Warner Bros.
Mutiny on the Bounty—Metro-Goldwyn-Mayer
My Geisha—Paramount
The Phantom of the Opera—British—Universal-International
Rome Adventure—Warner Bros.
Der Rosenkavalier—British—Independent
Samar—Warner Bros.
Sergeants 3—United Artists
The Singer Not the Song—British—Warner Bros.
The Story of the Count of Monte Cristo—French—Warner Bros.
The Tartars—Italian—Metro-Goldwyn-Mayer
Who's Got the Action?—Paramount
The Wonderful World of the Brothers Grimm—Pal/
Cinerama/Metro-Goldwyn-Mayer
The World By Night No. 2—Warner Bros.

*Academy Award winner for best Color Cinematography

1963

The Best of Cinerama—Cinerama Releasing Corp.
The Birds—Hitchcock/Universal
Captain Sinbad—Metro-Goldwyn-Mayer
The Cardinal—Preminger/Columbia
Charade—Universal-International
Come Blow Your Horn—Paramount
Critic's Choice—Warner Bros.
Diary of a Madman—United Artists
Doctor in Distress—British—Independent
Donovan's Reef—Ford/Paramount
The Fast Lady—British—Independent
55 Days at Peking—Bronston/Allied Artists
The Flying Clipper—German—Independent
From Russia With Love—United Artists
From Saturday to Monday—Italian—Independent
Fun in Acapulco—Wallis/Paramount
Ghost at Noon—French/Italian—Independent
Gudrun—Danish—Independent
How the West Was Won—Metro-Goldwyn-Mayer
Imperial Venus—Italian/French—Independent
The Incredible Journey—Disney/Buena Vista
Irma La Douce—Mirisch/United Artists
Island of Love—Warner Bros.
Love Is A Ball—United Artists
McLintock!—Batjac/United Artists
MacBeth—Independent
Man's Paradise—Italian—Independent
Mary, Mary—Warner Bros.
Miracle of the White Stallions—Disney/Buena Vista
My Six Loves—Paramount
A New Kind of Love—Paramount
The Nutty Professor—Paramount
Palm Springs Weekend—Warner Bros.
Papa's Delicate Condition—Paramount
PT 109—Warner Bros.
Rampage—Warner Bros./7 Arts
The Running Man—British—Columbia
Savage Sam—Disney/Buena Vista
Seige of the Saxons—Columbia
Spencer's Mountain—Warner Bros.
Summer Holiday—British—American International
Summer Magic—Disney/Buena Vista
The Sword in the Stone (animated)—Disney/Buena Vista
Three Lives of Thomasina—Disney/Buena Vista
The Threepenny Opera—German—Independent
Tommy the Toreador—British—7 Arts
Twice Told Tales—United Artists
Who's Been Sleeping in My Bed?—Paramount
Who's Minding the Store?—Paramount
Women of the World—Italian—Embassy
The World at Night No. 3—Italian—Independent

1964

The Bargee—British—Independent
Becket—Wallis/Paramount

The Carpetbaggers—Paramount
The Castle—Danish—Independent
The Chalk Garden—Universal
Cheyenne Autumn—Ford/Warner Bros.
Circus World—Bronston/Paramount
Code 7, Victim 5—British—Independent
Crooks in Cloisters—British—Independent
The Curse of the Mummy's Tomb—British—Independent
Dark Purpose—Universal
A Distant Trumpet—Warner Bros.
The Disorderly Orderly—Paramount
East of Sudan—British—Columbia
Emil and the Detectives—Disney/Buena Vista
Ensign Pulver—Warner Bros.
An Evening With the Royal Ballet—British—Independent
The Fall of the Roman Empire—Bronston/Paramount
Father Goose—Universal
The Finest Hours—British—Columbia
The First Men in the Moon—British—Columbia
A Fistful of Dollars—Italian/German/Spanish—United
    Artists
For Those Who Think Young—United Artists
Four for Texas—Warner Bros.
Germany Greets Kennedy—German—Independent
Gold for the Caesars—Metro-Goldwyn-Mayer
The Golden Arrow—Italian—Metro-Goldwyn-Mayer
Goldfinger—United Artists
The Gorgon—British—Independent
The Incredible Mr. Limpet—Warner Bros.
Law of the Lawless—Paramount
The Long Ships—Columbia
Lydia—Canadian—Independent
Mail Order Bride—Metro-Goldwyn-Mayer
The Man from Rio—French—Independent
Man's Favorite Sport?—Universal
Marnie—Hitchcock/Universal
Mary Poppins (part animation)—Disney/Buena Vista
Mediterranean Holiday—Independent
The Misadventures of Merlin Jones—Disney/Buena Vista
Mondo Pazzo (Mondo Cane No. 2)—Italian—Independent
The Moon Spinners—Disney/Buena Vista
My Fair Lady*—Warner Bros.
The Nasty Rabbit—Independent
Paris When It Sizzles—Paramount
The Patsy—Paramount
The Pink Panther—United Artists
The Prize—Metro-Goldwyn-Mayer
The Quick Gun—Columbia
Red Desert—Italian/French—Independent
Robin and the Seven Hoods—Warner Bros.
Robinson Crusoe on Mars—Paramount
Roustabout—Wallis/Paramount
Send Me No Flowers—Universal
The 7th Dawn—United Artists
Sex and the Single Girl—Warner Bros.
The Soldier's Tale—British—Independent
The Son of Captain Blood—Paramount
Strange Bedfellows—Universal
Taggert—Universal
Those Calloways—Disney/Buena Vista
Three Nights of Love—Italian—Independent
A Tiger Walks—Disney/Buena Vista

Voice of the Hurricane—Independent
Where Love Has Gone—Paramount
White Voices—French/Italian—Independent
Wonderful Life—British—Independent
Yesterday, Today and Tomorrow—Italian/French—
    Embassy
Zulu—Paramount
*Academy Award winner for best Color Cinematography

1965

An American Wife—Italian—Independent
The Amorous Adventures of Moll Flanders—Paramount
Arizona Raiders—Columbia
The Art of Love—Universal
Battle of the Bulge—Warner Bros.
The Battle of Villa Fiorita—Warner Bros.
Beach Ball—Paramount
Billie—United Artists
Black Spurs—Paramount
Blood and Black Lace—Allied Artists
Boeing Boeing—Wallis/Paramount
La Boheme—Italian—Warner Bros.
The Bounty Killer—Embassy
The Brigand of Kandahar—British—Independent
Casanova '70—Italian—Independent
Coast of Skeletons—British—Independent
The Collector—Wyler/Columbia
Crack in the World—Paramount
Dingaka—Embassy
Dr. Terror's House of Horrors—British—Independent
Dr. Who and the Daleks—British—Independent
Ecco!—Italian—Independent
The Face of Fu Manchu—British—Independent
The Family Jewels—Paramount
Genghis Kahn—Columbia
Git!—Independent
Go Go Mania—British—Independent
The Golden Head (Millie Goes to Budapest)—
    Hungarian/U.S.—Independent
The Great Race—Warner Bros.
The Great Sioux Massacre—Columbia
The Greatest Story Ever Told—Stevens/United Artists
The Hallelujah Trail—United Artists
Harlow—Paramount
The Heroes of Telemark—British—Independent
I'll Take Sweden—United Artists
The Ipcress File—British—Universal
I've Gotta Horse—British—Independent
Lord Jim—Columbia
Love and Kisses—Universal
The Love Goddess (sequence)—Independent
Marriage on the Rocks—Warner Bros.
The Merry Wives of Windsor—Austria—Independent
Mister Moses—United Artists
The Moment of Truth—Spanish/Italian—Independent
The Monkey's Uncle—Disney/Buena Vista
Never Too Late—Warner Bros.
None But the Brave—Warner Bros.
The Oil Prince—Italian—Independent
One Million Dollars—United Artists

A Pistol for Ringo—Italian/Spanish—Independent
Red Line 7000—Paramount
Revenge of the Gladiators—Paramount
Sands of the Kalahari—Paramount
Seven Guns for the Mac Gregors—Italian/Spanish—
    Columbia
Shenandoah—Universal
The Skull—Paramount
Slalom—Italian/French/Egyptian—Independent
The Sons of Katie Elder—Wallis/Paramount
A Swingin' Summer—Independent
Taboos of the World—Italian—Independent
The Tenth Victim—French/Italian—Levine/Independent
That Darn Cat—Disney/Buena Vista
That Funny Feeling—Universal
The Third Day—Warner Bros.
Three Faces of a Woman—Italian—Independent
Thunderball—United Artists
The Town Tamer—Paramount
The Truth About Spring—Universal
The Ugly Dachshund—Disney/Buena Vista
Up Jumped a Swagman—British—Independent
A Very Special Favor—Universal
The War Lord—Universal
What—Italian/British—Independent
Wild Wild Winter—Universal
Young Fury—Paramount

1966

Africa Addio—Italian—Independent
After the Fox—United Artists
Alfie—British—Paramount
An American Dream—Warner Bros.
And Now Miguel—Universal
Any Wednesday—Warner Bros.
The Appaloosa—Universal
Arabesque—Universal
Arrivederci, Baby—Paramount
Assault on a Queen—Paramount
Beau Geste—Universal
A Big Hand for the Little Lady—Warner Bros.
The Big T-N-T Show—American International
Blindfold—Universal
Bolshoi Ballet '67—Paramount
Born Free—Columbia
Chamber of Horrors—Warner Bros.
The Chase—Columbia
The Countess from Hong Kong—Chaplin/Universal
Daleks Invade Earth A.D.—British—American International
The Devil's Own (The Witches)—British—Twentieth
    Century-Fox
Every Day is a Holiday—Spanish—Independent
Farenheit 451—Universal
The Fighting Prince of Donegal—Disney/Buena Vista
A Fine Madness—Warner Bros.
Follow Me, Boys!—Disney/Buena Vista
For a Few Dollars More—Italian/German/Spanish—
    United Artists
For Love and Gold—French/Italian—Independent
Frankie and Johnny—United Artists

Funeral in Berlin—Paramount
Gambit—Universal
Goal! World Cup 1966—British—Independent
The Great Wall—Japanese—Independent
Gunpoint—Universal
Harper—Warner Bros.
The Hostage—Independent
Incident at Phantom Hill—Universal
Inside Daisy Clover—Pakula-Mulligan/Warner Bros.
Johnny Reno—Paramount
Johnny Tiger—Universal
Juliet of the Spirits—Italian—Fellini/Independent
Kaliedoscope—British—Warner Bros.
Khartoum—United Artists
Kill or Be Killed—Italian—Independent
Kiss the Girls and Make Them Die—Italian—Columbia
The Last of the Secret Agents?—Paramount
Let's Kill Uncle—Universal
Lt. Robin Crusoe, U.S.N.—Disney/Buena Vista
Madame X—Universal
Mademoiselle de Maupin—Italian/French/Spanish/Yugoslavian—Independent
A Man Could Get Killed—Universal
*A Man For All Seasons**—Columbia
A Matter of Honor—Italian/French—Independent
Maya—Metro-Goldwyn-Mayer
Moment to Moment—Universal

Munster Go Home—Universal
Murderer's Row—Columbia
Naked Prey—Paramount
Nashville Rebel—American International
The Night of the Grizzly—Paramount
Not With My Wife, You Don't—Warner Bros.
One Million Years, B.C.—British—Twentieth Century-Fox
Othello—British—Warner Bros.
Out of Sight—Universal
The Pad (and How to Use It)—Universal
Paradise, Hawaiian Style—Wallis/Paramount
The Professionals—Columbia
Promise Her Anything—Paramount
The Psychopath—British—Paramount
The Rare Breed—Universal
Rings Around the World—Columbia
Secret Agent Super Dragon—Italian/French/German—
    Independent
Seven Golden Men Strike Again—Italian—Independent
Stop the World—I Want to Get Off—Warner Bros.
The Sultans—Paramount
The Taking of Power by Louis XIV—Independent
Texas Across the River—Universal
Thank You Very Much—Italian—Independent
Thunderbirds Are Go—British—United Artists
Tobruk—Universal
The Torn Curtain—Hitchcock/Universal
Two Kouney Lemels—Israel—Independent
Up the MacGregors—Italian/Spanish—Columbia
A Virgin for the Prince—Italian/French—Independent
Waco—Paramount
Walk, Don't Run—Columbia
Warning Shot—Paramount
White, Red, Yelloe, Pink (sequence)—Italian—
    Independent
The Wrong Box—British—Columbia

*Academy Award winner for best Color Cinematography

1967

The Adventures of Bullwhip Griffin—Disney/Buena Vista
After You, Comrade—African—Independent
The Ambushers—Columbia
Banning—Universal
Barefoot in the Park—Wallis/Paramount
Berserk—Columbia
Billion Dollar Brain—United Artists
The Birds, the Bees and the Italians—Italian—Warner Bros.
Blood Fiend—British—Independent
The Bobo—British—Warner Bros.
Bonditis—Swiss—Independent
Bonnie and Clyde*—Warner Bros.
A Bullet for the General—Italian—Avco Embassy
The Busy Body—Paramount
Camelot—Warner Bros./7 Arts
Casino Royale—Columbia
Charlie, the Lonesome Cougar—Disney/Buena Vista
Clambake—United Artists
C'mon, Let's Live a Little—Paramount
Cool Hand Luke—Warner Bros.
The Cool Ones—Warner Bros.
The Corrupt Ones—German—Warner Bros.
A Covenant with Death—Warner Bros.
Deadlier Than the Male—French—Universal
The Deadly Affair—British—Columbia
The Deadly Bees—British—Paramount
Divorce, Italian Style—Columbia
Don't Lose Your Head—British—Independent
Easy Come, Easy Go—Wallis/Paramount
Eldorado—Paramount
The Family Way—British—Warner Bros.
First to Fight—Warner Bros.
Follow That Camel—Paramount
Frank's Greatest Adventure—Independent
Games—Universal
The Gnome-Mobile—Disney/Buena Vista
The Graduate—Levine/Embassy
Gunfire in Abilene—Universal
Gunn—Paramount
Half a Sixpence—Paramount
The Happening—Horizon/Columbia
The Happiest Millionaire—Disney/Buena Vista
Hell on Wheels—Independent
The Hills Run Red—Italian—United Artists
The Hippie Revolt—Independent
The Hired Killer—Italian—Paramount
The Honey Pot (It Comes Up Murder)—British/Italian/U.S.—United Artists
Hostile Guns—Paramount
Hotel—Warner Bros.
House of 1,000 Dolls—American International
Hurry Sundown—Preminger/Paramount
I'll Never Forget What's 'is Name—British—Independent
It!—British—Warner Bros.
The Jokers—Universal
The Jungle Book (animated)—Disney/Buena Vista
King's Pirate—Universal
Knives of the Avenger—Italian—Independent
The Last Safari—British—Paramount
Lightning Bolt—Italian/Spanish—Independent
Made in Italy—Italian/French—Independent
The Mikado—British—Warner Bros.

Misunderstood—French/Italian—Independent
Monkeys Go Home—Disney/Buena Vista
The Naked Runner—Warner Bros.
Navajo Joe—Italian/Spanish—United Artists
Night of the Generals—Columbia
Oedipus Rex—Italian—Independent
Oh, Dad, Poor Dad, Mamma's Hung You in the Closet and I'm Feeling So Sad—Paramount
The 1,000,000 Eyes of Su-Murn—American International
Operation Kid Brother—United Artists
The President's Analyst—Paramount
Privilege—British—Universal
The Projected Man—British—Universal
Red Dragon—Italian/German/U.S.—Independent
Reflections in a Golden Eye—Warner Bros.
The Reluctant Astronaut—Universal
The Ride to Hangman's Tree—Universal
A Rose for Everyone—Italian—Independent
Rough Night in Jericho—Universal
The Savage Eye—Italian—Independent
The Spirit is Willing—Paramount
The Taming of the Shrew—Columbia
Thoroughly Modern Millie—Universal
To Each His Own—Italian—Independent
To Sir With Love—Columbia
Triple Cross—Warner Bros.
Up the Down Staircase—Warner Bros.
Valley of Mystery—Universal
The Viscount—Warner Bros.
Wait Until Dark—Warner Bros.
War—Italian Style—Italian—American International
The War Wagon—Batjac/Universal
Waterhold No. 3—Paramount
What Am I Bid?—Independent
The Wild Rebels—Independent
You Only Live Twice—United Artists
The Young Girls of Rochefort—French—Warner Bros.
The Young Warriors—Universal

*Academy Award winner for best Cinematography (separate classifications for color and black-and-white were discontinued starting this year.)

1968

Ace High—Italian—Paramount
And There Came a Man—Italian/French—Independent
Any Gun Can Play—Italian/Spanish—Independent
Arizona Bushwackers—Paramount
Assignment K—British—Columbia
The Ballad of Josie—Universal
Barbarella—French/Italian—Paramount
Battle Beneath the Earth—British—Metro-Goldwyn-Mayer
Benjamin—French—Independent
Better a Widow—Italian/French—Universal
The Big Gundown—Italian/Spanish—Independent
Birds in Peru—French—Universal
The Birthday Party—British—Independent
Blackbeard's Ghost—Disney/Buena Vista
The Bliss of Mrs. Blossom—British—Paramount
Blue—Paramount
The Bofors Gun—British—Universal
Boom!—U.S./British—Universal
Bullitt—Warner Bros./7 Arts
Bye Bye Braverman—Warner Bros./7 Arts
Candy—U.S./French/Italian—Cinerama Releasing Corp.

185

The Champagne Murders—French—Universal
Charlie Bubbles—British—Universal
Charly—Cinerama Releasing Corp.
Chitty Chitty Bang Bang—British—United Artists
Chubasco—Warner Bros./7 Arts
The Cobra—Italian/Spanish—Independent
Coogan's Bluff—Universal
Corruption—British—Columbia
Countdown—Warner Bros./7 Arts
The Counterfeit Killer—Universal
Counterpoint—Universal
Custer of the West—U.S./Spanish—Cinerama Releasing Corp.
A Dandy in Aspic—British—Columbia
Danger: Diabolik—Italian/French—Paramount
The Devil in Love—Italian—Warner Bros./7 Arts
The Devil's Bride—British—Twentieth Century-Fox
Did You Hear the One About the Traveling Saleslady?—Universal
Doctor Faustus—British/Italian—Columbia
Don't Just Stand There!—Universal
Don't Raise the River, Lower the Bridge—British—Columbia
The Double Man—British—Warner Bros./7 Arts
Duffy—British—Columbia
Fever Heat—Paramount
Finian's Rainbow—Warner Bros./7 Arts
Firecreek—Warner Bros./7 Arts
Five Card Stud—Wallis/Paramount
Funny Girl—Columbia
Ghosts—Italian Style—Italian/French—Independent
The Girl on a Motorcycle (Naked Under Leather)—British/French—Warner Bros./7 Arts
The Good, the Bad and the Ugly—Italian—United Artists
Grand Slam—Italian/Spanish/German—Paramount
Great Catherine—British—Warner Bros./7 Arts
The Green Berets—Batjac/Warner Bros./7 Arts
Hammerhead—British—Columbia
Head—Columbia
The Heart is a Lonely Hunter—Warner Bros./7 Arts
Heidi—Austrian/German—Warner Bros./7 Arts
The Hell With Heroes—Universal
Here We Go Round the Mulberry Bush—British—Independent
The Horse in the Gray Flannel Suit—Disney/Buena Vista
The Hostage—Independent
House of 1,000 Dolls—German/Spanish/British—American International
How Sweet It Is!—National General
I Love You, Alice B. Toklas—Warner Bros./7 Arts
In Enemy Country—Universal
Interlude—British—Columbia
Isabel—Canadian—Paramount
Island of the Doomed—Spanish/German—Independent
Jigsaw—Universal
Journey to Shiloh—Universal
Kona Coast—Warner Bros./7 Arts
Knives of the Avenger—Italian—Independent
Listen, Let's Make Love—Italian/French—Lopert/7 Arts
The Long Day's Dying—British—Independent
A Lovely Way to Die—Universal
Madigan—Universal

A Maiden for the Prince—Italian/French—Independent
The Man Outside—British—Allied Artists
A Matter of Innocence (Pretty Polly)—British—Universal
The Murder Clinic—Italian/French—Independent
Negatives—British—Independent
Never A Dull Moment—Disney/Buena Vista
Nobody's Perfect—Universal
No Way to Treat A Lady—Paramount
The Odd Couple—Paramount
Oedipus the King—British—Universal
Oliver!—British—Columbia
The One and Only, Genuine, Original Family Band—Disney/Buena Vista
P.J.—Universal
Paper Lion—United Artists
Payment in Blood—Italian—Columbia
Petulia—Warner Bros./7 Arts
The Pink Jungle—Universal
A Place for Lovers—Italian/French—Metro-Goldwyn-Mayer
Poor Cow—British—National General
The Private Navy of Sgt. O'Farrell—United Artists
Project X—Paramount
Rachel, Rachel—Warner Bros./7 Arts
Rosemary's Baby—Paramount
Rosie—Universal
*Romeo and Juliet**—British/Italian—Paramount
Run Like A Thief—Spanish/U.S.—Independent
Sergeant Ryker—Universal
Sebastian—British—Paramount
Secret Ceremony—British—Universal
The Secret War of Harry Frigg—Universal
The Sea Gull—Warner Bros./7 Arts
The Shakiest Gun in the West—Universal
Shalako—British—Cinerama Releasing Corp.
The Shuttered Room—British—Warner Bros./7 Arts
Sky Over Holland—Warner Bros./7 Arts
The Spirit is Willing—Paramount
The Strange Affair—Paramount
Suddenly, A Woman!—Danish—Independent
Sweet November—Warner Bros./7 Arts
The Swimmer—Columbia
Tarzan and the Jungle Boy—U.S./Swiss—Paramount
30 is a Dangerous Age, Cynthia—British—Columbia
Three Guns for Texas—Universal
Torture Garden—British—Columbia
Track of Thunder—United Artists
La Traviata—Italian—Independent
Up the Junction—British—Independent
Uptight—Paramount
The Vengeance of She—British—Twentieth Century-Fox
Villa Rides—Paramount
The Violent Four—Italian—Paramount
What's So Bad About Feeling Good?—Universal
Will Penny—Paramount
The Young Girls of Rochefort—French—Warner Bros./7 Arts

*Academy Award winner for best Cinematography

1969

The Adding Machine—British/U.S.—Universal

All Heat in Black Stockings—British—National General
Angel in My Pocket—Universal
The April Fools—National General
The Arrangement—Warner Bros.
The Assassination Bureau—British—Paramount
Assignment to Kill—Warner Bros./7 Arts
Before Winter Comes—British—Columbia
The Big Bounce—Warner Bros./7 Arts
Bob & Carol & Ted & Alice—Columbia
The Brotherhood—Paramount
Buona Sera, Mrs. Campbell—United Artists
Camille 2000—Independent
Can Heironymus Merkin Ever Forget Mercy Humppe and Find True Happiness?—British—Universal
Castle Keep—Columbia
A Challenge for Robin Hood—British—Twentieth Century-Fox
A Change of Habit—Universal
Charro!—National General
Daddy's Gone-A-Hunting—Independent
Death of a Gunfighter—Universal
Death Rides A Horse—Italian—United Artists
80 Steps to Jonah—Warner Bros./7 Arts
Eye of the Cat—Universal
A Fine Pair—Italian—National General
Fraulein Doktar—Italian/Yugoslavian—Paramount
Goodbye, Columbus—Paramount
The Good Guys and the Bad Guys—Warner Bros./7 Arts
The Great Bank Robbery—Warner Bros./7 Arts
Hell in the Pacific—Cinerama Releasing Corp.
Hellfighters—Universal
Hell's Angels '69—Independent
Hook, Line and Sinker—Columbia
How to Commit Marriage—Cinerama Releasing Corp.
The Illustrated Man—Warner Bros./7 Arts
The Learning Tree—Warner Bros./7 Arts
The Lost Man—Universal
The Love Bug—Disney/Buena Vista
Love Feeling—British—Independent
The Love God?—Universal
The Loves of Isadora—British—Universal
MacKenna's Gold—Columbia
The Madwoman of Chaillot—Warner Bros./7 Arts
A Man Called Gannon—Universal
Mayerling—British—Metro-Goldwyn-Mayer
Medium Cool—Paramount
Midas Run—Cinerama Releasing Corp.
Mission Batangas—Independent
My Side of the Mountain—U.S./Canadian—Paramount
The Night of the Following Day—Universal
Oh! What A Lovely War—British—Paramount
Once Upon A Time in the West—Italian—Paramount
On My Way to the Crusades, I Met A Girl Who . . .—Italian—Warner Bros./7 Arts
Otley—British—Columbia
Pendulum—Columbia
Play Dirty—British—United Artists
The Rain People—Warner Bros./7 Arts
Ring of Bright Water—British—Cinerama Releasing Corp.
Riot—Paramount
Run Wild, Run Free—British—Columbia
The Sergeant—Warner Bros./7 Arts
Seven Golden Men—Italian—Warner Bros./7 Arts

Shock Troops—French/Italian—United Artists
Skidoo—Paramount
The Southern Star—French/British—Columbia
The Stalking Moon—National General
The Sterile Cuckoo—Paramount
Support Your Local Sheriff—United Artists
The Sweet Body of Deborah—Italian—Warner Bros./7 Arts
Sweet Charity—Universal
Take the Money and Run—Cinerama Releasing Corp.
They Came to Rob Las Vegas—French/Italian—Warner Bros./7 Arts
Those Daring Young Men in Their Jaunty Jalopies—Italian/French/British—Paramount
True Grit—Wallis/Paramount
The Trygon Factor—British—Warner Bros./7 Arts
Twisted Nerve—British—National General
2000 Years Later—Warner Bros./7 Arts
The Valley of Gwangi—Warner Bros./7 Arts
The Wild Bunch—Warner Bros./7 Arts
Winning—Universal
The Witches—Italian/French—United Artists
The Wrecking Crew—Columbia
Young Americans—Columbia

1970

Act of the Heart—Canadian—Universal
Adam at 6 A.M.—National General
The Adventurers—Paramount
Africa Blood and Guts—Italian—Independent
Airport—Universal
All the Way Up—British—Independent
And Soon the Darkness—Warner Bros./Pathe
The Aristocats (animated)—Disney/Buena Vista
The Babymaker—National General
The Ballad of Cable Hogue—Warner Bros.
The Body—British—EMI/Metro-Goldwyn-Mayer
The Boatniks—Disney/Buena Vista
The Buttercup Chain—British—Columbia
The Cannibals—Italian—Independent
Captain Milkshake—Independent
Catch-22—Paramount
The Cheyenne Social Club—National General
Chisum—Batjac/Warner Bros.
The Cockeyed Cowboys of Calico County—Universal
El Condor—National General
The Conformist—Italian/French—Paramount
Cromwell—British—Columbia
The Damned—Italian—Warner Bros.
Darker Than Amber—National General
Darling Lili—Paramount
Detective Belli—Italian—Independent
Diary of a Mad Housewife—Universal
The Executioner—British—Columbia
Eyewitness—British—EMI/Metro-Goldwyn-Mayer
Flap—Warner Bros.
The Forbin Project—Universal
Frankenstein Must Be Destroyed—British—Warner Bros.
The Grasshopper—National General
Hoffman—British—Warner Bros./Pathe
Homer—National General

The Horror of Frankenstein—British—EMI/Metro-Goldwyn-Mayer
I Love My Wife—Universal
Imago—Independent
In Search of Gregory—British/Italian—Universal
Just Another War—Italian/Yugoslavian—Independent
Kemek—German—Independent
King of the Grizzlies—Disney/Buena Vista
Last of the Mobile Hot Shots—Warner Bros.
Let It Be—British—United Artists
Little Big Man—National General
The Looking Glass War—Columbia
The Magic Christian—Commonwealth United/American International
A Man Called Horse—National General
The Man Who Haunted Himself—British—Warner Bros./Pathe
The Mercenary—Italian/Spanish—United Artists
The Mind of Mister Soames—British—Columbia
The Molly Maguires—Paramount
Monte Walsh—National General
Moon Zero Two—British—Warner Bros.
Most Beautiful Wife—Italian—Independent
Night of Counting the Years—Egyptian—Independent
Norwood—Paramount
The Olympics in Mexico—Columbia
On a Clear Day You Can See Forever—Paramount
The Out-of-Towners—Paramount
Performance—British—Warner Bros.
The Phynx—Warner Bros. (unreleased)
Pufnstuf—Universal
Rabbit, Run—Warner Bros.
The Railway Children—British—Universal
Red Desert—Italian—Independent
Rio Lobo—National General
The Rise and Fall of Michael Rimmer—British—Warner Bros.
Sabata—Italian/U.S.—United Artists
The Savage Wild—American International
The Scars of Dracula—British—EMI/Metro-Goldwyn-Mayer
Scrooge—British—National General
Skullduggery—Universal
The Spider's Strategy—Italian—Independent
Spring and Port Wine—British—Warner Bros./Pathe
Start the Revolution Without Me—Warner Bros.
Story of a Citizen Above All Suspicion—Italian—Independent
Story of a Woman—Italian/Swedish—Universal
Strogoff—Italian/German—Independent
Sunflower—Italian—Avco Embassy
Take a Girl Like You—British—Columbia
Taste the Blood of Dracula—British—Warner Bros.
Tell Me That You Love Me, Junie Moon—Preminger/Paramount
There Was a Crooked Man—Warner Bros.
Tomorrow—British—Rank
Trog—British—Warner Bros.
Twinky—British/Italian—Rank
Two Mules for Sister Sara—Universal
Under Cover Rogue—Italian—Independent
Upon This Rock—Independent
The Vampire Lovers—British—EMI/Metro-Goldwyn-Mayer

Waterloo—Italian/Russian—Paramount
Which Way to the Front?—Warner Bros.
Woodstock—Warner Bros.
W.U.S.A.—Paramount
You Can't Win 'Em All—British—Columbia

1971

Adios, Sabata—Independent
The African Elephant—National General
The Anderson Tapes—Columbia
The Andromeda Strain—Universal
And Soon the Darkness—British—Independent
The Barefoot Executive—Disney/Buena Vista
Bedknobs and Broomsticks (part animation)—Disney/Buena Vista
The Beguiled—Universal
Big Jake—National General
Billy Jack—Warner Bros.
Black Jesus—Italian—Independent
Bless the Beasts and Children—Kramer/Columbia
Blue Water, White Death—National General
The Body—British—Metro-Goldwyn-Mayer
Bora Bora—French/Italian—American International
The Brotherhood of Satan—Columbia
Captain Apache—British—Independent
Carnal Knowledge—Avco Embassy
The Cat O' Nine Tails—Italian/French/German—National General
A Clockwork Orange—British—Kubrick/Warner Bros.
The Clowns—Italian/French/German—Independent
The Conformist—Italian/French/German—Paramount
Creatures the World Forgot—British—Columbia
Dead of Summer—Italian/French—Independent
Death in Venice—Italian/French—Warner Bros.
The Decameron—Italian/French/West German—United Artists
The Deserter—Italian/Yugoslavian/U.S.—Paramount
The Devils—British—Warner Bros.
Diamonds Are Forever—British—United Artists
Dirty Harry—Warner Bros.
The Dirty Heroes—Italian/French/West German—Independent
$ (Dollars)—Columbia
A Drama of Jealousy—and Other Things (The Pizza Triangle)—Italian—Warner Bros.
Dusty and Sweets McGee—Warner Bros.
Five Bloody Graves—Independent
Fragment of Fear—British—Columbia
Friends—Paramount
Get to Know Your Rabbit—Warner Bros.
Glory Boy (My Old Man's Place)—Cinerama Releasing Corp.
The Go-Between—British—Columbia
A Gunfight—Paramount
Harold and Maude—Paramount
The Hired Hand—Universal
How to Frame a Figg—Universal
The Invincible Six—U.S./Iran—Independent
Julius Caesar—British—Commonwealth United/American International
Klute—Pakula/Warner Bros.
The Last Movie—Universal
The Last Rebel—Columbia

The Last Valley—British—Cinerama Releasing Corp.
Long Ago, Tomorrow—British—Independent
Lust for a Vampire—British—Independent
MacBeth—British—Columbia
Maddalena—Italian/Yugoslavian—Independent
Malcolm X—Warner Bros.
A Man Called Sledge—Italian—Columbia
Man in the Wilderness—Warner Bros.
The Man Who Haunted Himself—British—Independent
Medicine Ball Caravan—U.S./French—Warner Bros.
McCabe and Mrs. Miller—Warner Bros.
Million Dollar Duck—Disney/Buena Vista
Minnie and Moskowitz—Cassavettes/Universal
Nana—Swedish/French—National General
The Narco Men—Spanish/Italian—Independent
The Omega Man—Warner Bros.
On Any Sunday—Independent
One More Train to Rob—Universal
Percy—British—Metro-Goldwyn-Mayer
Peter Rabbit and Tales of Beatrix Potter—British—Metro-Golden-Mayer
Play Misty For Me—Universal
Plaza Suite—Paramount
The Priest's Wife—Italian/French—Ponti/Warner Bros.
The Projectionist—Independent
Punishment Park—Independent
Puzzle of a Downfall Child—Universal
Raid on Rommel—Universal
The Reckoning—British—Columbia
Red Sky at Morning—Wallis/Universal
The Red Tent—Italian/Russian—Paramount
Romance of a Horsethief—Allied Artists
Sacco & Vanzetti—Italian/French—Independent
A Safe Place—Columbia
Scandalous John—Disney/Buena Vista
The Scars of Dracula—British—Independent
A Severed Head—British—Columbia
Shoot Out—Universal
The Ski Bum—Avco Embassy (unreleased)
Skin Game—Warner Bros.
Story of a Woman—U.S./Italian—Universal
Sudden Terror—British—National General
Summer of '42—Warner Bros.
THX 1138—Warner Bros.
The Todd Killings—National General
A Town Called Hell—British/Spanish—Independent
T.R. Baskin—Paramount
200 Motels—British—United Artists
Two-Lane Blacktop—Universal
The Vampire Lovers—British—American International
Villan—British—Metro-Goldwyn-Mayer
Waterloo—Italian/Russian—Paramount
When Dinosaurs Ruled the Earth—British—Warner Bros.
The Wild Country—Disney/Buena Vista
Willy Wonka and the Chocolate Factory—Paramount
Zeppelin—British—Warner Bros.

1972

The Animals—Independent
The Assassination of Trotsky—French/Italian/British—Cinerama Releasing Corp.
Bad Company—Paramount
Baron Blood—Italian—American International

Battle of Neretva—Yugoslavian/German/Italian/U.S.—Independent
Blindman—Italian/U.S.—Twentieth Century-Fox
Blood from the Mummy's Tomb—British—American International
Bluebeard—French/Italian/German—Cinerama Releasing Corp.
Born to Boogie—British—Independent
*Cabaret**—Allied Artists
Cancel My Reservation—Warner Bros.
The Candidate—Warner Bros.
Captain Milkshake—Independent
Chato's Land—United Artists
Come Back, Charleston Blue—Warner Bros.
The Concert for Bangladesh—Twentieth Century-Fox
The Cowboys—Warner Bros.
Crescendo—British—Warner Bros.
Cross and the Switchblade—Independent
Dealing: or the Berkeley-to-Boston Forty-Brick Lost-Bag Blues—Warner Bros.
Deliverance—Warner Bros.
The Dirty Outlaws—Italian—Independent
Dr. Jekyll and Sister Hyde—British—American International
Dracula A.D. 1972—British—Warner Bros.
Duck, You Sucker (A Fistful of Dynamite)—Italian—United Artists
Dulcima—British—Independent
The Emigrants—Swedish—Warner Bros.
Fellini's Roma—Italian/French—United Artists
Fillmore—Twentieth Century-Fox
Four Flies on Grey Velvet—Italian/French—Paramount
Frenzy—British—Hitchcock/Universal
The Getaway—First Artists/National General
The Godfather—Paramount
The Great Northfield, Minnesota, Raid—Universal
The Groundstar Conspiracy—Canadian—Universal
Hands of the Ripper—British—Universal
Here Comes Every Body—British—Independent
Jeremiah Johnson—Warner Bros.
Joe Kidd—Universal
Johnny Hamlet—Italian—Independent
Last of the Red Hot Lovers—Paramount
Last Tango in Paris—Italian/French—United Artists
The Legend of Boggy Creek—Independent
The Life and Times of Judge Roy Bean—First Artists/National General
Limbo—Universal
The Little Ark—National General
Lizard in a Woman's Skin (Schizoid)—Italian/French/Spanish—American International
Lola—British/Italian—American International
Mary, Queen of Scots—British—Wallis/Universal
Napoleon and Samantha—Disney/Buena Vista
The Nightcomers—British—Avco Embassy
The Night Evelyn Came Out of the Grave—Italian—Independent
No Drums, No Bugles—Cinerama Releasing Corp.
Now You See Him, Now You Don't—Disney/Buena Vista
Outback—Australian—United Artists
Pete 'n' Tillie—Universal
Play It Again, Sam—Paramount
Play It As It Lays—Universal
Pocket Money—National General

Portnoy's Complaint—Warner Bros.
Prime Cut—National General
The Public Eye—U.S./British—Universal
Puppet on a Chain—British—Cinerama Releasing Corp.
Red Sun—French/Italian/Spanish—National General
Return of Sabata—Italian/French/West German—United Artists
Silent Running—Universal
Slaughterhouse-Five—Universal
Snoopy, Come Home—National General
Snow Job—Warner Bros.
Snowball Express—Disney/Buena Vista
Something Big—National General
Sometimes a Great Notion—Universal
Super Fly—Warner Bros.
Ten Days' Wonder—French—Independent
Trick Baby—Universal
Ulzana's Raid—Universal
Up the Sandbox—First Artists/National General
The Valachi Papers—Italian/French—De Laurentiis/Columbia
The War Between Men and Women—National General
Wednesday's Child—British—Independent
Weekend Murders—Italian—Metro-Goldwyn-Mayer
What's Up, Doc?—Warner Bros.
You'll Like My Mother—Universal

*Academy Award winner for best Cinematography

1973

Alfredo, Alfredo—Italian—Paramount
The All-American Boy—Warner Bros.
Alpha Beta—British—Independent
American Graffiti—Universal
Ash Wednesday—Paramount
The Assassin of Rome—Italian—Columbia
Battle of the Amazons—Italian/Spanish—American International
Baxter—British—National General
Blume in Love—Warner Bros.
The Boy Who Cried Werewolf—Universal
Breezy—Universal
Brother Sun Sister Moon—Italian/British—Paramount
Cahill, United States Marshall—Batjac/Warner Bros.
Charley and the Angel—Disney/Buena Vista
Charley Varrick—Universal
Class of '44—Warner Bros.
Cleopatra Jones—Warner Bros.
Contact—Italian—Independent
The Day of the Dolphin—Avco Embassy
The Day of the Jackal—Universal
The Deadly Trackers—Warner Bros.
Deaf Smith & Johnny Ears—Italian—Metro-Goldwyn-Mayer
Diary of a Cloistered Nun—Italian—Independent
The Don is Dead—Wallis/Universal
Don't Look Now—British/Italian—British Lion
Enter the Dragon—Warner Bros.
Fear is the Key—British—Independent
The Friends of Eddie Coyle—Paramount
Giordano Bruno—Italian—Independent

Girls Are For Loving—Independent
High Plains Drifter—Universal
Hit—Paramount
The Iceman Cometh—American Film Theater
I Did It—Italian—Dear/Warner Bros.
Jesus Christ Superstar—Universal
Jimi Hendrix—Warner Bros.
The Last of Sheila—Warner Bros.
Lialeh—Independent
The Long Goodbye—United Artists
Loveland—Independent
The MacKintosh Machine—Warner Bros.
Magnum Force—Warner Bros.
The Man Called Noon—British—National General
Massacre in Rome—Italian—Independent
Maurie—National General
Mean Streets—Warner Bros.
The Naked Ape—Universal
The Nelson Affair—British—Wallis/Universal
Night Watch—British—Brut/Avco Embassy
Number One—Italian—Independent
The Nuns of Sant'Arcangelo—Italian—Independent
O Lucky Man!—British—Warner Bros./Columbia
One Little Indian—Disney/Buena Vista
Papillon—Allied Artists
Re: Lucky Luciano—Italian—Independent
Robin Hood (animated)—Disney/Buena Vista
The Sacred Knives of Vengeance—Chinese—Warner Bros.
Scalaway—Paramount
Scarecrow—Warner Bros.
Serpico—De Laurentiis/Paramount
Showdown—Seaton/Universal
Sssssss—Zanuck-Brown/Universal
Steel Arena—Independent
The Sting—Zanuck-Brown/Universal
The Stone Killer—Columbia
Summer Wishes, Winter Dreams—Columbia
Teresa the Thief—Italian—Independent
That Man Bolt—Universal
That'll Be the Day—British—Independent
A Touch of Class—Brut/Avco Embassy
Two People—Universal
Visions of Eight—Wolper/Cinema 5
A Warm December—First Artists/National General
Whatever Happened to Miss September—Independent
The World's Greatest Athlete—Disney/Buena Vista

1974

The Abdication—British—Warner Bros.
Airport '75—Universal
Alice Doesn't Live Here Anymore—Warner Bros.
Alicia—Dutch—Independent
Always A New Beginning—Independent
Amarcord—Italian—Fellini/Warner Bros.
The Arabian Nights—Italian—United Artists
The Bears and I—Disney/Buena Vista
The Beast—Italian/French—Warner Bros.
The Beast Must Die—British—Cinerama Releasing Corp.
Beautiful People—Warner Bros.
Black Eye—Warner Bros.

Black Sampson—Warner Bros.
The Black Windmill—Universal
Blazing Saddles—Warner Bros.
The Castaway Cowboy—Disney/Buena Vista
Chinatown—Paramount
The Conversation—Paramount
Coonskin—Paramount
Craze—British—Warner Bros.
Dakota—Dutch—Independent
Death Wish—De Laurentiis/Paramount
Digby, the Biggest Dog in the World—Cinerama Releasing Corp.
The Dove—British—EMI
Earthquake—Universal
La Faro da Padre—Italian—Independent
Freebie and the Bean—Warner Bros.
The Front Page—Universal
The Girl from Petrovka—Zanuck-Brown/Universal
The Godfather Part II—Paramount
Gold—British—Allied Artists
Herbie Rides Again—Disney/Buena Vista
How Long Can You Fall?—Italian—Independent
The Island at the Top of the World—Disney/Buena Vista
It's Alive—Warner Bros.
The Klansman—Paramount
Li'l Scratch—Independent
The Little Prince—Paramount
The Longest Yard—Paramount
Lords of Flatbush—Columbia
Lost in the Stars—American Film Theater
Mahler—British—Independent
Mame—Warner Bros.
Man on a Swing—Paramount
Mc Q—Warner Bros.
Murder on the Orient Express—Paramount
The Mutation—British—Columbia
My Name is Nobody—Italian—Independent
My Way—South African—Independent
Newman's Law—Universal
The Night Porter—Italian—United Artists
Our Time—Warner Bros.
The Parallax View—Paramount
Paul and Michelle—French/British—Paramount
Phase IV—Paramount
Return of the Dragon—Independent
The Savage Is Loose—Independent
Sonny & Jed—Italian—Independent
Star Dust—Italian—Independent
Stardust—British—Columbia
The Sugarland Express—Zanuck-Brown/Universal
Superdad—Disney/Buena Vista
Swallows and Amazona—British—Independent
Swept Away . . .—Italian—Independent
The Terminal Man—Warner Bros.
That Midnight Man—Universal
Three Tough Guys—Italian—De Laurentiis/Paramount
Torso—Italian—Independent
Truck Stop Women—Independent
Uptown Saturday Night—First Artists/Warner Bros.
Venial Sin—Italian—Independent
Verdi—Independent
A Very Natural Thing—Independent
Willie Dynamite—Zanuck-Brown/Universal

Zandy's Bride—Warner Bros.

1975

Abduction—Independent
The Apple Dumpling Gang—Disney/Buena Vista
The Arena—Independent
Bigfoot: The Mysterious Monster—Independent
Black Christmas—Warner Bros.
A Boy and His Dog—Independent
Brother, Can You Spare A Dime? (sequences)—Independent
Children of Rage—Independent
Cleopatra Jones and the Casino Of Gold—Warner Bros.
Conduct Unbecoming—British Lion/Allied Artists
Coonskin—Independent
The Day of the Locust—Paramount
Doc Savage . . . the Man of Bronze—Pal/Warner Bros.
Dog Day Afternoon—Warner Bros.
Drifter—Independent
The Drowning Pool—Warner Bros.
The Eiger Sanction—Universal
Escape to Witch Mountain—Buena Vista
Farewell, My Lovely—Avco Embassy
Fire in the Flesh—Independent
The Fortune—Columbia
Galileo—British—American Film Theater
Give 'em Hell, Harry!—Independent
Hedda—British—Independent
The Hindenburg—Universal
The Human Factor—Independent
Inside Out—British—Warner Bros.
Jacques Brel Is Alive and Well and Living in Paris—French/Canadian—American Film Theater
Janis (sequences)—Universal
Jaws—Zanuck-Brown/Universal
Journey Back to Oz (animated)—Independent
The Land That Time Forgot—British—American International
The Last Days of Man on Earth—British—Independent
Let's Do It Again—First Artists/Warner Bros.
Lisztomania—Warner Bros.
Lord Shango—Independent
Love and Energy—Italian—Independent
The Maids—British—American Film Theater
Mandingo—De Laurentiis/Paramount
The Man Who Would Be King—Allied Artists/Columbia
Messiah of Evil—Independent
Midnight Pleasures—Italian—Independent
Mitchell—Allied Artists
Mr. Quilp—British—Avco Embassy
Night Moves—Warner Bros.
One of Our Dinosaurs Is Missing—Disney/Buena Vista
The Other Side of the Mountain—Universal
Out of Season—Independent
Paper Tiger—British—Independent
Permission to Kill—European—Avco Embassy
Posse—Bryna/Paramount
The Prisoner of Second Avenue—Warner Bros.
Rafferty and the Gold Dust Twins—Warner Bros.
The Reincarnation of Peter Proud—American International
Ride A Wild Pony—Disney/Buena Vista

Rollerball—United Artists
Rooster Cogburn—Wallis/Universal
Salo or the 120 Days of Sodom—Italian—United Artists
Scent of Woman—Italian—Twentieth Century-Fox
Shampoo—Columbia
Sheila Levine Is Dead and Living In New York—
    Paramount
Sidecar Racers—Universal
The Strongest Man in the World—Disney/Buena Vista
Those Were the Years—Italian—Independent
Three Days of the Condor—Paramount
When the North Wind Blows—Independent
White, Yellow, Black—Italian/Spanish/French—Indepen-
    dent
The Yakuza—Warner Bros.

The Ritz—Warner Bros.
Robin and Marion—British—Columbia
Seven Nights in Japan—Anglo/French—Paramount
The Seven Per-Cent Solution—British—Universal
The Shaggy D.A.—Disney/Buena Vista
Shoot—Canadian—Avco Embassy
The Shootist—DeLaurentiis/Paramount
Shout at the Devil—British—American International
The Slipper and the Rose—British—Universal
The Song Remains the Same—British—Warner Bros.
Sparkle—Warner Bros.
St. Ives—Warner Bros.
Swashbuckler—Universal
To the Devil a Daughter—British/German—EMI
Treasure of Matecumbre—Disney/Buena Vista
Two-Minute Warning—Universal
W.C. Fields and Me—Universal
Winterhawk—Independent
Won Ton Ton, The Dog Who Saved Hollywood—
    Paramount

1976

Aces High—British—EMI/Cine Artists
Alfie Darling—British—EMI
Allegro non Troppo (sequences—animated)—Italian—
    Independent
All the President's Men—Warner Bros.
The Bawdy Adventures of Tom Jones—British—Universal
Best of Walt Disney's True-Life Adventures
    (compilation)—Disney/Buena Vista
The Bingo Long Traveling All-Stars & Motor Kings—
    Universal
Car Wash—Universal
Carry on England—British—Rank/Independent
The Context—Italian—United Artists
Crime and Passion—American International
The Enforcer—Warner Bros.
Escape from the Dark—Disney/Buena Vista
Face to Face—Swedish—DeLaurentiis/Paramount
Family Plot—Hitchcock/Universal
Fellini's Casanova—Italian—Grimaldi/Universal
Freaky Friday—Disney/Buena Vista
Gable and Lombard—Universal
The Genius—Italian/French/German—Titanus
The Great Scout & Cathouse Thursday—American
    International
The Gumball Rally—First Artists/Warner Bros.
Gus—Disney/Buena Vista
How Funny Can Sex Be?—Italian—Independent
The Incredible Sarah—British—Independent
It Shouldn't Happen to a Vet—British—EMI
Jim, the World's Greatest—Universal
Julia—West German—Independent
The Last Tycoon—Paramount
Lipstick—DeLaurentiis/Paramount
Mackintosh & T.J.—Independent
Massacre in Rome—Italian—Ponti/Independent
Midway—Mirisch/Universal
Moses—British/Italian—Avco Embassy
Mustang Country—Universal
The Next Man—Allied Artists
No Deposit No Return—Disney/Buena Vista
Obsession—Columbia
Ode to Billy Joe—Warner Bros.
Operation Daybreak—Warner Bros.

1977

Airport '77—Universal
Bishop's Bedroom (La Stanza del Vescovo)—Italian—
    Independent
Candleshoe—Disney/Buena Vista
The Car—Universal
The Choirboys—Universal
Cross of Iron—British/West German—Avco Embassy
Dynasty—Hong Kong—Independent
Exorcist II: The Heretic—Warner Bros.
Greased Lightning—Warner Bros.
The Great Day (Una Giornata Speciale)—Italian—
    Independent
The Great Gundown—Independent
Herbie Goes to Monte Carlo—Disney/Buena Vista
Heroes—Universal
It's Alive—Warner Bros.
Jabberwocky—British—Columbia
The Last Remake of Beau Geste—Universal
MacArthur—Universal
March or Die—British—Columbia
Nasty Habits—Brut/Independent
1900—Italian—Paramount
Oh, God!—Warner Bros.
One on One—Warner Bros.
Orca—Paramount
Outlaw Blues—Warner Bros.
The Pack—Warner Bros.
Pete's Dragon—Disney/Buena Vista
The Prince and the Pauper—British—Warner Bros.
The Rescuers—Disney/Buena Vista
Rollercoaster—Universal
September 30, 1955—Universal
The Sentinel—Universal
The Sex Machine—Independent
Silver Bears—Columbia
Slap Shot—Universal
Smokey and the Bandit—Universal
Sorcerer—Universal
The Squeeze—British—Warner Bros.

Stand Up Virgin Soldiers—British—Warner Bros.
Stormtroopers (Sturmtruppen)—Italian—Independent
Submission (Scandalo)—Italian—Independent
Sweeney—British—EMI
Tentacles—Italian—American International
Thieves—Brut/Paramount
Torso—Italian—Ponti/Independent
The Town That Dreaded Sundown—American International
25 Years-Impressions—British—EMI
Twilight's Last Gleaming—Allied Artists
The Violation of Claudia—Independent
Viva Knievel!—Warner Bros.
Which Way Is Up?—Universal
White Rock—British—Independent

1978

Alice, Sweet Alice (Communion)—Allied Artists
All Things Bright and Beautiful—Independent
Almost Summer—Motown/Universal
The Betsy—Allied Artists
Beyond and Back—Sunn Classic
The Big Fix—Universal
Bloodbrothers—Warner Bros.
Blue Collar—Universal
Born Again—Avco Embassy
The Boys In Company C—Columbia
The Brink's Job—DeLaurentiis/Universal
Caravans—Universal
The Cat From Outer Space—Disney/Buena Vista
Comes a Horseman—United Artists
Crossed Swords—British—Warner Bros.
Death on the Nile—Paramount/EMI
The Deer Hunter—Universal/EMI
The End of the World in Our Usual Bed in a Night Full of Rain—Warner Bros.
F.I.S.T.—United Artists
FM—Universal
Force 10 From Navarone—American International
Gray Lady Down—Mirisch/Universal
The Greek Tycoon—Universal
Halloween—Independent
Hot Lead and Cold Feet—Disney/Buena Vista
House Calls—Universal
I Wanna Hold Your Hand—Universal
If Ever I See You Again—Columbia
Interiors—United Artists
Invasion of the Body Snatchers—United Artists
It Lives Again—Warner Bros.
Jaws 2—Universal
King of the Gypsies—DeLaurentiis/Paramount
Laserblast—Independent
Message from Space—Japanese—United Artists
The Medusa Touch—British—Independent
Metamorphoses—Independent
Moment by Moment—Universal
Movie, Movie—Warner Bros.
National Lampoon's Animal House—Universal
Nunzio—Universal
The Other Side of the Mountain, Part 2—Filmways/Universal

Paradise Alley—Universal
Return from Witch Mountain—Disney/Buena Vista
Revenge of the Pink Panther—United Artists
Same Time, Next Year—Universal
Sgt. Pepper's Lonely Hearts Club Band—Universal
Silver Bears—Columbia/EMI
Skateboard—Universal
Slow Dancing in the Big City—United Artists
Straight Time—First Artists/Warner Bros.
Stevie—First Artists
Superman—Warner Bros.
The Swarm—Warner Bros.
Sweeney 2—British—EMI
Take All of Me—Independent
Uncle Joe Shannon—United Artists
Warlords of Atlantis—Columbia/EMI
Watership Down (animated)—Avco Embassy
The Wiz—Motown/Universal
The Wild Geese—British—Allied Artists

1979

Agatha—First Artists/Warner Bros.
Americathon—Lorimar/United Artists
Apocalypse Now—Coppola/United Artists
The Apple Dumpling Gang Rides Again—Disney/Buena Vista
Being There—Lorimar/United Artists
The Bermuda Triangle—Sunn Classic
Beyond Death's Door—Sunn Classic
The Black Hole—Disney/Buena Vista
The Black Stallion—United Artists
Boulevard Nights—Warner Bros.
Buck Rogers—Universal
The Concorde–Airport '79—Universal
Cuba—United Artists
Dawn of the Dead—Independent
Dracula—Mirisch/Universal
The Fall of the House of Usher—Sunn Classic
Firepower—Independent
The Frisco Kid—Warner Bros.
Game of Death—Columbia
Going in Style—Warner Bros.
Hair—United Artists
Hanover Street—Columbia
Head Over Heels—United Artists
Hurricane—DeLaurentiis/Paramount
The In-Laws—Warner Bros.
In Search of Historic Jesus—Sunn Classic
The Jerk—Universal
Jesus—Warner Bros.
Last Embrace—United Artists
The Legend of Sleepy Hollow—Sunn Classic
A Little Romance—Orion/Warner Bros.
Lost and Found—Columbia
The Main Event—Warner Bros.
Moonraker—United Artists
More American Graffiti—Universal
1941—Universal/Columbia
The North Avenue Irregulars—Disney/Buena Vista
Old Boyfriends—Avco Embassy
Over the Edge—Orion/Warner Bros.

The Passage—United Artists
Phantasm—Avco Embassy
The Prisoner of Zenda—Mirisch/Universal
Promises in the Dark—Orion/Warner Bros.
Rich Kids—United Artists
Rocky II—United Artists
Running—Universal
The Seduction of Joe Tynan—Universal

Soldier of Orange—Dutch—Rank
Summer Camp—Independent
Sunburn—Paramount
10—Orion/Warner Bros.
Tilt—Warner Bros.
Walk Proud—Universal
The Wanderers—Orion/Warner Bros.
Yanks—Universal

2

Technicolor and the Academy Awards

1929-30 *King of Jazz*, winner for best Set Decoration—by Herman Rosse (first Technicolor film to win an Academy Award)

1931-32 Class II Academy Award (plaque) to the Technicolor Motion Picture Corp. for its Color Cartoon Process

1931-32 *Flowers and Trees* wins first Oscar for Walt Disney

1936 Special Academy Award (plaque) to W. Howard Greene for the Color Photography of *The Garden of Allah*

1937 Special Academy Award (plaque) to W. Howard Greene for the Color Photography of *A Star Is Born*—recommended by a committee of leading cinematographers after viewing all color pictures made during the year.

1938 Special Academy Award (plaques) to Oliver Marsh and Allen Davey for the Color Cinematography of *Sweethearts*

Special Academy Award (plaque) to J. Arthur Ball for his outstanding contribution to the advancement of Color in Motion Picture Photography

1939 *Gone With the Wind*, winner for best Color Cinematography—by Ernest Haller and Ray Rennahan (first Technicolor film to win in this newly created Academy Award classification)

Special Academy Award (plaque) to William Cameron Menzies for outstanding achievement in the use of color for the enhancement of dramatic mood in the production of *Gone With the Wind*

Special Academy Award (statuette) to the Technicolor Corp. for its contributions in successfully bringing three-color feature production to the screen

Class III Academy Award (citation) to Winton Hock and Technicolor for an Auxiliary Optical System

1940 *The Thief of Bagdad* (British), winner for best Color Cinematography—by George Perinal

1941 *Blood and Sand*, winner for best Color Cinematography—by Ernest Haller and Ray Rennahan

1942 *The Black Swan*, winner for best Color Cinematography—by Leon Shamroy

1943 *Phantom of the Opera*, winner for best Color Cinematography—by Hal Mohr and W. Howard Greene

1944 *Wilson*, winner for best Color Cinematography—by Leon Shamroy

1945 *Leave Her To Heaven*, winner for best Color Cinematography—by Leon Shamroy

1946 *The Yearling*, winner for best Color Cinematography—by Charles Rosher, Leonard Smith and Arthur Arling

1947 *Black Narcissus* (British), winner for best Color Cinematography—by Jack Cardiff

1948 *Joan of Arc*, winner for best Color Cinematography—by Joseph Valentine, William V. Skall and Winton Hock

1949 *She Wore A Yellow Ribbon*, winner for best Color Cinematography—by Winton Hock

1950 *King Solomon's Mines*, winner for best Color Cinematography—by Robert L. Surtees

Cinematography—by Robert L. Surtees

1951 *An American In Paris*, winner for best Color Cinematography—by Alfred Gilks and John Alton

1952 *The Quiet Man*, winner for best Color Cinematography—by Winton Hoch and Archie Stout

Class II Academy Award (plaque) to Technicolor for an improved method of color motion picture photography under incandescent light

1953 *Shane*, winner for best Color Cinematography—by Loyall Griggs

1955 *To Catch A Thief*, winner for best Color Cinematography—by Robert Burks

1956 *Around the World in 80 Days*, winner for best Color Cinematography—by Lionel Lindon

1957 *Bridge on the River Kwai*, winner for best Color Cinematography—by Jack Hildyard

1959 *Ben-Hur*, winner for best Color Cinematography —by Robert L. Surtees

Class II Academy Award (plaques) to Wadsworth E. Pohl, William Evans, Werner Hopf, S.E. Howse, Thomas P. Dixon, Stanford Institute and Technicolor for the design and development of the Technicolor electronic printing timer

Class II Academy Award (plaques) to W.E. Pohl, Jack Alford, Henry Imus, Joseph Schmit, Paul Fassnacht, Al Lofquist and Technicolor for the development and practical application of equipment for wet printing

1960 *Spartacus*, winner for best Color Cinematography—by Russell Metty

1961 *West Side Story*, winner for best Color Cinematography—by Daniel L. Fapp

Class II Academy Award (plaques) to James Dale, S.Wilson, H.E. Rice, John Rude, Laurie Atkin, W.E. Pohl, H. Peasgood and Technicolor for a process of automatic selective printing

Class III Academy Award (citations) to W.E. Pohl and Technicolor for an integrated sound and picture transfer process

1962 *Lawrence of Arabia*, winner for best Color Cinematography—by Fred A. Young

1964 *My Fair Lady*, winner for best Color Cinematography—by Harry Stradling

Class I Academy Award (statuettes) to Petro Vlahos, W.E. Pohl (Technicolor) and Ub Iwerks for the conception and perfection of techniques for color traveling matte composite cinematography

1966 *A Man For All Seasons*, winner for best Color Cinematography—by Ted Moore

1967 *Bonnie and Clyde*, winner for best Cinematography—by Burnett Guffey (separate classifications for color and black-and-white were discontinued starting this year)

1968 *Romeo and Juliet*, winner for best Cinematography—by Pasqualino DeSantis

1972 *Cabaret*, winner for best Cinematography—by Geoffrey Unsworth

1976 Class II Academy Award (plaques) to William Graham, Geoffrey Norman, Manfred Mitchelson and Siegfried Seibert for developing and engineering Technicolor's new high speed continuous contact printing system

(Class Awards are presented for SCIENTIFIC or TECHNICAL achievements)

3

Technicolor Milestones

1915   Technicolor Motion Picture Corp. established by Dr. Herbert T. Kalmus (November 19)

1916   "Technicolor Process Number One," a two-component additive system, developed for Technicolor by Kalmus, Comstock & Westcott, Inc.

1917   First Technicolor feature, *The Gulf Between,* produced in Jacksonville, Florida; serviced in the first Technicolor laboratory, a railway car

1922   "Technicolor Process Number Two," a two-component subtractive system, developed

Technicolor, Inc. formed

Technicolor's first Hollywood laboratory established

1924   *Cytherea* filmed with artificially lit interiors; Technicolor's first experience in photographing an interior set on a dark stage

1925   Douglas Fairbanks' *The Black Pirate* filmed in Technicolor

1926   "Technicolor Process Number Three," a two-component subtractive imbibition process, developed

1928   First Technicolor picture with music and sound effects, *The Viking*

1929   First Technicolor all-talking picture, *On With The Show*

1930   Technicolor's main Hollywood plant completed

1931   Dr. Troland issued patents for his Monopack process (applied for in 1921)

1932   "Technicolor Process Number Four," a three-component imbibition process, developed

First film in Technicolor three-component process, *Flowers and Trees,* produced in animation by Walt Disney

1934   First live action three-color picture, *La Cucaracha*

1935   First full-length three-color feature, *Becky Sharp*

Technicolor, Ltd. organized in London

1937   First Technicolor feature filmed in England, *Wings of the Morning*

Technicolor entered non-theatrical film field

Snow White and the Seven Dwarfs, Disney's first full-length animated feature, premiered (first general release; 1938)

1938   Developed a continuous developing machine for processing three-strip negative

1939   *Gone With the Wind* released

Introduced three-strip negative three times the speed of previous negatives for use in Technicolor cameras

1941   Technicolor Monopack process introduced with aerial shots in *Dive Bomber* (remained in use for special purposes until 1952)

1944   Optical printer introduced by Technicolor which enabled fades, dissolves and special effects to be printed in color

1948   Technichrome, a special purpose product, introduced for photography of the Olympic Games held in England

1950   Technicolor introduced a three-strip photographic system using uncorrected incandescent illumination and with a substantially lower light level

1953   Developed and built a contact printer with additive color for use in wide screen processes

1954   With lenses from Superscope and Panavision, set up printers for first making anamorphic prints from flat negatives and flat prints from Cinema-Scope negatives

1955   "Technicolor Process Number Five," a method of achieving improved definition of imbibition prints working from new Eastman color negative, introduced

Technicolor Italiana launched in Rome

Developed Technicolor-Technirama, a multi-purpose photography and print system that provided flexibility in the preparation of negatives and a wide choice of high quality color release prints suited to large screen exhibition in 35mm or 70mm sizes or smaller audience requirements in 16mm. First used on *Night Passage* (1957)

1956-57   Development of the wet printing process to permit making high quality reduced grain, dirt-free prints from 35mm and 16mm color-reversal films. First full feature wet printed: *Pal Joey*

1956-58   With the introduction of Todd-AO and Camera 65, developed and manufactured optical printers for handling 65mm negatives and printing enlargement to 70mm or reduction to 35mm—anamorphic or flat—and 16mm anamorphic

1960   Introduced Super Technirama 70

Technicolor's founder, Dr. Herbert T. Kalmus, retired

1961   Made Cinemiracle extractions (three panel) from Camera 65 and Technirama. Location shots for *How The West Was Won* were filmed in 65mm then converted to Cinerama to be compatible with the three-camera studio cinematography

Introduced an integrated transfer process in which the sound track is printed and the picture image is colored in a continuous operation

Introduced a predetermined distance counter which electronically programmed effects and light changes during the printing of matrices

Introduced auto-selective printing, allowing dissolves and fades from original negatives without the cost and quality loss of using internegatives and using an assembled original negative for printing many versions

1963   Introduced Techniscope as well as a new system for printing 35mm negatives in 70mm release prints for road show potential

Dr. Kalmus died on July 11 at age 81

1963-64   Built optical printers for making 70mm "rectified" prints from 65mm Ultra-Panavision negatives for Cinerama to be shown on a curved screen. First pictures were *It's A Mad, Mad, Mad, Mad World* and *The Greatest Story Ever Told*

1964   Developed improved method of traveling matte

photography and processing, enabling background scenes to be photographed abroad with a relatively small crew, with the action subsequently performed in Hollywood before a blue screen

Engaged by the National Aeronautics and Space Administration to administer photographic operations at Kennedy Space Center in Florida

1965   Technicolor television film processing plant opened at Universal City

1965-70   Introduction of new dye systems to improve quality and quality control

1966   The desaturation process first developed for *Moby Dick* (1956) was substantially improved for *Reflections In A Golden Eye*

Designed and installed a triple rank manufacturing system to produce super-8mm Technicolor dye transfer prints

Development of a technique making possible production of full color television prints from television color tapes of both feature shows and commercials

1967   Technicolor Fotografica, S.A., the Spanish affiliate, initiated in Barcelona

1968   Awarded the prime contract for all photographic work at the Air Force Eastern Test Range, for the United States Air Force and NASA at Cape Kennedy

Technicolor Ltd., Television Division facility, began operations in London

Technicolor Techniscope System selected for recording the summer Olympic Games in Mexico by the Mexican Organizing Committee

1969   Development of a Pan-Scan printer for producing television aspect prints from anamorphic negatives, with effects, overlay titles in one pass through the printer

Technicolor cameras recorded departure and early flight of Saturn V as it carried three astronauts to man's first landing on the moon

First color television spot commercial broadcast in Great Britain, processed by Technicolor, Ltd., London (Television Division)

1972   Technicolor introduced Full-Vue color prints (silk finish, rounded corners, borderless) for the consumer market

1974-75   Installation and utilization of a process control computer for answer print scene-to-scene timing and conversion of light points

1975   Technicolor processed its last domestic film in the three-strip process (a reprint order of Walt Disney's *Swiss Family Robinson*) and closed its dye transfer plant in Hollywood

Opened new film processing complex at Universal City

1976   Developed and engineered new high speed continuous contact printing system

Technicolor's graphic services subsidiary awarded

long-term contract by Department of Interior for technical services to the Earth Resources Observation Systems (Sioux Falls, S.D.), bringing company's government contracts, in the United States and abroad, to six.

1977   Landmark Technicolor plant in Hollywood sold to Television Center Studios; executive offices opened in Century City.

4

The Technicolor Technique

For ten years, beginning in 1915, Dr. Kalmus divided his energies between Technicolor and other Kalmus, Comstock & Westcott clients. In 1925, he made a decision to break away from the engineering firm and devote full time to the color company. With Dr. Kalmus went Dr. Leonard Troland and Joseph Arthur Ball.

While Dr. Daniel Comstock was responsible for the majority of patents issued on the two-color process, it was Mr. Ball, one of Dr. Comstock's students at M.I.T. who is credited with the unique method of making prints which grew into Technicolor's three-component system. And, together with Henry Prouch, a German mechanic, and George Alfred Mitchell, the originator of the famous Mitchell camera, he designed and built three of the original new Technicolor three-strip cameras. By May, 1932, the entire three-color "package" was ready to make its debut.

Color printing procedures begin with white light. Optically speaking, white light consists of three primary colors: red, blue and green. This is one way of saying that when proper amounts of red, blue and green are subtracted from white light, any color visible to the human eye will be reproduced.

THE CAMERA
(1932-1955)

The Technicolor three-strip camera exposed three separate black-and-white negatives simultaneously through a single lens. Immediately behind this lens was a beam-splitter made by two prisms of optical glass which were gold coated (later silver flecked) to produce a slight mirrored effect. The purpose of the beam-splitter was to reflect part of

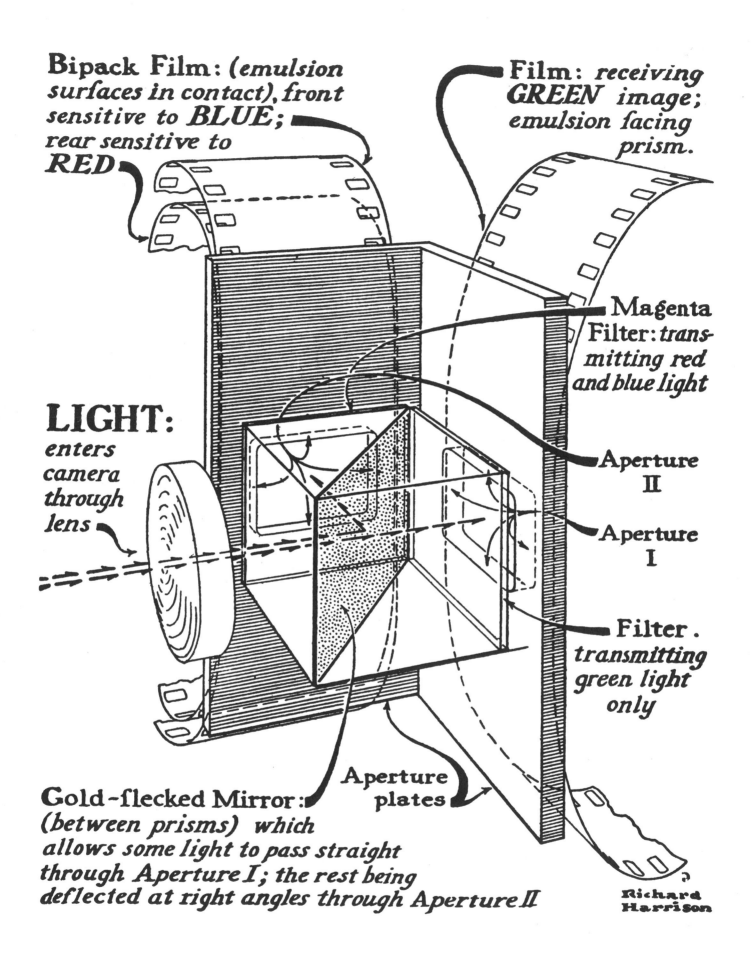

Bipack Film: *(emulsion surfaces in contact), front sensitive to* **BLUE;** *rear sensitive to* **RED**

Film: *receiving* **GREEN** *image; emulsion facing prism.*

LIGHT: *enters camera through lens*

Magenta Filter: *transmitting red and blue light*

Aperture II

Aperture I

Filter. *transmitting green light only*

Gold-flecked Mirror: *(between prisms) which allows some light to pass straight through Aperture I; the rest being deflected at right angles through Aperture II*

Aperture plates

Richard Harrison

Three separate black-and-white negatives (the red, green and blue records) are shown threaded on sprockets within the Technicolor three-strip camera.

the light to an aperture to the left. The remaining light passed directly through to a normally positioned aperature.

The ray of light that passed directly through the prism reached a green filter that allowed only green light (or a green image) to reach the negative behind it. The reflected beam of light was directed to a standard bi-pack containing two negatives. The front film carried a red-orange dye which absorbed the blue light and filtered out the red rays. These rays passed through to register on the rear film of the pair.

In the early days (left), negatives were dried on giant open-slot cylinders. At right, removing rolls of color negative from later drying method.

Using this camera, suppose one takes a picture of a red balloon on green grass against a blue sky. Since the balloon reflects only red light, it must register on the red negative. In the same way, the green grass sends its reflected light to the green negative and the blue sky leaves its impression on the blue negative. Although it is necessary to identify the negatives by color, it must be remembered that they were not actually colored. The red negative, for instance, had no capacity for turning red when the light hit it. It was simply a black-and-white record of the red element and offered an orthodox photograph of the red portions in the camera's field. The three negatives also embodied the intensity of the light that struck them.

The next step was to preserve these values in a special positive that would absorb and print the dyes.

THREE-STRIP RELEASE PRINTS
Imbibition or Dye Transfer
(1932-1955)

The exposed film from the Technicolor three-strip camera, when developed, produced negatives that were silver in color. Held up to the light, however, they appeared the same as black-and-white negatives. These strips of negative were then run through a matrix printer, a device in which special matrix film was exposed to light coming through a negative.

In photography, matrix means what it does in other forms of printing: a relief image from which multiple copies are made. In effect, the matrices were the "plates" from which the films were developed. Because the original negatives were used so infrequently—only to make new sets of matrices when necessary—they remained in excellent condition.

The matrix positive, a special gelatin-coated film, was capable of absorbing (or imbibing) and printing dyes. Through a special chemical process, the gelatin on it was hardened in proportion to the light that hit it when exposed to the original negative. Using the red image as an example, wherever the object photographed was the reddest, the hardening of the gelatin was thinnest. That was because the red light blackened the negative and therefore kept the light from the gelatin on the matrix. When the red matrix was washed, the soft gelatin flushed away. The remaining hard gelatin formed a relief of the red record. In this relief, the red portions of the scene were represented by valleys; the blue and green portions by hills.

While the matrices were being made, a special dye-receptive blank film was prepared. If the customer wanted prints with optical sound tracks,* the silver sound record was incorporated in the blank film at this stage. If the customer's prints were to carry magnetic sound tracks,* the silver sound record was omitted and the magnetic tracks were applied after the dye transfer.

Each matrix was dyed on a dye transfer machine with its complementary, or opposite, color. The red matrix was brought into contact with a blue-green dye called cyan (blue-green being complementary to red). The green matrix was dyed with a magenta dye (complementary to green) and the blue matrix was dyed with a yellow dye (complementary to blue).

Again, using the red record as an example, when the red matrix was brought into contact with the blue-green dye, the dye was imbibed only in proportion to the thickness of the matrix. Therefore, the hills on the matrix, which act like type in printing, got a great deal of dye and the valleys got little or none. Since the red balloon was a valley on the red matrix, the spot where the balloon registered did not get any blue-green color. Conversely, the low spots on the red matrix were high spots on the other two matrices. So on the blue and green matrices, the places where the balloon did not register became hills. Because of that, in those spots, they absorbed ample amounts of yellow and magenta dyes.

When each of the three matrices had been processed through the dye transfer machine, the once blank film contained all the colors necessary for excellent reproduction of the color scene and was ready for delivery to exhibitors for projection. Where yellow dye was present, blue light was subtracted from the projector's white light source. Similarly, red was subtracted where cyan was present and green where

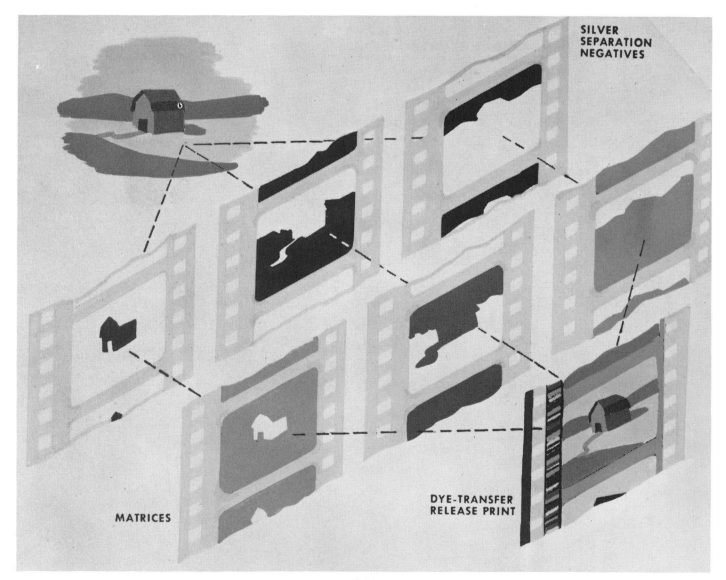

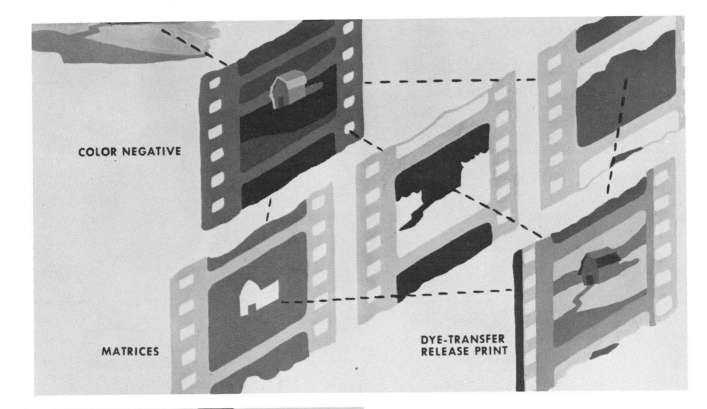

COLOR NEGATIVE

MATRICES

DYE-TRANSFER
RELEASE PRINT

COLOR NEGATIVE

COLOR POSITIVE
RELEASE PRINT

magenta occured. Absence of all dyes resulted in white light on the screen. The presence of all dyes in sufficient quantities created an absence of light, or a black image.

• • •

Beginning in the early 1950s, Technicolor began processing dye transfer prints from the then recently introduced Eastman and Ansco color negatives. The printing process—working with red, blue, and green matrices—was essentially the same as for the three-strip process, which used three separate negatives exposed by the Technicolor camera. The main difference was in step number one. Instead of working from three negatives, matrices were made from a single strip of color negative which contained three emulsion layers—one for each of the three primary colors—superposed on a cellulose acetate base. These three emulsion layers were differently sensitive to different colors of light. This means that the photo-sensitive silver halide particles in the separate emulsions were exposed by different colors of light. Generally, color negative films had a filter layer between the top two emulsions. Where the color sensitivity was not complete, this filter aided in separating unwanted colors from a particular emulsion.

COLOR POSITIVE RELEASE PRINTS
(1955-today)

(1) Color positive release prints are manufactured only from color negative.

(2) Color positive stock is similar to color negative in that it has three superposed emulsion layers.

(3) Color positive stock is contact-printed by light coming through the color negative, which has different colors correlated to the sensitivity of color positive emulsion layers.

(4) Color positive stock records one color image aspect in each of its three emulsion layers and, after printing, is developed. When optical sound tracks* are required for

color positive release prints, the picture images are printed first. The sound track image is then printed and developed. Development of the picture image is the last step.

When magnetic sound tracks* are required, they are placed on the release prints after printing and developing.

*Most motion pictures today use an optical sound track. Few use magnetic tracks; even fewer use a combination of the two. This was not the case during the 1950s when stereophonic sound was at its peak in films. In those days, magnetic four-track stereo systems were used to a high degree in conjunction with the then new wide screen processes, particularly CinemaScope and VistaVision.

Warner Bros. was the first studio to experiment with stereophonic sound in two pre-World War II pictures, *Four Wives* (1939) and *Santa Fe Trail* (1940). The system, called Vitasound, was not successful as few theater owners were willing to spend the money to install special sound equipment.

In late 1940, Walt Disney introduced Fantasound with his Technicolor *Fantasia*. It was generally well received but, again, exposure was limited to a handful of major theaters during its roadshow run.

It wasn't until 1952, with the release of *This Is Cinerama*, that stereophonic sound—and magnetic sound tracks—began to receive wide attention. Over the following few years, films featuring stereophonic sound became immensely popular with movie audiences.

Following a low period during the 1960s, Universal successfully featured Sensurround with *Earthquake* (1974), *Midway* (1976) and *Rollercoaster* (1977). Currently, there is renewed interest in multi-channel sound spearheaded by the Dolby system.

Bibliography

Most of the research for *Glorious Technicolor* was extracted from the archives of the Technicolor Corporation, personal memos and correspondence between company principals, technicians and industry executives, as well as interviews with primary sources who have worked with the company either in processing or film production.

Also examined were the journals and publications prepared by Technicolor personnel, including:

An Outline of the History of the Beginning of the Technicolor Development in Boston—1914-1925 by Dr. Daniel F. Comstock (date unknown)

The Technicolor Process of Three-Color Photography by James A. Ball (1935)

Color Consciousness by Natalie Kalmus (1935)

Technicolor Adventures in Cinemaland by Dr. Herbert T. Kalmus (1938)

Mobile Photography by the Technicolor Method by George Cave (1939)

Technicolor Cinematography by Winton Hoch (1942)

Technicolor Today by Dr. Herbert T. Kalmus (1952)

Technicolor News & Views (house organ, various issues)

The following books were particularly helpful either in giving an overview of the motion picture industry, past or present, or in substantiating details relating to specific motion picture productions:

Eames, John D. *The MGM Story.* New York: Crown, 1975.

Film Daily Year Book. New York: Arno Press.

Finch, Christopher. *The Art of Walt Disney.* New York: Abrams, 1973

Friedman, Joseph S. *History of Color Photography.* Boston: American Photographic Publishing Co., 1944.

Griffith, Richard, and Mayer, Arthur. *The Movies.* New York: Simon & Schuster, 1957.

Harmetz, Aljean. *The Making of the Wizard of Oz.* New York: Knopf, 1977.

Huntley, John. *British Technicolor Films.* London: Skelton Robinson, 1949.

International Motion Picture Almanac. New York: Quigley Publications.

Jacobs, Lewis. *The Rise of the American Film.* New York: Harcourt, Brace, 1939.

LeRoy, Mervyn, and Kleiner, Dick. *Take One.* New York: Hawthorn Books, 1974.

Limbacher, James L. *Four Aspects of the Film.* New York: Brussel and Brussel, 1968.

Manvell, Roger. *Love Goddesses of the Movies.* New York: Crescent Books, 1975.

The New York Times Directory of the Film. New York: Arno Press/Random House, 1971

The New York Times Film Reviews, 1913-1970. New York: Arno Press/Quadrangle, 1971.

Osborne, Robert. *Academy Awards Illustrated.* La Habra: ESE California, 1969.

Parish, James Robert. *The Fox Girls.* New Rochelle: Arlington House, 1972.

Parish, James Robert, and Bowers, Ronald L. *The Golden Era: The MGM Stock Company.* New Rochelle: Arlington House, 1973.

Powdermaker, Hortense. *Hollywood the Dream Factory.* Boston: Little, Brown, 1950.

Pratt, William, and Bridges, Herb. *Scarlett Fever.* New York: Collier Macmillian, 1977.

Rhode, Eric. *A History of the Cinema.* New York: Hill and Wang, 1976.

Rosten, Leo. *Hollywood.* New York: Harcourt Brace, 1941.

Schickel, Richard. *The Disney Version*. New York: Simon & Schuster, 1968.

Stine, Whitney, and Davis, Bette. *Mother Goddam*. New York: Hawthorn Books, 1974.

Taylor, Deems. *A Pictorial History of the Movies*. New York: Simon and Schuster, 1943.

Taylor, John Russell. *The Hollywood Musical*. New York: McGraw-Hill, 1971.

Trent, Paul. *Those Fabulous Movie Years: The 30s*. Barre: Barre Publishing, 1975.

Wilson, Arthur (editor). *The Warner Bros. Golden Anniversary Book*. New York: Dell/Film and Venture Corp., 1973.

Among the periodicals consulted were: *American Cinematographer, Business Screen, Daily Variety, Film Facts, Films In Review, Fortune, Hollywood Citizen News, Hollywood Reporter, Journal of the SMPTE, Motion Picture Daily, Motion Picture Herald, Motion Picture News, Moving Picture World, The Photographic Journal, Popular Mechanics, Saturday Evening Post, Stage, Views & Reviews* and *Village Voice*.

Index

208